Exam Ref DP-500 Designing and Implementing Enterprise-Scale Analytics Solutions Using Microsoft Azure and Microsoft Power BI

D1282072

Daniil Maslyuk
Justin Frébault

Exam Ref DP-500 Designing and Implementing Enterprise-Scale Analytics Solutions Using Microsoft Azure and Microsoft Power BI

Published with the authorization of Microsoft Corporation by:
Pearson Education, Inc.

ISBN-13: 978-0-13-809737-0
ISBN-10: 0-13-809737-2

Library of Congress Control Number: 2023938072

1 2023

TRADEMARKS

Microsoft and the trademarks listed at http://www.microsoft.com on the "Trademarks" webpage are trademarks of the Microsoft group of companies. All other marks are property of their respective owners.

WARNING AND DISCLAIMER

SPECIAL SALES

For information about buying this title in bulk quantities, or for special sales opportunities (which may include electronic versions; custom cover designs; and content particular to your business, training goals, marketing focus, or branding interests), please contact our corporate sales department at corpsales@pearsoned.com or (800) 382-3419.

For government sales inquiries, please contact governmentsales@pearsoned.com.

For questions about sales outside the U.S., please contact intlcs@pearson.com.

EDITOR-IN-CHIEF
Brett Bartow

EXECUTIVE EDITOR
Loretta Yates

DEVELOPMENT EDITOR
Songlin Qiu

MANAGING EDITOR
Sandra Schroeder

SENIOR PROJECT EDITOR
Tracey Croom

COPY EDITOR
Liz Welch

INDEXER
Timothy Wright

PROOFREADER
Donna E. Mulder

TECHNICAL EDITOR
Owen Auger

EDITORIAL ASSISTANT
Cindy Teeters

COVER DESIGNER
Twist Creative, Seattle

COMPOSITOR
codeMantra

To Dasha, Leonard, and William, who served as a great source of motivation and support.

—DANIIL MASLYUK

To my wife Phaedra, who doesn't have much to do with data analytics but who has everything to do with enriching the rest of my life.

—JUSTIN FRÉBAULT

Contents at a glance

Contents

Introduction

Exam DP-500 focuses on designing and implementing enterprise-scale analytics solutions using Microsoft Azure and Microsoft Power BI. About a quarter of the book examines implementing and managing a data analytics environment, which includes both Azure and Power BI. Another quarter of the book reviews the query and data transformation by using Azure and Power BI. One more quarter of the book is dedicated to tabular data modeling in Power BI. The remainder of the book reviews the data visualization skills in Azure and Power BI.

This book was written for business intelligence developers, business intelligence architects, data engineers, and data architects. Before reading this book, you should be familiar with Azure, Power BI, the basics of Power Query, and DAX. It helps if you've passed the PL-300 exam already.

This book covers every major topic area found on the exam, but it does not cover every exam question. Only the Microsoft exam team has access to the exam questions, and Microsoft regularly adds new questions to the exam, making it impossible to cover specific questions. You should consider this book a supplement to your relevant real-world experience and other study materials. If you encounter a topic in this book that you do not feel completely comfortable with, use the "Need more review?" links you'll find in the text to find more information and take the time to research and study the topic. Great information is available on MSDN, TechNet, and in blogs and forums.

Organization of this book

This book is organized by the "Skills measured" list published for the exam. The "Skills measured" list is available for each exam on the Microsoft Learn website: *microsoft.com/learn*. Each chapter in this book corresponds to a major topic area in the list, and the technical tasks in each topic area determine a chapter's organization. If an exam covers six major topic areas, for example, the book will contain six chapters.

Preparing for the exam

Microsoft certification exams are a great way to build your résumé and let the world know about your level of expertise. Certification exams validate your on-the-job experience and product knowledge. Although there is no substitute for on-the-job experience, preparation through study and hands-on practice can help you prepare for the exam. This book is *not* designed to teach you new skills.

We recommend that you augment your exam preparation plan by using a combination of available study materials and courses. For example, you might use the *Exam Ref* and another study guide for your at-home preparation and take a Microsoft Official Curriculum course for the classroom experience. Choose the combination that you think works best for you. Learn more about available classroom training, online courses, and live events at *microsoft.com/learn*.

Note that this *Exam Ref* is based on publicly available information about the exam and the authors' experience. To safeguard the integrity of the exam, authors do not have access to the live exam.

Microsoft certifications

Microsoft certifications distinguish you by proving your command of a broad set of skills and experience with current Microsoft products and technologies. The exams and corresponding certifications are developed to validate your mastery of critical competencies as you design and develop, or implement and support, solutions with Microsoft products and technologies both on-premises and in the cloud. Certification brings a variety of benefits to the individual and to employers and organizations.

> **NEED MORE REVIEW?**   **ALL MICROSOFT CERTIFICATIONS**
>
> For information about Microsoft certifications, including a full list of available certifications, go to *microsoft.com/learn*.

Quick access to online references

Throughout this book are addresses to webpages that the authors have recommended you visit for more information. Some of these links can be very long and painstaking to type, so we've shortened them for you to make them easier to visit. We've also compiled them into a single list that readers of the print edition can refer to while they read.

Download the list at *MicrosoftPressStore.com/ERDP500/downloads*.

The URLs are organized by chapter and heading. Every time you come across a URL in the book, find the hyperlink in the list to go directly to the webpage.

Errata, updates, & book support

We've made every effort to ensure the accuracy of this book and its companion content. You can access updates to this book—in the form of a list of submitted errata and their related corrections—at:

MicrosoftPressStore.com/ERDP500/errata

If you discover an error that is not already listed, please submit it to us at the same page.

For additional book support and information, please visit *MicrosoftPressStore.com/Support*.

Please note that product support for Microsoft software and hardware is not offered through the previous addresses. For help with Microsoft software or hardware, go to *support.microsoft.com*.

Stay in touch

Let's keep the conversation going! We're on Twitter: *twitter.com/MicrosoftPress*.

Acknowledgments

Daniil Maslyuk: I would like to thank Loretta Yates for continuing to trust me to write the official Power BI exam reference books, Malobika Chakraborty for handling the project, the editing team for making this book a better read, and everyone else at Pearson who worked on this book to make it happen. This book wouldn't be possible without Justin, who made me realize that co-authoring doesn't have to be difficult.

Justin Frébault: I would like to thank Harry Misthos, my Pearson editor, for his continuous support during the writing process. I would also like to thank Loretta Yates, and the whole Microsoft Press team at Pearson, for all their hard work. Without you, the book wouldn't be a reality. Finally, Daniil Maslyuk, my co-author. It really was a delight collaborating with him on this book. Thank you!

About the authors

 DANIIL MASLYUK is an independent business intelligence consultant, trainer, and speaker who specializes in Microsoft Power BI. Daniil blogs at xxlbi.com and tweets as @DMaslyuk.

 JUSTIN FRÉBAULT MCT, is an independent data solutions architect and trainer who specializes in Microsoft data products. He blogs at lafreb.com and is active on LinkedIn.

## CHAPTER 1

Implement and manage a data analytics environment

Data is the most important asset of a company. Data analysts wanting to scale their practice at the enterprise level need the right tools and practices. Just like a fine restaurant, where kitchen staff puts in a tremendous amount of work to deliver beautiful dishes, insight from data only comes from a tremendous amount of work in data governance, data modeling, and the entire analytics lifecycle.

Skills covered in this chapter:

- Skill 1.1: Govern and administer a data analytics environment
- Skill 1.2: Integrate an analytics platform into an existing IT infrastructure
- Skill 1.3: Manage the analytics development lifecycle

Skill 1.1: Govern and administer a data analytics environment

In the last few years, data governance has become an important topic of data analytics. After growing their data landscapes, companies have needed tools and practices to bring clarity to their data assets. It's all too easy to create more and more data assets. But without governance data silos, duplication of metrics and incoherences start to emerge. Governance solutions are necessary to maintain order in the data landscape of an enterprise.

> **This skill covers how to:**
> - Manage Power BI assets by using Azure Purview
> - Identify data sources in Azure by using Azure Purview
> - Recommend settings in the Power BI admin portal
> - Recommend a monitoring and auditing solution for a data analytics environment, including Power BI REST API and PowerShell cmdlets

Manage Power BI assets by using Azure Purview

At the enterprise level, as the number of teams working with Power BI increases, governance tools become necessary to keep track of all the data assets of the company. Data will keep growing, so to maintain clarity and avoid silos and duplication, specialized tools that allow you to catalog and research data assets are required. Microsoft Purview will help you manage Power BI assets.

Data governance is becoming an important topic, a sign of a healthy data strategy. If anything, it is increasingly necessary for compliance and privacy purposes. But also in line with data observability, data governance ensures that the quality of the data is of the highest degree. Progress in data governance hasn't been as fast as in other areas of data analytics, so a tool like Microsoft Purview can really be a game changer for your organization.

What is Microsoft Purview?

Microsoft Purview is a data-governance solution. It doesn't duplicate the data, but rather catalogs the data assets and their metadata. It shows the data lineage. It doesn't require a lot of configurations. Rather, it is intended to work out of the box with your data stack. Microsoft Purview will give visibility to the data assets that are already in the organization.

> **NOTE   METADATA**
>
> Metadata is a set of data that gives information about other data.

To review the skills needed to manage Power BI assets by using Microsoft Purview, let's start by creating an instance of Microsoft Purview, as seen in Figure 1-1.

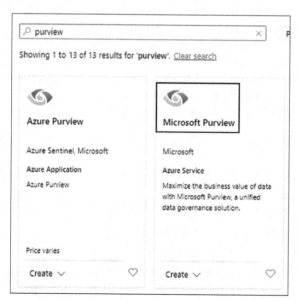

FIGURE 1-1 Creating a new Microsoft Purview instance via the Azure portal

Once the deployment is complete, go to the resource and launch the web portal, as shown in Figure 1-2.

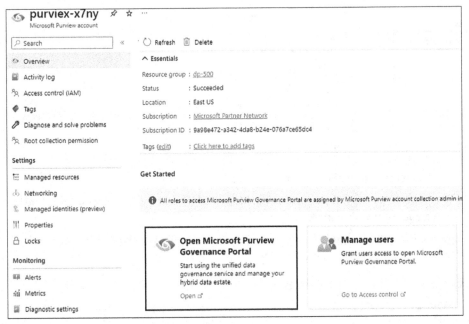

FIGURE 1-2 Microsoft Purview Governance Portal

Registering a data asset

We will register two data sources: an Azure SQL Database and an Azure Data Lake.

The first step to registering a data asset is to give the proper rights to Microsoft Purview. This can be done at the resource, resource group, or subscription level. The higher levels give access to the child levels. The following steps are for the subscription level. The same steps apply for the other levels.

1. Go to your subscription in the Azure portal.

2. Select **Access control (IAM)** from the left menu.

3. Select **+ Add** ,as shown in Figure 1-3, then select **Add role assignment**.

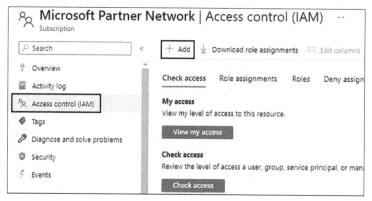

FIGURE 1-3 Adding new rights at the subscription level

4. On the first tab, **Role**, select the **Reader role**.

5. On the second tab, **Assignment**, select **Managed Identity**, **+Select members**, and select your Microsoft Purview account.

6. Select **Review + assign** to finish the role assignment. This will allow Microsoft Purview to list resources under the subscription.

CONNECT A NEW SOURCE: AZURE SQL DATABASE

After granting the proper rights to Microsoft Purview, we can register the data source in the web portal.

1. In the Azure portal, go to the Microsoft Purview resource.

2. Open the Microsoft Purview Governance Portal.

3. On the left tab, select **Data map**, then select **Sources > Register**, as shown in Figure 1-4.

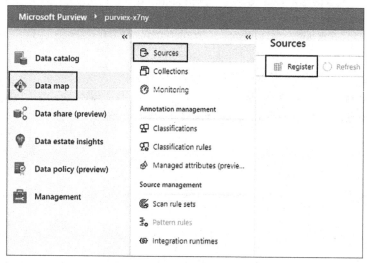

FIGURE 1-4 Registering a new source in Microsoft Purview

4. Select **Azure SQL Database**, as shown in Figure 1-5.

FIGURE 1-5 Registering an Azure SQL Database

NEED MORE REVIEW? **CONNECTING AN AZURE SQL DATABASE**

If you want to learn more about the process, see the step-by-step tutorial here: *https://learn. microsoft.com/en-us/azure/purview/register-scan-azure-sql-database*.

CONNECT A NEW SOURCE: AZURE DATA LAKE

Similarly, you can connect to other data sources, like Azure Data Lakes. When registering the data source you need to select Azure Data Lake Storage Gen2, as shown in Figure 1-6.

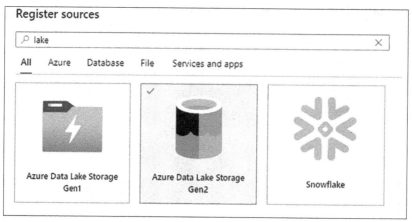

FIGURE 1-6 Registering Azure Data Lake Storage Gen2

NEED MORE REVIEW? **CONNECTING AN AZURE DATA LAKE**

If you want to learn more about the process, see the step-by-step tutorial here: *https://learn.microsoft.com/en-us/azure/purview/register-scan-adls-gen2.*

Register and scan a Power BI tenant

Microsoft Purview can register a Power BI workspace in the same tenant or across tenants. The security is different than with other data sources. First, you must authenticate Microsoft Purview to the Power BI tenant. Second, you need to configure the Power BI tenant to grant read rights to Microsoft Purview. Finally, you can register and scan the Power BI tenant.

The first step is to create a new security group in Azure Active Directory (Azure AD) containing the Microsoft Purview Managed Identity.

1. In your **Azure portal,** expand the menu icon at the top left and select **Azure Active Directory**, as shown in Figure 1-7.
2. Select **Overview** > **+ Add** > **Group.**
3. Leave **Group type** as **Security**.
4. For **Group name**, specify a name of your choice, like **purview**.
5. Select **No owners selected** and add your account.
6. Select **No members selected** and search for your **Microsoft Purview** account name. Select **Create** to create a new **Group**, as shown in Figure 1-8.

FIGURE 1-7 Azure Active Directory in the Azure portal

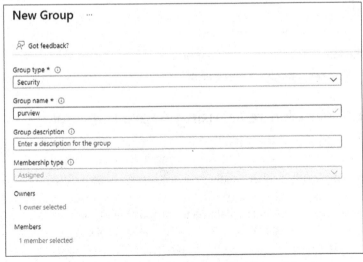

FIGURE 1-8 New Group in Azure Active Directory for Microsoft Purview

The next step is to configure the Power BI tenant to enable access to the read-only admin API. To do that:

1. Sign into app.powerbi.com and navigate to **Settings** > **Admin portal**.
2. In the **Tenant settings** section, scroll down to **Admin API settings**.
3. Select **Allow service principals to use read-only admin APIs.**
4. Select **Specific security groups** in the **Apply to:** section.
5. Select your Azure AD group containing Microsoft Purview Managed Identity, as seen in Figure 1-9.
6. Select **Apply**.

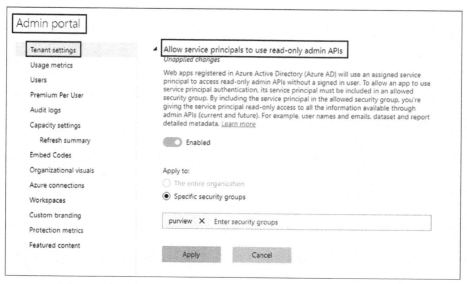

FIGURE 1-9 Select Admin API settings in Power BI

The last step is to register and scan the Power BI tenant:

1. Navigate back to the **Microsoft Purview** web portal.
2. Select **Data Map** > **Sources** > **Register** > **Power BI**.

Identify data sources in Azure by using Azure Purview

Registering data sources is a preliminary step to leveraging the other functionalities of Microsoft Purview: automated data discovery, end-to-end data lineage, and data classification.

In any data project, the first step after understanding the business requirements is to understand what data is needed and available. Microsoft Purview allows you to identify the right data, search and browse the catalog, and validate via the lineage that the right dataset is used to meet the business requirements. Microsoft Purview is an enabler of one of the most important tasks in any data project.

Browse and search data catalog assets

A straightforward way to search for data assets is to use the search bar in the web portal, as shown in Figure 1-10.

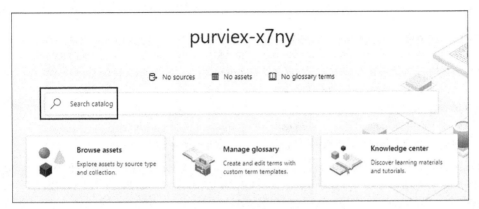

FIGURE 1-10 Search bar in Microsoft Purview web portal

After a search, additional filters become available, like source type, object type, collection, classification, contact, label, and assigned term.

Sometimes, though, we don't know what assets are available or what to look for. That's where browsing becomes interesting. To access the browsing feature, select **Browse assets**, as shown in Figure 1-11.

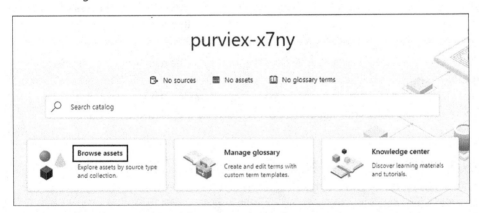

FIGURE 1-11 Browse feature in Microsoft Purview web portal

You can browse data assets by collection or by source type, depending on what is most efficient.

Browsing by collection is ideal when some work has been done to curate collections that align with the business. You can only browse the collections you have access to.

NEED MORE REVIEW?   **COLLECTIONS**

You can review how to create and manage collections here: *https://learn.microsoft.com/en-us/ azure/purview/how-to-create-and-manage-collections.*

Browsing by source type is particularly intuitive. The interface presents the various data sources, and when selecting one you see a hierarchy of the data assets. As data analysts are generally acquainted with the technology of the underlying data sources, browsing by source type can be an effective way to find data assets.

When you're selecting a data asset, different tabs are available. The Overview tab contains the asset description. It can be edited to something meaningful that will help other data analysts understand the importance of that asset for their business requirements.

Below the asset description is the Classification menu. Classification in Microsoft Purview allows you to tag specific classification labels to the data asset, like Credit Card Number or Person's Name, reflecting the sensitivity of the data.

On the right side of the Overview pane is the collection path. The collection path represents where the asset is within Microsoft Purview, not where it is in your data platform. You can modify that by creating more collections and moving the asset from one collection to another.

The Schema and Lineage tabs are particularly useful for data analysts, due to their deep integration with Power BI.

On the Schema tab you find all the tables and field names of your data model, as well as their data type, sensitivity label, and description. When you select a field, additional information is displayed about whether the field is a measure or whether it is hidden. The Schema tab allows data analysts to get a thorough understanding of the Power BI asset.

The Lineage tab is also crucial, as it displays the journey of the data, from the original sources to the final Power BI asset, through the various intermediate transformations, datasets, or reports. As the data landscape becomes increasingly complex, it is important to have the full picture of where the data is coming from and how it is reused by other data products.

Use data assets with Power BI

A couple of extra features are available to data analysts that can be extremely useful: requesting access to a new data asset and creating a report based on a data asset.

When browsing data assets that you need to meet your business requirements, Microsoft Purview offers the ability to directly request access to the data asset if you don't have access. As shown in Figure 1-12, when you select a data asset, the option **Request access** is available if you have not already been granted access.

FIGURE 1-12 Request access to a data asset

Additionally, the **Open in Power BI Desktop** feature allows you to start a report straight from the Microsoft Purview explorer. The button will trigger the download of a Power BI Data Source (PBIDS) file, which is essentially a file defining the data source connection. When opening that file, you will be prompted to log into the data source with your credentials and then you can start creating your report. Having a PBIDS file simplifies the workflow, as you no longer have to look for the data source type or the data source name.

Use Microsoft Purview in Azure Synapse Studio

Finally, Microsoft Purview can be used to identify data sources directly within Azure Synapse Studio. This can be useful because Azure Synapse Studio is already the tool used by data analysts to run their notebooks or reports.

To review this skill, let's do the following:

1. Open **Azure Synapse Studio.**
2. Navigate to the **Data** pane.
3. Locate the search bar at the top.
4. Select **Purview** from the drop-down menu next to the search bar.
5. Search for a data asset.
6. Filter on **Object Type** or **Collections**, just like in the Microsoft Purview web portal.

> **NEED MORE REVIEW?** **CONNECTING YOUR AZURE SYNAPSE TO MICROSOFT PURVIEW**
>
> This step requires some more work to get the permissions right; see *https://learn.microsoft.com/en-us/azure/synapse-analytics/catalog-and-governance/quickstart-connect-azure-purview.*

Recommend settings in the Power BI admin portal

Global, Power Platform, and Power BI admins can access the admin portal in Power BI by selecting **Settings** > **Admin portal** in the Power BI service. Figure 1-13 shows the **Tenant settings** section of the portal.

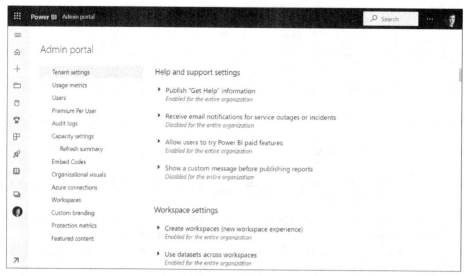

FIGURE 1-13 Power BI tenant settings

Ideally, those who have access to Power BI admin portal should be familiar with Power BI; otherwise, it might be difficult for admins to understand the users.

For optimal governance and security, it's important for admins to set and periodically review the settings to ensure that the settings are in line with the enterprise policies. The Power BI team releases new features and admin settings from time to time, so it's a good idea to review the settings on a regular basis—for example, once a quarter.

Unlike in the Microsoft 365 admin center, there's no "global reader" role; therefore, it's recommended that you document the applied settings and make the documentation available for others to view. If Power BI tenant settings documentation is available in your organization, your Power BI users won't have to guess which settings are applied. Additionally, to keep track of who updates the admin settings, you can use audit logs, as discussed later in this chapter.

The default tenant settings vary; some options are enabled, while some are disabled. Furthermore, some settings can be enabled or disabled for specific security groups, whereas others apply to the entire organization. Most often, a tenant setting can be applied in one of the following ways:

- Disabled for the entire organization
- Enabled for the entire organization
- Enabled for some users

When enabling a setting for some users, you can specify the security groups to enable the setting for, as well as the security groups for which you want to disable the setting.

As mentioned previously, tenant settings can be added and sometimes removed by the Power BI team. The following are recommendations relevant for most enterprise environments.

Help and support settings

- **Publish "Get Help" information**—If your company has some internal resources, such as training documentation, discussion forums, or a dedicated help desk, you should use this setting to promote the resources.

- **Receive email notifications for service outages or incidents**—You should use a mail-enabled security group to get notifications about issues and resolutions.

- **Allow users to try Power BI paid features**—You may want to disable this setting in some cases. For example, if your company uses Power BI Premium, then there may be little reason for users to try Power BI Premium Per User.

- **Show a custom message before publishing reports**—If you want your users to see a specific message when they attempt to publish a report, you can use this setting.

Workspace settings

- **Create workspaces**—You may want to restrict the creation of workspaces to only some Power BI Pro users so there's less deviation in naming. At the same time, you should ensure that the workspace creation turnaround time is reasonable; otherwise, users may tend to put too much into existing workspaces.

- **Use datasets across workspaces**—There are very few cases where this setting should be disabled. Allowing datasets to be used across workspaces promotes data reusability and consistency. This setting must be enabled if you want to have workspaces that contain datasets only; otherwise, you won't be able to make use of them. Note that building reports from datasets requires the Build permission.

Information protection

- **Allow users to apply sensitivity labels for content**—This setting should be the same as for files and email in Office.

- **Apply sensitivity labels from data sources to their data in Power BI**—This setting should be enabled if your company uses sensitivity labels on its data sources. Inheriting sensitivity labels will remind the dataset owner of the underlying data sensitivity, and if there are multiple degrees of sensitivity, then the most restrictive is used.

- **Automatically apply sensitivity labels to downstream content**—When used together with other information protection settings, enabling this setting will ensure that the data remains protected end-to-end.

- **Allow workspace admins to override automatically applied sensitivity labels**—You can enable this setting to avoid situations when nobody has the usage rights to pre-set sensitivity labels, making some workspace items inaccessible.

- **Restrict content with protected labels from being shared via link with everyone in your organization**—You may want to enable this setting if you want to prevent people from sharing protected content by using links.

Export and sharing settings

- **Allow Azure Active Directory guest users to access Power BI**—If users aren't expected to collaborate with external users, then this setting should be disabled.

- **Invite external users to your organization**—Again, this should be disabled if it's unusual for users to work with external users. Otherwise, you should align this setting with your company's security policies, since this setting is tied to Azure AD.

- **Allow Azure Active Directory guest users to edit and manage content in the organization**—This setting should be enabled in case your company is working with external users who are frequent collaborators, such as consultants.

- **Show Azure Active Directory guests in lists of suggested people**—This setting should be aligned with your company's security policies.

- **Publish to web**—This setting should be disabled by default because publishing to web isn't secure by design. You may want to enable it only for the group of users who have real needs to publish to web.

- **Copy and paste visuals**—Since in most cases it's possible to take a screenshot anyway, this setting should be enabled, as it will improve productivity.

- **Export to Excel**—This setting should be enabled, especially if your company uses sensitivity labels. You can disable export of data for each report individually in case of highly sensitive reports if you don't use sensitivity labels.

- **Export to .csv**—If your company uses sensitivity labels and there are concerns about data security, you may want to disable this setting since the labels aren't included in CSV files.

- **Download reports**—This setting should be enabled because in some cases it allows users to retrieve reports if they lost PBIX files.

- **Allow live connections**—This setting should be enabled as it promotes the dataset reusability and data consistency.

- **Export reports as PowerPoint presentations or PDF documents**—This setting should be enabled in most cases, since PowerPoint and PDF files can make use of the sensitivity labels.

- **Export reports as MHTML documents**—You may want to apply the same setting as Export to CSV, since MHTML documents aren't supported by Azure Information Protection.

- **Export reports as Word documents**—You may want to apply the same setting as Export to Excel, since Word documents support sensitivity labels.

- **Export reports as XML documents**—You may want to apply the same setting as Export to CSV, since XML files aren't supported by Azure Information Protection by default.

- **Export reports as image files**—You may want to apply the same setting as Export to CSV, since images aren't supported by Azure Information Protection by default.

- **Print dashboards and reports**—Unless there's some restriction on printing, this setting should be enabled. Audit logs capture information on who's printing too much.

- **Certification**—This setting should be enabled for a small group of users who are trusted to certify content. Ideally there should also be a documented procedure that explains the criteria for certification of content.

- **Create email subscriptions**—This setting should be enabled as it improves productivity. Subscriptions are captured in audit logs.

- **Allow email subscriptions to be sent to external users**—Similar to other settings related to external users, this setting should be disabled if your data shouldn't be shared with external users.

- **Featured content**—You may want to either disable this setting or enable it for a small group of users because it determines who can feature content on the home page for all users to see.

- **Allow connections to featured tables**—This setting should be enabled as it promotes access to the featured tables in your organization.

- **Allow shareable links to grant access to everyone in your organization**—You may want to disable this setting if most reports should not be shared throughout the organization.

- **Enable Microsoft Teams integration in the Power BI service**—This setting should be enabled for improved productivity and to promote collaboration.

- **Install Power BI app for Microsoft Teams automatically**—This setting should be enabled for improved productivity and to promote collaboration.

- **Enable Power BI add-in for PowerPoint**—This setting should be enabled as it can drastically increase productivity by saving time spent on copying and pasting visuals between Power BI and PowerPoint.

- **Allow DirectQuery connections to Power BI datasets**—This setting should be enabled for maximum productivity, as it allows users to build composite models and promotes reusability and data consistency, just like Live Connections.

Discovery settings

- **Make promoted content discoverable**—This setting should be enabled unless promoted content should not be as widely used as certified content.

- **Make certified content discoverable**—This setting should be enabled to promote the dataset reusability and data consistency.

- **Discover content**—This setting should be enabled to promote the dataset reusability and data consistency.

Content pack and app settings

- **Publish content packs and apps to the entire organization**—You may want to enable this setting only for a small set of users, like the central business intelligence team, to avoid accidental oversharing.

- **Create template organizational content packs and apps**—The same as publishing apps to the entire organization, this setting should usually be enabled only for the central business intelligence team, since template apps are organizationwide.

- **Push apps to end users**—This setting should be enabled in most cases. If there are many apps in your organization, you may want to enable this setting only for those users who usually publish widely distributed content; otherwise, users may see more content in Power BI than they want to see.

Integration settings

- **Allow XMLA endpoints and Analyze in Excel with on-premises datasets**—This setting should be enabled to promote the use of your data models as data sources for analysis.

- **Dataset Execute Queries REST API**—This setting should be enabled again to promote the dataset reusability. If there's concern about too much querying, you can analyze the audit logs and train users to write more efficient queries.

- **Use ArcGIS Maps for Power BI**—This setting should be disabled unless your organization uses Esri mapping services, because Power BI sends data to Esri for processing.

- **Use global search for Power BI**—This setting should be enabled in most cases to make it easier to find content.

- **Use Azure Maps visual**—You should note that Azure Maps may process the data outside of your tenant region, law boundaries, and so forth and align this setting with your company's security policy.

- **Map and filled map visuals**—The same as with Azure Maps, you should align this setting with your company's security policy.

- **Integration with SharePoint and Microsoft Lists**—This setting should be enabled in most cases, especially when you use Microsoft SharePoint for version control (covered in Skill 1.3: Manage the analytics development lifecycle).

- **Snowflake SSO**—This option should be enabled if your company uses Snowflake and you'd like to use single sign-on, because your data will be sent to Snowflake for authentication.

- **Redshift SSO**—Like Snowflake, this option should be enabled if your company uses Redshift and you'd like to use single sign-on, because your data will be sent to Redshift for authentication.

- **Azure AD Single Sign-On (SSO) for Gateway**—This setting should be enabled if your company uses an on-premises data gateway, and you'd like to use single sign-on for some data sources.

- **Power Platform Solutions Integration**—This setting should be enabled if your company uses other Power Platform products.

Power BI visuals

- **Allow visuals created using the Power BI SDK**—This setting should be disabled unless your company does not use any sensitive data. You may want to restrict the use of custom visuals only to those visuals that were approved in your organization.
- **Add and use certified visuals only (block uncertified)**—Again, this setting should be disabled unless your company does not use any sensitive data. Even if a visual isn't certified, it can be on-boarded as an organizational visual, making it available for use in Power BI.
- **Allow downloads from custom visuals**—The decision to allow custom visuals to have access to any data in your Power BI datasets should be aligned with your company's security policy.

R and Python visuals settings

- **Interact with and share R and Python visuals**—This setting should usually be disabled unless you have strong reasons for using R or Python visuals in the Power BI service, because R and Python visuals may pose security concerns.

Audit and usage settings

- **Create audit logs for internal activity auditing and compliance**—This setting should always be enabled, since auditing data is necessary for the well-being of any Power BI implementation.
- **Usage metrics for content creators**—This setting should be enabled because it will allow content creators to understand the usage patterns and popularity of their content.
- **Per-user data in usage metrics for content creators**—This setting should usually be enabled because in many cases it can be useful for content creators to talk to content users to improve the content.
- **Azure Log Analytics connections for workspace administrators**—This setting should be enabled if your company uses Azure Log Analytics.

Dashboard settings

- **Web content on dashboard tiles**—In most cases this setting should be enabled for richer dashboard functionality, unless accessing external content is restricted by company policy.

Developer settings

- **Embed content in apps**—This setting should be enabled for a group of users who have legitimate needs to make Power BI content available outside of the Power BI service.

- **Allow service principals to use Power BI APIs**—This setting should only be enabled for a group of service principals that are under proper governance.
- **Allow service principals to create and use profiles**—This setting should only be enabled for those service principals that have legitimate needs to create and use profiles.
- **Block ResourceKey Authentication**—This setting should be aligned with the enterprise security policies specifying whether or not authentication by ResourceKey is allowed.

Admin API settings

- **Allow service principals to use read-only admin APIs**—This setting should only be enabled for a group of service principals that are under proper governance.
- **Enhance admin APIs responses with detailed metadata**—This setting should be enabled if it's desirable to get information such as table and column names from GetScanResult APIs; otherwise, the setting should be disabled for better performance.
- **Enhance admin APIs responses with DAX and mashup expressions**—This setting should be enabled if it's desirable to get DAX and M expressions from GetScanResult APIs; otherwise, the setting should be disabled for better performance.

Dataflow settings

- **Create and use dataflows**—This setting should be enabled to promote the reusability of data in your organization unless there's a well-maintained and popular data warehousing solution already in place.

Template app settings

- **Publish template apps**—This setting should usually be disabled unless your company is a software vendor that develops and publishes template apps.
- **Install template apps**—This setting should usually be enabled to enhance the reporting offerings already in place in your company.
- **Install template apps not listed in AppSource**—This setting should usually be disabled unless there's a legitimate need to install a template app from a trusted vendor that's not on AppSource.

Q&A settings

- **Review questions**—This setting should always be enabled to make it possible for dataset owners to improve the Q&A experience.
- **Synonym sharing**—This setting should usually be enabled to make Q&A easier to use; in case of poor synonym quality, you can train users or improve the naming conventions of your datasets.

Dataset Security

- **Block republish and disable package refresh**—In general, this tenant-wide setting should be disabled because it will only allow dataset owners to publish updates, hindering collaboration. Another option to limit who can publish reports and update datasets is by controlling the workspace membership.

Advanced networking

- **Azure Private Link**—This setting should be aligned with your company's security policies. If you want to allow people to use a Private Link to access your Power BI tenant, you'll need to enable this companywide setting.
- **Block Public Internet Access**—Again, this setting should be aligned with your company's security policies. If you enable this setting, only people with a Private Link will be able to access your Power BI tenant.

Metrics settings

- **Create and use Metrics**—This setting should be enabled to enhance the reporting offerings in your organization.

User experience experiments

- **Help Power BI optimize your experience**—In most cases, you want to keep this setting enabled, since it will help prepare your users for upcoming changes to the Power BI service.

Share data with your Microsoft 365 services

- **Allow Microsoft 365 services to access Power BI metadata**—This setting should be aligned with your security policies; note that if your Power BI and Microsoft 365 tenant services are in different regions, some metadata may flow between different regions.

Insights settings

- **Receive notifications for top insights**—In most cases, this setting should be enabled to make use of the insights found in the Power BI service.
- **Show entry points for insights**—Again, this setting should be enabled in most cases.

Datamart settings

- **Create Datamarts**—The same as dataflows, this setting should be enabled to promote the reusability of data in your organization unless there's a well-maintained and popular data warehousing solution already in place.

Quick measure suggestions

- **Allow quick measure suggestions**—You may want to enable this setting to help new users with creating measures.
- **Allow user data to leave their geography**—This setting should be aligned with the enterprise security policies.

Recommend a monitoring and auditing solution for a data analytics environment, including Power BI REST API and PowerShell cmdlets

Monitoring and auditing are two pillars of a modern data analytics solution. The concept of monitoring comes from the DevOps practices, with the end goal of improving the quality of software services. Similarly, monitoring and auditing your data solution will improve the quality of the data products for the users. There are few things worse than end users alerting you that a data product is down or broken.

Power BI offers some capabilities for monitoring. We will first review the Usage Metrics report feature, and then how to monitor in an automated way with the Power BI REST API and the PowerShell cmdlets.

Leveraging the Usage Metrics Dashboards

The Usage Metrics report feature is an easy, albeit limited, tool for monitoring. It is available in the Power BI Service for Reports and Dashboards. Select the option to view the Reports Metrics from the menu for a data asset, as shown in Figure 1-14.

FIGURE 1-14 Option in Power BI Service to view the Usage Metrics report

The Usage Metrics report contains useful information such as the number of **Views per day** and **Unique viewers per day**, or the number of **Views by user**.

> **NOTE**   **HIDING PERSONALLY IDENTIFIABLE INFORMATION**
>
> If you need to hide personally identifiable information from the Usage Metrics reports, follow the documentation here: *https://learn.microsoft.com/en-us/power-bi/collaborate-share/service-modern-usage-metrics#exclude-user-information-from-usage-metrics-reports*.

At the top right of the Usage Metrics report is a button that allows you to switch to the new Usage Metrics report experience. The new Usage Metrics offers performance metrics in addition to the usage metrics.

Automating monitoring and auditing

For an enterprise solution, monitoring and auditing cannot be left to a manual process. You need something more than having to consult the usage metrics report. Power BI offers an API that allows you to programmatically extract activity events. It is called the *activity log*.

To query the activity log, the first option is to use the REST API:

```
https://api.powerbi.com/v1.0/myorg/admin/activityevents
```

A **startDateTime** and **endDateTime** need to be passed as parameters in UTC format. This API call will return all user activity for one day. If the amount of data returned is large, you will need to add pagination logic with a continuation token. The user activity can then be stored in a monitoring database on a daily basis. Finally, custom alerting and monitoring can be built on top of that datastore.

A second way to query the event log is to use the built-in PowerShell cmdlet:

```
Get-PowerBIActivityEvent
```

The cmdlet also takes a **startDateTime** and **endDateTime** and handles pagination if the number of entries is large. For example, you could use it as follows:

```
Get-PowerBIActivityEvent -StartDateTime '2023-02-01T00:00:00' -EndDateTime
'2023-02-01T23:59:59'
```

Skill 1.2: Integrate an analytics platform into an existing IT infrastructure

The analytics platform doesn't exist on its own—it usually comes later as an organization gains in maturity. That's why it is important to be able to integrate it with the existing IT infrastructure. Historically, the other IT systems have been on-premises, so we need a way to connect them with Power BI. Today it is important to integrate easily with other cloud services. Power BI does integrate seamlessly with other core data analytics products like Azure Data Lake Storage Gen2 or Azure Synapse Analytics.

This skill covers how to:

- Identify requirements for a solution, including features, performance, and licensing strategy
- Configure and manage Power BI capacity
- Recommend and configure an on-premises gateway in Power BI
- Recommend and configure a Power BI tenant or workspace to integrate with Azure Data Lake Storage Gen2
- Integrate an existing Power BI workspace into Azure Synapse Analytics

---

Identify requirements for a solution, including features, performance, and licensing strategy

You should consider two high-level types of licenses for Power BI when examining requirements for a solution: per-user license and organizational subscription.

- Per-user licenses can be Free, Pro, or Premium Per User (sometimes referred as PPU).
- An organizational subscription, also referred as capacity-based, can either be standard or premium. This will significantly affect what users can do with Power BI assets.

Let's start by breaking down the functionalities available to users when the organizational subscription is standard. Free users will be able to access assets they created themselves. Pro users will be able to publish and collaborate with other Pro users. Similarly, PPU users will be able to publish and collaborate with other PPU users.

Now when the organization has a Premium subscription—again, also called Premium capacity—the paradigm is different. Pro and PPU users can share and collaborate with all users, including Free ones.

For example, if the price for a Pro license is $10, a PPU license $20, and a Premium capacity $5,000, at what point would it make sense, from a cost perspective, to switch to a Premium capacity? If you have more than 500 users who need to consume reports, it would automatically make sense to switch to Premium capacity.

Performance

Besides cost, there are differences in performance when the workspace is in a Premium capacity, or a Shared capacity (with the standard subscription).

Essentially, with a Shared capacity your workload will run on a Power BI compute shared with other customers. With a Premium capacity, you get a dedicated compute. If your use case requires dependable and consistent performance, consider a dedicated compute with a Premium capacity.

The user license will also dictate some performance aspects: the number of data refreshes available per day and the maximum size of a model.

Features

Finally, each license comes with a set of features. For example, a Pro license will not allow you to use paginated reports, dataflows, or datamarts (among others)—a Premium license will be needed for that. Also, a Pro or Premium license is needed to link an Azure Synapse Analytics resource to Power BI.

> **NEED MORE REVIEW?** **FEATURES FOR EACH LICENSE**
>
> The list of features for each license can be found here: *https://powerbi.microsoft.com/en-us/ pricing*.

EXAM TIP

It is important to understand the different licensing types and to be ready to recommend a solution based on a set of features, performance, and cost requirements.

Configure and manage Power BI capacity

Once you purchase Premium or Embedded capacity, you can configure and manage it in the capacity settings section of the admin portal. Figure 1-15 shows the Embedded section as an example.

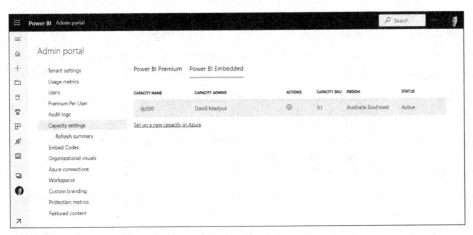

FIGURE 1-15 Power BI capacity settings

To manage a capacity, you select its name from the list of available capacities, where you'll see several sections, including these:

- **Capacity usage report**—You can view the report to track usage, identify patterns, and make capacity management decisions.

- **Notifications**—You can get notified when you're about to exceed the available capacity, and you can specify the capacity usage level at which you want to be notified as well as who should be notified.

- **Contributor permissions**—You can specify the people who can add or remove workspaces in this capacity.

- **Workloads**—In this section, you can set various limits and options for the capacity, such as the query memory limit, query timeout, and XMLA endpoint availability.

- **Workspaces assigned to this capacity**—You can search for, add, or remove workspaces assigned to the capacity.

Additionally, for Premium capacities, you can change the capacity name and admins or delete a capacity by selecting Settings. You can manage Embedded capacities in the Azure portal.

Recommend and configure an on-premises gateway in Power BI

In most cases, to share a report you created in Power BI Desktop, you need to publish it to the Power BI service. Once you publish your report, the mechanics of connecting to data change, which means the cloud, not your machine, needs to have access to your data sources—it's true for imported data, as well as DirectQuery and Live Connection.

Making on-premises data available from the cloud can be achieved by using a *data gateway*, which is covered in this section. Most cloud data sources can be refreshed in the Power BI service without a gateway—one notable exception is the **Web.Page** function in Power Query.

In this section, "on-premises" loosely refers to a corporate network, which can include

- On-premises data sources
- Cloud data sources that reside in IaaS (Infrastructure-as-a-Service) virtual machines
- Cloud data sources that reside within a virtual network (VNet)

A gateway is an agent that is installed in your corporate network and acts as a bridge between the Power BI service and your corporate network. Additionally, a gateway handles credentials and authentication.

Note that a Power BI Report Server instance does not require a gateway because it already resides within a corporate network.

Figure 1-16 shows a simplified data refresh diagram when using on-premises data sources.

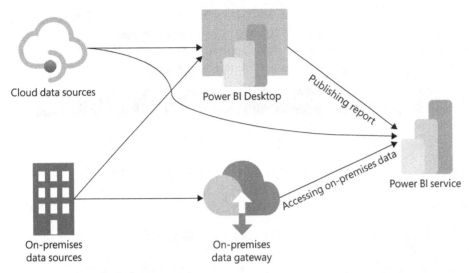

Cloud data sources

Power BI Desktop

Publishing report

Power BI service

On-premises
data sources

On-premises
data gateway

Accessing on-premises data

FIGURE 1-16 Data refresh diagram

When working in the Power BI Desktop, you're supposed to have all the necessary access to the data sources you're working with—cloud or on-premises. Once you publish your report to the Power BI service, the cloud data sources may reach the Power BI service directly, whereas the on-premises data will need to go through a gateway for data to be refreshed in the Power BI service.

Tenant administration for gateways

Before you install a gateway, you need to ensure that you're allowed to install one, which depends on whether tenant administration for gateways is enabled in your tenant. You can change the setting in the Power BI service by going to **Settings** > **Manage connections and gateways** > **On-premises data gateways**.

If the **Tenant administration for gateways** toggle is switched to **On**, you'll see the **Manage gateway installers** option, which allows you to restrict users in your organization from installing gateways and specify the users who can install gateways. You can see the setting in Figure 1-17. Note that to be a gateway administrator, a user does not have to be allowed to install gateways. Gateway roles are discussed later in this section.

Install a gateway

To install a gateway, select **Download** > **Data Gateway** in the Power BI service, which takes you to the gateway download page. The Power BI gateway is available in two modes:

- **Standard**—This gateway can be used by multiple users for all supported services, such as Power Automate. It's preferred in enterprise environments when several people are going to use the same data sources. Dataflows and paginated reports that connect to on-premises data also require standard mode.

- **Personal**—Only you can use a gateway in personal mode, and you can use it only for scheduling a refresh in Power BI. A gateway in personal mode may be appropriate when you don't need to share data sources with others. R and Python scripts as data sources require a personal gateway. You can install only one personal gateway.

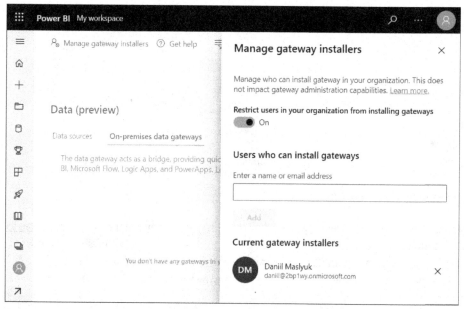

FIGURE 1-17 Manage gateway installers

EXAM TIP

Be aware of the functionality difference between the two gateway installation modes and be prepared to decide which one is appropriate in any given situation.

Additionally, there's also the virtual network (VNet) gateway, which is a Microsoft managed service. It doesn't need to be installed, and like an on-premises gateway in standard mode, it also allows you to share data sources with others. VNet gateways are outside the scope of this book.

In general, a data gateway should be installed on a machine that is always on and connected to the internet, because a gateway cannot access on-premises data sources from a machine that is powered off. You can install up to one gateway in each mode on the same computer, and you can manage multiple gateways from the same interface in the Power BI service. Installing Power BI gateways together with a self-hosted integration runtime (used for Azure Data Factory, for example) is not recommended.

If you want to practice working with a gateway, you need to install an on-premises data gateway. During the installation process, you must sign into your Power BI account, and you have to give your gateway a name. You also need to specify a recovery key that you can use to move or recover the gateway. Once you have finished installing the gateway, you must add data sources and users to it.

Note that when installing a gateway in standard mode, you can make it part of a *cluster*, which is the term that the Power BI service uses to call one or more nodes grouped for high availability (avoiding having a single point of failure) and load balancing (automatic distribution of load across all nodes in a cluster). In general, it's recommended to have more than one gateway node in enterprise scenarios, as well as separate development or testing clusters. Even if there's only one node in a gateway cluster, the Power BI service will still call it a gateway cluster. For simplicity, in this section we're using the term *gateway* instead of gateway cluster.

> **NOTE   ON-PREMISES GATEWAY INSTALLATION INSTRUCTIONS**
>
> For more details on the data gateway installation process, including requirements and considerations, see "Install an on-premises data gateway" at *https://learn.microsoft.com/en-us/data-integration/gateway/service-gateway-install*.

Manage gateway settings

Once you install a gateway, you'll be able to see it in the list of available gateways by selecting **Settings > Manage connections and gateways > On-premises data gateways**. From there, you can select your gateway and then select **Settings** to change the gateway settings:

- **Name**—The gateway name that users will see.
- **Department**—The users will see the department next to the gateway name.
- **Description**—The description seen mostly by gateway admins.
- **Contact information**—A free text field that can contain an email address or other useful information that users will see.
- **Distribute requests across all active gateways in this cluster**—Required for load balancing.
- **Allow user's cloud data sources to refresh through this gateway cluster**—This setting allows merging and appending cloud and on-premises data sources together.
- **Allow user's custom data connectors to refresh through this gateway cluster**—This setting allows custom connectors to be used with the gateway. Custom connectors are outside the scope of this book.

Manage gateway users

To manage the users with whom a gateway is shared, select a gateway from the list of available gateways and then select **Manage users**.

When sharing a gateway with other users, you can select one of the following roles:

- **Connection Creator**—Allows the user to create data sources and connections on the gateway.

- **Connection Creator with resharing**—Allows the user to create data sources and connection on the gateway and reshare gateway access.
- **Admin**—Allows the user to create data sources and connections on the gateway, and manage gateway access, configurations, credentials, and updates.

At the very least, a gateway should have more than one administrator to avoid dependence on one person. You can see the gateway sharing options in Figure 1-18.

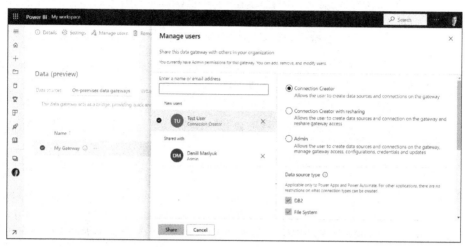

FIGURE 1-18 Manage gateway users

Add a data source to a gateway

After you have a gateway installed, you can add data sources to it in the Power BI service. To start, select **Settings > Manage connections and gateways**. At this point, you should see the page shown in Figure 1-19.

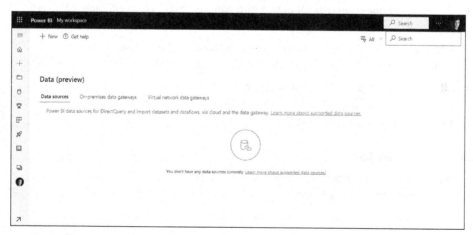

FIGURE 1-19 Data sources

You can start adding a new data source by selecting **New**. You'll then be prompted to select the gateway to add the data source to, assign a name to the data source, select the data source type, and so on. An example is shown in Figure 1-20.

FIGURE 1-20 New data source

Note that data source specifics, such as the server address, need to be the same in the list of gateway data sources and within the dataset or dataflow. For example, if you can access a shared drive by typing either *sdrv01* or *sdrv01.internal.yourcompany.com* in Windows Explorer and in the gateway, you specify the address as *sdrv01.internal.yourcompany.com*, then you'll need to use *sdrv01.internal.yourcompany.com* in Power Query when authoring your queries.

Manage data source users

For a user to successfully use a gateway for accessing on-premises data, they need to be specified as a user for all on-premises data sources used in a dataset or dataflow, and all data sources must be added to one gateway, because you can use no more than one gateway for data refreshes.

To manage users of a data source, go to the list of data sources (**Settings** > **Manage connections and gateways**), select a data source, and then select **Manage users**. Three roles are available for users of data sources:

- **User**—Allows the user to use the data source
- **User with resharing**—Allows the user to use the data source and reshare with others
- **Owner**—Allows the user to use the data source, as well as manage data source configurations and credentials

You can see the data source sharing options in Figure 1-21.

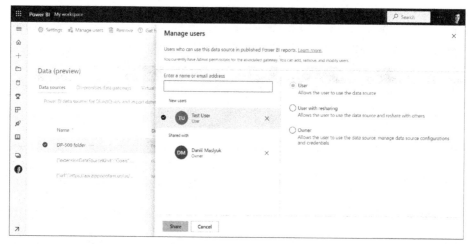

FIGURE 1-21 Manage data source users

Note that being a gateway administrator does not automatically make you a user of its data sources. To use a data source, you still need to be listed as its user, regardless of your gateway role.

Use a gateway

If you want to schedule a refresh of a report that uses on-premises data sources, you'll need to use a gateway. Figure 1-22 shows the **Gateway connection** section in dataset settings.

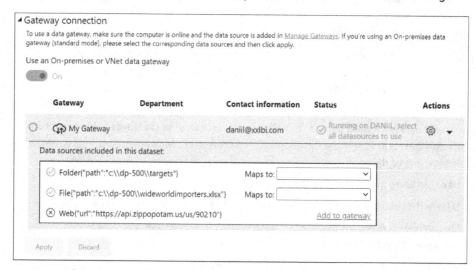

FIGURE 1-22 Gateway connection

To use a gateway, you'll need to select data sources from the **Maps to** drop-down lists and select **Apply**. If you're also using web data sources, you may have to enter credentials in the **Data source credentials** section in dataset settings. Once all credentials are in place, you can use your gateway to refresh your dataset.

Recommend and configure a Power BI tenant or workspace to integrate with Azure Data Lake Storage Gen2

By default, the data used in the Power BI service is kept in the storage provided by Power BI. By integrating with Azure Data Lake Storage Gen2 (ADLS Gen2), instead of using the default storage provided by Power BI, you can store data from dataflows in your organization's ADLS Gen2 account.

When you use your own storage for dataflows, Power BI stores data in the Common Data Model (CDM) model, which includes both data and metadata. The main benefit of using your own storage is that you're no longer restrained to using the dataflows connector, and any tool that can read data from ADLS Gen2 will be able to read your dataflows data, which allows you to build solutions for more scenarios than possible with Power BI alone.

Another benefit to using your own storage is that the Power BI service only writes data, and you'll have access to all past versions of data in your storage account, which can be convenient for audit purposes, for example.

ADLS Gen2 integration is possible at the tenant and the workspace levels.

Configure storage at the tenant level

Before you connect your own storage to the Power BI service, ensure that the following requirements are met:

- You've got the Owner, Storage Blob Data Owner, and Storage Blob Data Reader roles at the storage account level, scoped to *This resource*.
- The storage account has Hierarchical namespace enabled.
- The storage account and the Power BI service are in the same Azure Active Directory and region.
- The minimum TLS version of the storage account is set to Version 1.2.

Note that storage accounts behind MFA and firewall scenarios are currently not supported.

To connect your Azure Data Lake Storage Gen2 account in the Power BI service, perform the following steps:

1. Go to **Settings** > **Admin portal** > **Azure connections** > **Tenant-level storage**. You'll be presented with the options shown in Figure 1-23.

Connect to Azure resources

▲ Tenant-level storage

Connect an Azure Data Lake Gen2 storage account. <u>Learn more</u>

[Connect to Azure]

Subscription

Select an Option ⌄

Resource group

Select an Option ⌄

Storage account

Select an Option ⌄

Save   Cancel

FIGURE 1-23 Tenant-level storage

2. Select **Connect to Azure**.

3. Select your subscription, resource group, and storage account.

4. Select **Save**.

Once connected, you'll see the **Disconnect from Azure** option in case you want to disconnect your storage account. To disconnect the tenant storage account, you'll need to ensure that all workspaces have been disconnected from the tenant storage account. Workspace-level connections are covered next.

Configure storage at the workspace level

At the workspace level, workspace admins can be allowed to use either the default tenant connection or a separate account. To allow admins to use separate storage accounts for each workspace, go to **Settings** > **Admin portal** > **Azure connections** > **Workspace-level storage permissions** and ensure the **Allow workspace admins to connect their own storage account** option is checked.

You can configure the workspace-level storage by selecting **Settings** in a workspace, then **Azure connections** > **Storage**, where you'll see the options presented in Figure 1-24.

In the workspace storage settings, you can select the **Use the default Azure connection** option to use the tenant storage account, if it's been configured, or select **Connect to Azure** to use another storage account. Once connected, you'll see the **Disconnect from Azure** option. To disconnect a storage account from a workspace, you'll need to delete all dataflows in the workspace first. Note that the underlying data isn't automatically deleted upon disconnection; you'll need to delete the data manually from the storage account.

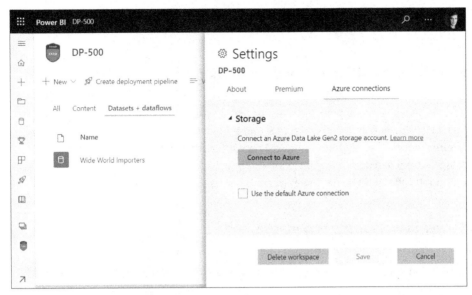

FIGURE 1-24 Workspace storage settings

Integrate an existing Power BI workspace into Azure Synapse Analytics

The amount of data generated by systems has been growing, and so has its use by businesses. More data to process means new tools needed to deliver. That's what sparked the transition from the data warehouse to the data lake, and now to the Lakehouse.

Processing vast amounts of data has become possible thanks to distributed computing and parallel processing. One of the foremost engines for parallel processing is Apache Spark. Apache Spark takes your code and executes it on multiple machines, in-memory, without you having to deal with the complexity of the task. Everything that you do in traditional ETL is made available in parallel. Not only that, but Apache Spark also includes streaming capabilities and machine learning (ML) libraries.

What is Azure Synapse Analytics?

Azure Synapse Analytics is the modern data analytics product from Microsoft. It bundles together a couple of technologies and capabilities: SQL Server and Apache Spark. Azure Synapse Analytics allows you to create notebooks and write code in all languages supported by Apache Spark, plus C#. Alternatively, there are no-code tools within Azure Synapse Analytics. They also leverage the two engines: Apache Spark or SQL Server.

Azure Synapse Analytics is a great solution for modern data analytics because of its pace of innovation and its integration with other Azure and Microsoft products. We have already reviewed the integration between Azure Synapse Analytics and Microsoft Purview. Another important integration is between Azure Synapse Analytics and Power BI.

The integration between Power BI and Synapse

Integrating Azure Synapse Analytics with Power BI gives you the ability to do data processing in parallel, as well as streaming and machine learning, and to get actionable insights from your data. Once Power BI is linked to Azure Synapse Analytics, it becomes possible to create and consume reports directly from Synapse. The SQL Server engine of Synapse—either via a serverless SQL pool or a dedicated SQL pool—is responsible for querying the data lake. One of the benefits is having multiple data roles working on the same platform.

Link Power BI workspace to Synapse

To link a Power BI workspace to Azure Synapse Analytics, follow these steps:

1. Starting in Azure Synapse Analytics, go to **Manage** > **Linked Services** > **+ New**, as shown in Figure 1-25.

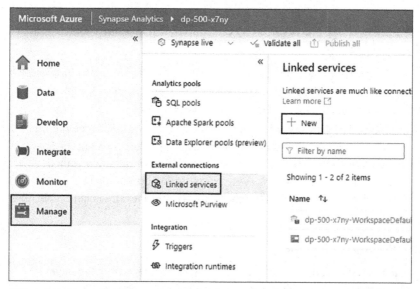

FIGURE 1-25 Screenshot of Azure Synapse Analytics menu to create a new Linked Services

2. Select **Power BI** and then **Continue**, as shown in Figure 1-26.

3. Enter a name and an optional description.

4. Select the Power BI workspace from the **Workspace name** drop-down menu and select **Create**.

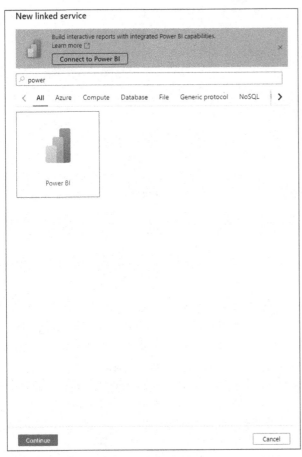

FIGURE 1-26 Screenshot of Azure Synapse Analytics selection of Linked Services, with a focus on Power BI

Skill 1.3: Manage the analytics development lifecycle

To industrialize your data analytics platform, you will have to embrace automation and DevOps practices. This will translate into source control for Azure Synapse Analytics and Power BI. It will also mean introducing automated deployment pipelines, and administration will have to be done programmatically with templates, the Power BI REST API, and the XMLA endpoint.

Commit code and artifacts to a source control repository in Azure Synapse Analytics

Historically, data analysts haven't been preoccupied by DevOps. DevOps is a practice known by software engineers when they write code. Data analysts can write SQL, but they don't necessarily keep track of it. And when it comes to no-code solutions, like no-code ETLs, or simply creating reports, tracking changes is kept manual and error prone.

However, there is a lot of value in DevOps practices for all the data roles. The goal of DevOps is to increase the quality of the software product. For us data analysts, it will mean increasing the quality of the data product. One of the few principles of DevOps is CI/CD (continuous integration/continuous delivery). It is the idea of introducing automation at every stage of the software development process: code changes, testing, validation, build, release, deployment. The first step of CI/CD is to track code changes in a version control system.

Azure Synapse Analytics doesn't track code changes by default. But you can enable it, as a first step, to increase the quality of your data products.

Connecting a source control repository to Azure Synapse Analytics

You can connect Azure Synapse Analytics either to GitHub or to Azure DevOps Git. Let's look at both ways.

GITHUB

1. In Synapse Studio, in the **Data**, **Develop**, or **Integrate** section, from the **Synapse Live** drop-down menu, select **Set up code repository**, as shown in Figure 1-27.

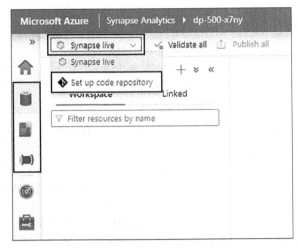

FIGURE 1-27 The Synapse Live drop-down menu

2. For **Repository type** select GitHub.

3. Enter your GitHub account that owns the repository in **GitHub repository owner**, as shown in Figure 1-28.

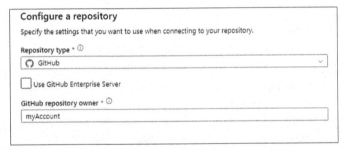

FIGURE 1-28 GitHub parameters for integration with Azure Synapse Analytics

4. Select **Continue**. You will be prompted to give Synapse access to your GitHub repository.

AZURE DEVOPS GIT

1. In Synapse Studio, in the **Data**, **Develop**, or **Integrate** section, from the **Synapse Live** drop-down menu, select **Set up code repository**, as shown in Figure 1-27.

2. For **Repository type** select Azure DevOps Git.

3. Select your **Azure Active Directory** from the drop-down list.

4. Select your repository from the drop-down list, or use a repository link directly.

5. Click **Apply**.

Recommend a deployment strategy for Power BI assets

The simplest deployment strategy for Power BI assets would include a Power BI report developer publishing their report from Power BI Desktop and subsequently overwriting the same report by publishing new report versions. This strategy may be sufficient in small organizations or small teams, where report changes are infrequent, and the same people rarely work on the same assets at the same time. In such cases, a "master" version of a PBIX file may be kept somewhere as the latest version—we'll review source control strategies later in this chapter.

In many enterprises, a more elaborate deployment strategy may be preferable. For example, a business user may request a change to a report, and while you're developing a new version of the report, the original version should still be accessible to users. Furthermore, you may want to have someone test the new version, and again, the original version should remain in use until the changes are accepted. A deployment strategy can help address the issues associated with multiple versions of Power BI assets.

Large organizations often use application lifecycle management (ALM) to minimize the effort associated with development and deployment of Power BI assets. In practice this means that large organizations often have the following three deployment stages:

1. **Development**—This is the initial stage, where Power BI developers publish the updated versions of Power BI assets that they intend to test later. This stage is usually available only to developers of Power BI assets. It's important to always start with this stage and not skip it, especially in team environments, because if you make changes in a subsequent stage and someone else deploys to the development stage first, your changes may be lost. At this stage, you usually load minimum amounts of data.

2. **Test**—This stage is designed to get a small number of testers or business users to test the new versions of Power BI assets. The assets that successfully pass tests are deployed to the final—production—stage, and the assets that don't meet the requirements are developed further in the development stage. Again, when making changes, it's important to start in the development stage instead of making changes directly in the test or even production stage. This stage is usually accessible to developers and those business users who are designated to perform testing. Usually you load larger volumes of data in this stage compared to the development stage.

3. **Production**—This is the final stage that contains Power BI assets that have been tested and accepted. Usually, this is the stage that's visible to most business users.

Figure 1-29 shows the workflow diagram with three stages of ALM.

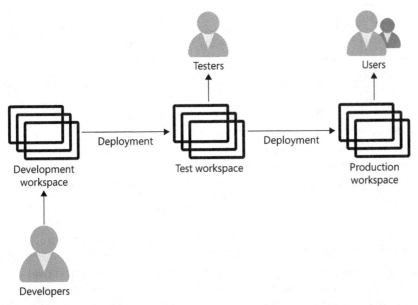

Testers

Users

Deployment

Deployment

Development
workspace

Test workspace

Production
workspace

Developers

FIGURE 1-29 ALM workflow

The names of stages may vary in different companies—for example, you may encounter Dev/UAT/Prod, which often means the same as Development/Test/Production.

In the Power BI service, you can use deployment pipelines that will help you manage different stages effectively. By using deployment pipelines, you can avoid keeping several copies of each Power BI asset outside of the Power BI service. Furthermore, deployment pipelines can show you which assets differ between deployment stages. We'll review deployment pipelines later in this chapter.

If your organization often uses the same datasets for different reports, you should consider using shared datasets to minimize data duplication. It's best practice to publish shared datasets in a separate workspace from reports. We'll cover shared datasets later in this chapter.

Recommend a source control strategy for Power BI assets

When you publish a report to the Power BI service, there's no version control, so when you publish a new version of a report, it will overwrite the old version and the old version will be lost. Especially in corporate environments, where keeping multiple versions of the same assets is not trivial, you should have a source control strategy.

Source control, also known as version control, is a system for tracking changes. Source control can be used to prevent work from being lost and to enable you to recover previous versions of your Power BI assets. Some of the tools you may choose include SharePoint and various Git solutions, and there are a few factors to consider.

First, you should consider the background of your Power BI developers. If most of your
Power BI developers do not have a coding background and usually use PBIX files, then you may
find SharePoint easier to use than a Git implementation. SharePoint will store file versions, and
you'll be able to recover prior versions of your PBIX files. If there are conflicting changes, you'll
need to merge the changes manually. To minimize the conflicts, you can check in and check
out files in SharePoint.

On the other hand, if your developers use BIM files created in Tabular Editor or Visual
Studio, then you may want to use a Git solution. Git allows its users to pull the code behind a
dataset, make changes to it, push the changes, and merge. In this way, you can have multiple
developers working on one dataset at the same time. Note that Power BI reports, which are
PBIX files, are binary, and you can't track changes within files by using Git alone, so you may
want to avoid storing PBIX files in Git. You can use a combination of SharePoint and Git: store
PBIX files on SharePoint and BIM files in Git.

In your organization, the choice of a source control strategy should depend on the project:

- Use SharePoint if you develop PBIX files only so that you can track versions.
- Use Git for BIM files and SharePoint for PBIX files if your team develops datasets in Tabular Editor or Visual Studio.

Again, the Power BI service by itself should not be used as the only repository for your
reports. Although there's little you can do in case of dataflows, you can export dataflow
models in JSON and use Git to track changes. You can also use deployment pipelines for both
dataflows and datamarts, covered next.

Implement and manage deployment pipelines in Power BI

As mentioned previously in the chapter, deployment pipelines in the Power BI service allow you
to improve the process of developing, testing, and making the content available to end users

by reducing the amount of manual work and possibility of inconsistency. Deployment pipelines offer the following benefits:

- **A single view of all stages**—There's a separate workspace for development, test, and production stages. For each stage, you can create or update the corresponding app.
- **Automatic change of data sources and parameters**—You can set up rules that will be followed when deploying from one stage to the next.
- **Selective deployment**—For scenarios where you have multiple reports in the development stage and only some are ready to be tested, you can select those in the deployment pipeline and deploy only them to the next stage. Alternatively, you can deploy all content.
- **Refreshing all datasets at once**—You can refresh all datasets within a single stage with a single click.
- **Content comparison**—You can compare two stages and see the differences between them. Note that you'll be comparing metadata only, not the underlying data.

> **NOTE DEPLOYMENT PIPELINES LICENSING AND PERMISSIONS**
> To create a deployment pipeline, all workspaces need to reside in Premium capacity, and you need to be an admin in workspaces.

Using deployment pipelines can be divided into four stages:

1. Create a pipeline.
2. Assign workspaces.
3. Develop and test content.
4. Share with users.

Create a pipeline

You can create a pipeline in one of two ways:

- From a workspace by selecting **Create deployment pipeline**
- From the **Deployment pipelines** menu in the Power BI service by selecting **Create a pipeline**

When creating a pipeline, you'll need to specify a name and, optionally, provide a description. Figure 1-30 shows a newly created deployment pipeline.

FIGURE 1-30 Deployment pipeline

You can share a pipeline with other content developers by selecting **Access** when viewing a deployment pipeline, as shown in Figure 1-31.

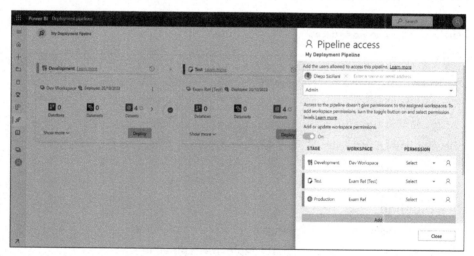

FIGURE 1-31 Deployment pipeline access

Note that access to a deployment pipeline is managed separately from access to each workspace, and you can grant access to workspaces at the same time that you give access to a deployment pipeline. While you can grant access to individual users, Microsoft recommends using security groups to manage pipeline and workspace access instead of adding specific users.

The next step is to assign workspaces to stages.

Assign workspaces

Initially, you'll need to select one workspace and assign it to a deployment stage (development, test, or production). It's most common to start by assigning a workspace to the *Development* stage. After you select a workspace, you'll need to confirm your choice by selecting **Assign a workspace**.

Workspaces for other stages can be created automatically from the pipeline when you deploy content, or you can assign existing workspaces to stages. If you do not see a workspace in the list of available workspaces to assign, it could be due to one of the following issues:

- You aren't a workspace admin.
- The workspace isn't in Premium capacity.
- The workspace is already assigned in another deployment pipeline.
- The workspace is a template app workspace.

Note that you don't necessarily need to have all three stages assigned—you can use two adjacent stages, too.

You can view the workspace content in a deployment pipeline by selecting **Show more** under a workspace. You can also unassign a workspace from a stage by selecting **Unassign workspace** in the deployment stage options.

Once you assign the workspaces, you can use your deployment pipeline.

Develop and test content

Typically, you'll publish to the development workspace first, then deploy to testing once the content is ready. Note that you deploy metadata only; you'll need to refresh datasets to populate them with data after deployment.

When deploying, you can deploy all content in the current workspace to the next stage by selecting **Deploy**. Figure 1-32 shows the Deploy buttons under the Development and Test stages. The final stage, Production, has the **Update app** button instead of **Deploy**.

FIGURE 1-32 Deploy options

Alternatively, you can deploy the content selectively. Deployment pipelines allow you to compare content between adjacent stages, so you can see what changed by selecting **Compare**, as shown in Figure 1-33.

FIGURE 1-33 Compare content

Once you see the list of content, you can select the content you want to deploy. There are two things to note about selective deployment:

- You cannot deploy content to a stage that does not have the artifacts the content depends on. For example, you cannot deploy a report if its dataset isn't available in the target stage.

- If you deploy dependent content without the artifacts the content depends on, you may get unexpected results. For example, if you added a new table in a dataset and create visuals based on the new table and you deploy the report only, you'll get errors.

Whichever way you choose to deploy, you'll have an option to add a note to your deployment, which will be visible in the deployment history. To view deployment history, select **Deployment history** when viewing a pipeline (see Figure 1-34).

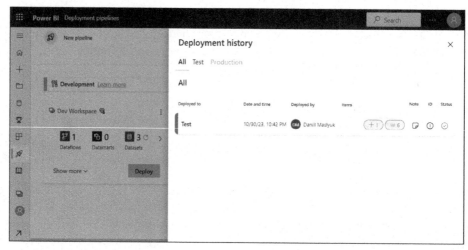

FIGURE 1-34 Deployment history

Another useful feature of deployment pipelines is deployment rules, which allow you to update data sources or parameter values when deploying. For example, you can update the data source from a dev to a test environment, or you can increase the number of rows to import after deployment; you may use a small subset of your fact table for development and a full table for testing. Deployment rules are available for dataflows, datasets, datamarts, and paginated repots.

Deployment rules are only available for the Test and Production stages. To edit deployment rules, select **Deployment settings** (the thunderbolt and cog icon) in the upper-right corner of the deployment stage where you want to apply deployment rules. Figure 1-35 shows an example of a deployment rule, where a parameter's value is updated.

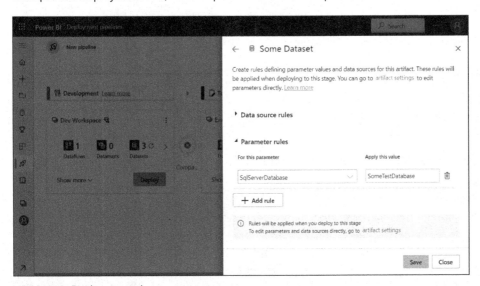

FIGURE 1-35 Deployment rules

There are a few things to note when working with deployment rules:

- Not all data sources are supported.
- You must be the owner of the artifact that you create deployment rules for.
- If you delete an artifact or unassign a workspace, the relevant deployment rules will be lost.

Share with users

The final step is to deploy from testing to production. Again, you'll have to refresh the datasets, dataflows, and datamarts after deployment. You'll also need to update the app.

Perform impact analysis of downstream dependencies from dataflows and datasets

For content you share, such as datasets or dataflows, it may be useful to know what other reports or dashboards use a specific artifact. Since Power BI allows you to use some content across different workspaces, the dependent artifacts that use the shared content may reside outside of their home workspace, and the owner of the shared content may not always have access to the workspace. This information is contained in the artifact's impact analysis. For example, to see the impact analysis, from the dataset menu select **View lineage**. You'll see the information shown in Figure 1-36.

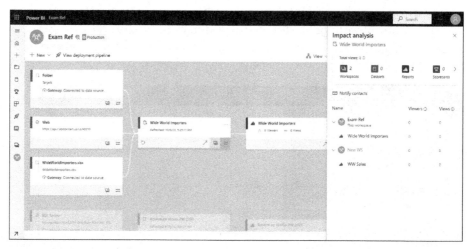

FIGURE 1-36 Impact analysis

Note how impact analysis shows the list of reports and dashboards across all workspaces related to the dataset. For each item, you can see how many viewers and views it had in the last 30 days, excluding today, and which workspace it's in. Impact analysis is particularly useful when you're making potentially breaking changes to the dataset because you know which items are going to be affected, as well as how popular those items are. You can notify contacts of the affected reports and dashboards by selecting **Notify contacts**.

Recommend automation solutions for the analytics development lifecycle, including Power BI REST API and PowerShell cmdlets

The Power BI REST API is a web service that allows the Power BI admin to programmatically manipulate Power BI resources. The cmdlets are commands executable in Windows Power-Shell. The PowerShell cmdlets allow you to do operations similar to the Power BI REST API. In fact, if there isn't an equivalent command in a PowerShell cmdlet, it is possible to simply call the Power BI REST API via PowerShell cmdlets. You must install the PowerShell cmdlets in PowerShell with this:

```
Install-Module -Name MicrosoftPowerBIMgmt
```

These commands allow you to automate the analytics development lifecycle. The primary way is by using pipelines.

Pipelines

The pipeline tool requires a Premium capacity. Pipelines are a concept anchored in DevOps, specifically CI/CD. They help to manage the lifecycle of organizational content. They allow you to deploy and work on Power BI assets in isolated environments before the end users are affected by the changes. They also include automated transition to each stage. The overall goal is to eliminate manual actions, and therefore errors, in the deployment process.

A pipeline consists of three stages:

1. **Development**—This stage is for the Power BI developers, sometimes called a sandbox, where they can look at their design for the first time in the Power BI service.

2. **Test**—This stage usually involves other users than the Power BI developers; sometimes dedicated testers, or some power users are involved in testing the quality of the reports and other Power BI assets. It's also where performance can be assessed against production load.

3. **Production**—This is the final stage of the pipeline, where the end users will be able to consume the Power BI assets.

There is no manual intervention to move an asset from one stage to another. That ensures that the quality of the assets is optimal.

In the Power BI REST API, a number of operations can be executed over pipelines. Here are some common ones:

- **Create Pipeline**—Creates a new pipeline. The command is

```
POST https://api.powerbi.com/v1.0/myorg/pipelines
```

- **Deploy All**—Deploy all assets from one stage to the next. The command is

```
POST https://api.powerbi.com/v1.0/myorg/pipelines/{pipelineId}/deployAll
```

- **Selective Deploy**—Deploy specific assets from one stage to the next. The command is

```
POST https://api.powerbi.com/v1.0/myorg/pipelines/{pipelineId}/deploy
```

> **NEED MORE REVIEW?** **OPERATIONS AVAILABLE ON PIPELINES**
>
> For a list of all the operations available on pipelines, please visit *https://learn.microsoft.com/en-us/rest/api/power-bi/pipelines.*

Deploy and manage datasets by using the XMLA endpoint

When you use a Power BI Premium or Embedded capacity, you can use the XML for Analysis (XMLA) endpoint to connect to your datasets. By using XMLA endpoints, you can get data from a Power BI dataset and use a client tool other than Power BI to interact with the data. For example, you can visualize the data in Excel, or you can use a third-party tool to edit your dataset.

To use the XMLA endpoints for deployment and management of datasets, the option **Allow XMLA endpoints and Analyze in Excel with on-premises datasets** must be enabled in the Power BI admin portal. The **XMLA Endpoint** setting in the capacity settings must also be set to **Read Write**.

When making a connection by using the XMLA endpoint, you connect to a Power BI workspace as if it were a server, with datasets acting as databases. To get the workspace connection address, go to the workspace settings and select **Premium** > **Workspace Connection** > **Copy**, as shown in Figure 1-37.

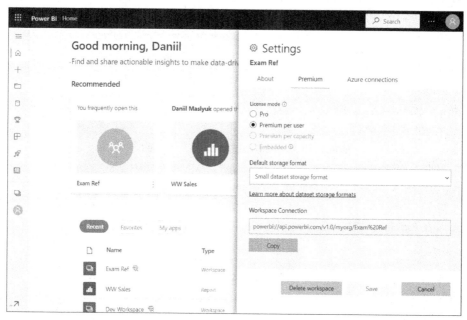

FIGURE 1-37 The Premium section of workspace settings

The address will have the following format:

```
powerbi://api.powerbi.com/v1.0/myorg/Your Workspace Name
```

You can then use the address as a server address when making a connection in your client tool. Most client tools will allow you to select a dataset after you connect to your workspace. Some client tools require setting an initial catalog—in this case, use the name of a dataset you want to connect to.

> **NOTE USING AZURE B2B AND XMLA ENDPOINT**
>
> If you're a B2B user in someone's tenant and want to connect to their dataset by using the XMLA endpoint, you'll need to replace *myorg* with their domain name, so the workspace connection string will look like *powerbi://api.powerbi.com/v1.0/contoso.com/Your Workspace Name*.

When you connect to a workspace from Tabular Editor, you can select a dataset and edit it. You can also deploy a new dataset to a workspace by using Tabular Editor if you perform the following steps:

1. Create a new model or open an existing one from a file, database, or a folder, and make edits as necessary.
2. Select **Model** > **Deploy**.
3. Enter the workspace connection string in **Server** and select **Next**.
4. Select an existing dataset or enter the new dataset name in **Database Name** and select **Next**.
5. Select the elements you want to deploy and select **Next**, then **Deploy**.
6. Refresh your dataset.

Tabular Editor will only deploy metadata, which is why you need to refresh your dataset as the last step if your changes include more than measure updates.

Note that you can use other tools, such as Visual Studio, to deploy and manage datasets. A description of all these tools is outside the scope of this book.

Create reusable assets, including Power BI templates, Power BI data source (PBIDS) files, and shared datasets

When you work in an organization with multiple report developers, often you need to develop reports in a consistent fashion. In this section, we'll explore several tools available in Power BI:

- Templates
- Power BI data source files
- Shared datasets

Templates

You can create templates in Power BI Desktop so that others can use your template as a starting point for their own reports. Besides the time that can be saved by using a template, greater consistency will exist between reports in the organization.

Power BI templates (PBIT files) contain the following:

- Queries, including parameters
- Data model, including DAX formulas, relationships, etc.
- Report pages, visuals, bookmarks, etc.

Power BI templates don't include the data or credentials.

To create a Power BI template from an existing report, select **File** > **Export** > **Power BI template**. You'll be prompted to enter an optional template description and save the file.

To use a Power BI template, you can open its file as you normally would, or you can open Power BI Desktop first, then select **File** > **Import** > **Power BI template**. Either way, you'll be prompted to specify the parameter values, if any, and then Power BI will load the data and create a report for you, which you can then edit further, save, and publish to the Power BI service.

PBIDS files

If you've already connected to data in Power BI Desktop, you can export PBIDS files, which have data source connection details embedded in them. They can be useful when you want to make it easier for report creators to connect to specific data sources.

To export a PBIDS file in Power BI Desktop, start by going to data source settings by selecting **Transform data** > **Data source settings**. You'll see a list of data sources like the one in Figure 1-38.

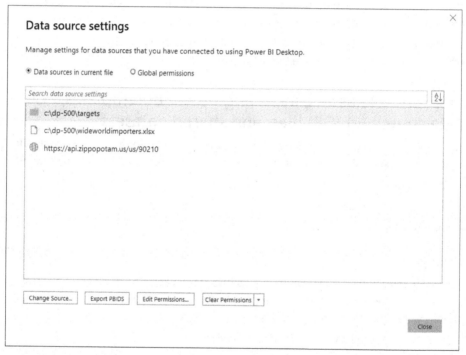

FIGURE 1-38 Data source settings

To export a PBIDS file for a data source, select the data source from the list and then select **Export PBIDS**, which will prompt you to save the new PBIDS file.

For example, if we export a folder data source, we'll get a PBIDS file with code similar to the following:

```
{
    "version": "0.1",
    "connections": [
        {
```

```
    "details": {
      "protocol": "folder",
      "address": {
        "path": "c:\\dp-500\\targets"
      },
      "authentication": null,
      "query": null
    },
    "options": {},
    "mode": null
  }
]
}
```

When you open a PBIDS file, the experience is the same as when you connect to the data source in a new Power BI Desktop file.

> **NOTE CREDENTIALS**
>
> PBIDS files do not contain credentials, so users still need to be able to access the data sources.

Shared datasets

A shared dataset is a dataset in the Power BI service used by a report from a different workspace. A dataset creator can allow others to build reports from their dataset by using the Build permission. Using shared datasets has several benefits:

- You ensure consistent data across different reports.
- When connecting to a shared dataset, you are not copying any data needlessly.
- You can create a copy of an existing report and modify it, which takes less effort than starting from scratch.

> **NOTE USING SHARED DATASETS**
>
> Sometimes different teams want to see the same data by using different visuals. In that case, it makes sense to create a single dataset and different reports that all connect to the same dataset.

You can connect to a shared dataset from either Power BI Desktop or the Power BI service:

- In Power BI Desktop, select **Data hub** > **Power BI datasets** on the **Home** tab.
- In the Power BI service, when you are in a workspace, select **New** > **Report** > **Pick a published dataset**.

Either way, you will then see a list of shared datasets you can connect to, as shown in Figure 1-39.

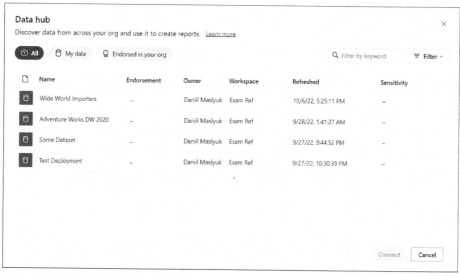

FIGURE 1-39 List of available datasets

After you are connected to a shared dataset in Power BI Desktop, some user interface buttons will be grayed out or missing because this connectivity mode comes with limitations. For example, when you connect to a shared dataset, Power Query Editor is not available and the Data view is missing. In the lower-right corner, you'll see the name and workspace you're connected to, as shown in Figure 1-40.

> Connected live to the Power BI dataset: Wide World Importers in Exam Ref

FIGURE 1-40 Power BI Desktop connected to a Power BI dataset

To change the dataset you are connected to, you can select the **Transform Data** label and then **Data source settings**, which will bring you back to the list of datasets available to you.

Note that you can still create measures, and they will be saved in your PBIX file but not in the shared dataset itself. That means other users who connect to the same shared dataset will not see the measures you created. These measures are known as *local* or *report-level* measures.

Chapter summary

- Add governance to your data platform by registering and scanning data assets in Microsoft Purview.
- Add observability to your data platform by searching and browsing data assets in Microsoft Purview. Also, the integration between Microsoft Purview and Power BI will provide a central point for data governance.

- For optimal Power BI governance and administration, periodically review the tenant settings, preferably letting users know which settings are currently applied.

- Monitor and audit your data platform in a programmatic way. By using the Power BI REST API and the PowerShell cmdlets, as well as the integrated reports offered in Power BI, you can make sense of who is doing what in your platform.

- Translate requirements into a licensing strategy when it comes to number and types of users, as well as performance and features.

- You can manage Power BI Premium capacities in the admin portal to oversee the utilization of your resources and apply settings that suit your usage patterns better.

- When working with on-premises data, you need to install and use an on-premises data gateway. For data behind corporate virtual networks (VNets), you can use a VNet gateway, which is an online service from Microsoft.

- Power BI dataflows can write data to your own Azure Data Lake Storage Gen2, allowing you to reuse dataflows outside of Power BI. You can also view data snapshots when using your own storage.

- Integrate Power BI with Azure Synapse Analytics. That allows you to leverage the ETL capabilities of Azure Synapse Analytics, and its parallel processing, with the data analysis capabilities of Power BI. You can effectively bring together your data engineers, data scientists, and data analysts on this integrated platform.

- Make the first step toward DevOps for data product by connecting a source control repository to your Azure Synapse Analytics.

- For scenarios when there are multiple report developers, you should have a deployment strategy that includes several stages, such as development, test, and production.

- Depending on your project, you may want to store PBIX files on SharePoint and BIM files in Git, because the Power BI service does not keep any versions or track changes.

- Deployment pipelines in the Power BI service allow you to streamline content deployment, having three different stages: development, test, and production.

- When your content, such as datasets and dataflows, are reused across different workspaces, you can use the lineage view to understand the impact analysis, especially if you're about to deploy potentially breaking changes.

- Manage programmatically your development lifecycle by using the Power BI REST API and PowerShell cmdlets.

- The XMLA endpoint offers a way to deploy and manage datasets by using third-party tools such as Tabular Editor.

- Power BI Desktop allows you to create reusable content, such as templates and data source files. Datasets that are used for more than one report or across workspaces become shared datasets, leading to improved data consistency and less data duplication.

Thought experiment

In this thought experiment, demonstrate your skills and knowledge of the topics covered in this chapter. You can find the answers in the section that follows.

You are an enterprise data analyst at Contoso responsible for creating and distributing Power BI reports, as well as administrating the analytics environments. Contoso uses Power BI Premium. Management requested that you build and share some of your reports with a wider audience.

Based on background information and business requirements, answer the following questions:

1. Your team would like to collaborate more closely with the data engineers in the organization. Which tool for ETL processing should you integrate with Power BI?

   A. Microsoft Purview

   B. Azure Synapse Analytics

   C. GitHub

   D. Azure DevOps

2. Your team would like to increase the quality of their data products in Azure Synapse Analytics. What is the first DevOps step you should recommend in order to meet that goal?

   A. Increase data quality checks in Power BI.

   B. Integrate a version control tool like GitHub.

   C. Enable deployment pipelines in Power BI.

   D. Register the data source in Microsoft Purview.

3. In your team of six, there are five members who don't create reports but need to consult them. Additionally, you need to be able to use the datamart feature of Power BI. Which licensing plan should you recommend? Your solution should minimize cost.

   A. 6 Pro licenses

   B. 6 Premium Per User licenses

   C. 1 Pro license

   D. 5 Premium Per User licenses and 1 Pro license

4. Your team mainly uses PBIX files and does not currently use BIM files for data models. Which tool should you use for source control?

   A. SharePoint

   B. Git

   C. SharePoint and Git

   D. Power BI service

5. Your organization has a brand team that dictates the style of reports, and you want all new reports to use the same Date table. Which tool you should use to improve the adherence to the brand team's guidelines?

   A. Power BI templates

   B. Power BI report themes

   C. Power BI data source files

   D. Shared datasets

6. You create a report based on data from Azure SQL Database. You publish the report to the Power BI service, and you need to ensure that the dataset is updated every day at midnight. Contoso does not use any special network configuration. Which gateway configuration do you need to use? Your solution must minimize the configuration effort.

   A. On-premises data gateway (personal mode)

   B. On-premises data gateway (standard mode)

   C. VNet gateway

   D. No gateway is necessary.

7. You often get requests for changes in your reports, and you need the original changes to be available via apps until your changes are approved by a report tester. How can you make your changes visible to a report tester? Your solution must minimize the data duplication and manual effort.

   A. Send the report tester a PBIX file with changes.

   B. Publish a version of the report with the UAT suffix and add it to the app.

   C. Use a deployment pipeline.

Thought experiment answers

1. The answer is **B**. Azure Synapse Analytics is the ETL tool used by data engineers that integrates with Power BI. Microsoft Purview is not an ETL tool, so option A is incorrect. GitHub and Azure DevOps are version control systems, not ETLs, so options C and D are incorrect.

2. The answer is **B**. Enabling version control is the first DevOps step to increase the quality of the data.

3. The answer is **C**. Contoso is using Power BI Premium, so the capacity license includes the datamart feature and the ability for all to consult reports; you would just need 1 Pro license to create them. Options A, B, and D would work but they don't minimize the cost and so they are incorrect.

4. The answer is **A**. For PBIX files, SharePoint works well when BIM files aren't used. Git is best for BIM files since it's not a good choice for large binary files, and PBIX files are binary, so B and C are both incorrect. Option D is incorrect because the Power BI service does not keep any version history of reports or datasets.

5. The answer is **A**. Power BI templates can hold Power BI themes and have some predefined data model elements, such as the Date table. Power BI report themes can only be used for styling, and a data source file cannot contain any styling elements, so options B and C are wrong. A shared dataset can contain a Date table, although it won't contain a theme, so option D is also wrong.

6. The answer is **D**. Since Contoso has no special network configuration in place, the Azure SQL Database can be accessed without a gateway. Options A, B, and C are incorrect because they suggest using a data gateway.

7. The answer is **C**. A deployment pipeline will reduce the manual effort by streamlining the deployment of your content. It will also allow a report tester to see a test version of the report and keep the current production app as is until you decide to deploy your changes to production. Option A is incorrect because the report tester may not be a user of Power BI Desktop, and you'll be sending a report duplicate with all necessary data, which may be against security policies. Option B would be acceptable if you couldn't use deployment pipelines; publishing different versions involves more effort than deploying by using deployment pipelines.

Query and transform data

Data duplication is natural in an organization. Data needs to be queried and transformed in a format that is most suitable for the use case. This is true even at the lowest level, in a database, where data is duplicated in the form of indexes to optimize reads.

Similarly, in an organization data will be queried and transformed from the operational to the analytical system(s), and queried and transformed again through the various layers of the analytical stack. In this chapter we will review how this is done with Azure Synapse and Power BI.

Skills covered in this chapter:

- 2.1: Query data by using Azure Synapse Analytics
- 2.2: Ingest and transform data by using Power BI

Skill 2.1: Query data by using Azure Synapse Analytics

There is no doubt that the amount of data generated and used by businesses is growing. And so are the requirements for near-real-time analytics; we want more insight and sooner. On top of that, the complexity of the analysis is increasing. With predictive and prescriptive solutions, we go beyond descriptive and diagnostic analytics.

To meet all these increasingly demanding requirements, data tools are multiplying. But there is value in a single platform: ease of training, reduced cognitive load, easier cross-team collaboration, fewer silos in the organization. . . . Azure Synapse Analytics is all about bringing together data engineers, data scientists, and data analysts in order to achieve more with your data.

> **This skill covers how to:**
> - Identify an appropriate Azure Synapse pool when analyzing data
> - Recommend appropriate file types for querying serverless SQL pools
> - Query relational data sources in dedicated or serverless SQL pools, including querying partitioned data sources
> - Use a machine learning PREDICT function in a query

Identify an appropriate Azure Synapse pool when analyzing data

Azure Synapse Analytics is an extremely rich platform (see Figure 2-1). As the requirements around data become more and more complex, so does the need for features. Azure Synapse Analytics can be seen as a one-stop shop for data in your organization, bringing together data engineers, data scientists, and data analysts.

Overall architecture of Azure Synapse Analytics

In Chapter 1, we reviewed the tight integration with Microsoft Purview, and with Power BI. Azure Synapse Analytics comes with a default data store: the Azure Data Lake Storage Gen2, although it is possible to link more data stores to your Azure Synapse Analytics. The default data store supports Delta Lake, an open source storage layer that comes on top of the Data Lake Storage and brings ACID transactions to Apache Spark.

> **NOTE ACID**
>
> ACID is the acronym for Atomicity, Consistency, Isolation, and Durability. One database implementation of ACID is not necessarily equivalent to another. For example, there are many levels of consistency possible in a data store. Nonetheless, ACID still provides more guarantees than BASE (Basically Available, Soft state, Eventual consistency).

Azure Synapse Analytics offers two query engines: Apache Spark and SQL. We will review both technologies and their various flavors in this chapter. These query engines allow for batch processing, parallel processing, stream processing, and machine learning workload. The beauty of Azure Synapse Analytics is also the variety of languages you can work with. SQL is the first to come to mind, but there is also Scala, Python, R, and last but not least, C#. Finally, Synapse Pipelines enables data transformations, even in a parallel computing fashion, with a low code tool.

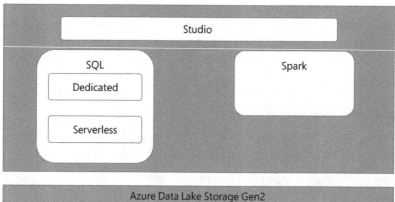

FIGURE 2-1 Overall architecture diagram of Azure Synapse Analytics

Concepts about Spark Pool

Apache Spark is a framework for in-memory parallel processing. It was first released in 2014, with the goal to provide a unified platform for data engineering and data science, as well as batch and streaming—a mission that resonates with Azure Synapse Analytics. Apache Spark is originally written in Scala, but also available in Python, SQL, and R. In Azure Synapse Analytics, Apache Spark is also available in C#.

Apache Spark runs on a cluster, as you can see in Figure 2-2.

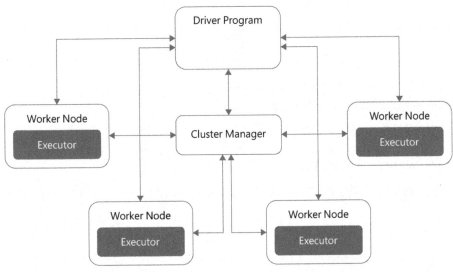

FIGURE 2-2 High-level overview of a Spark cluster

A Spark application is coordinated by the *driver program*. On a cluster, the *driver program* connects to the *cluster manager* to coordinate the work. In Azure Synapse Analytics, the *cluster manager* is YARN. The *cluster manager* is responsible for allocating resources (memory, cores, etc.) in the cluster. Once the *driver* is connected to the *cluster manager*, it acquires resources to create *executors*. *Executors* will be the ones doing the work: running in-memory computations and storing data.

An Azure Spark pool is not just a Spark instance on a cluster. Azure Synapse provides peripheral features:

- **Auto-Scale capabilities**—The Auto-Scale feature automatically scales up and down the number of nodes in a cluster. You can set a minimum and maximum number of nodes when creating a new Spark pool. Every 30 seconds, Auto-Scale monitors the number of CPUs and the amount of memory needed to complete all pending jobs, as well as the current total CPUs and memory, and scales up or down based on these metrics.

- **Apache Livy**—Apache Livy is a REST API for Apache Spark. Conveniently, it is included in Azure Spark pools. Apache Livy can be used to submit programmatically Spark jobs to the cluster.

- **Preloaded Anaconda libraries**—Apache Spark is great for parallel computing, but sometimes we don't need all that computing power, but instead want some more specialized functionalities for machine learning or visualization. Particularly during exploratory analysis, having Anaconda libraries preloaded in Azure Spark pools comes in handy.

An Azure Spark pool is a great tool when dealing with a large amount of data and when performance matters. Should it be data preparation, machine learning, or streaming data, a Spark pool is the right tool if you want to work in Python, SQL, Scala, or C#.

EXAMPLE OF HOW TO USE IT

To review how to use an Azure Spark pool, we will start by creating an Azure Synapse Analytics resource.

1. In your Azure portal, select **Create a resource**.
2. Search for and select **Azure Synapse Analytics**.
3. Select **Create**.
4. Once the resource is created, navigate to the resource and select **Open Synapse Studio**, as shown in Figure 2-3.

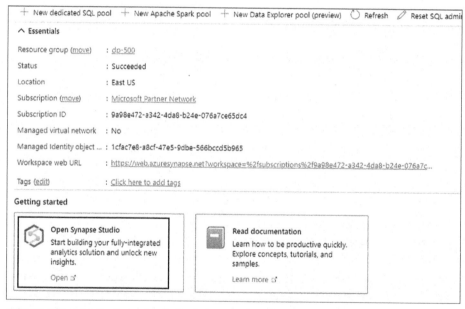

FIGURE 2-3 Synapse Resource view in the Azure portal

Now that we have our resource, let's create the Spark pool.

1. Go to **Manage**, as shown in Figure 2-4.
2. Navigate to **Apache Spark pools** > **+ New**.
3. Enter a name in **Apache Spark pool name**, like dp500.

FIGURE 2-4 The Manage menu in Azure Synapse Analytics Studio

4. Set **Isolated compute** to Disabled.

5. Set **Node size family** as Memory Optimized.

6. Set **Node size** to Small.

7. Set **Autoscale** to Enabled.

8. Set **Number of nodes** to 3 and 5.

9. Review that you have the same configuration as Figure 2-5.

10. Select **Review + create**.

11. Select **Create**.

Now that we have our compute, we can use it to query and analyze some data. To do that, we first need to get some data.

1. Navigate to https://www.nyc.gov/site/tlc/about/tlc-trip-record-data.page and download the January 2022 Green Taxi Trip Records.

2. In the Synapse Studio, navigate to the Data menu, as shown in Figure 2-6.

New Apache Spark pool

Basics •   Additional settings *   Tags   Review + create

Create an Synapse Analytics Apache Spark pool with your preferred configurations. Complete the Basics tab then go to Review + Create to provision with smart defaults, or visit each tab to customize.

Apache Spark pool details

Name your Apache Spark pool and choose its initial settings.

Apache Spark pool name *	dp500
Isolated compute * ⓘ	○ Enabled ⦿ Disabled
Node size family *	Memory Optimized ⌄
Node size *	Small (4 vCores / 32 GB) ⌄
Autoscale * ⓘ	⦿ Enabled ○ Disabled
Number of nodes *	3 ◯———————— 5
Estimated price ⓘ	**Est. cost per hour** 1.40 to 2.33 EUR View pricing details
Dynamically allocate executors * ⓘ	○ Enabled ⦿ Disabled

FIGURE 2-5 Configuration parameters for the Apache Spark pool

FIGURE 2-6 Data menu in Synapse Studio

3. Select the **Linked** tab and then select **Azure Data Lake Storage Gen2**.

4. Expand your primary container and select your primary file store.

5. Upload your Parquet file.

6. Right-click on the uploaded file and from the context menu select **New notebook** > **Load to Dataframe**.

7. In the new notebook, attach the Spark pool you created previously.

8. Run the first cell.

After a few minutes, the time for the Spark pool to spin up, you should see a table with the first 10 rows of the dataset, as shown in Figure 2-7. The data is now loaded in memory in a Spark DataFrame, so the analysis can proceed.

View	Table	Chart	— Export results ∨				
VendorID	**lpep_pickup_datetime**		**lpep_dropoff_datetime**	**store_and_fwd_flag**	**RatecodeID**	**PULocationID**	
2	2022-01-01 00:14:21		2022-01-01 00:15:33	N	1.0	42	
1	2022-01-01 00:20:55		2022-01-01 00:29:38	N	1.0	116	
1	2022-01-01 00:57:02		2022-01-01 01:13:14	N	1.0	41	
2	2022-01-01 00:07:42		2022-01-01 00:15:57	N	1.0	181	
2	2022-01-01 00:07:50		2022-01-01 00:28:52	N	1.0	33	
1	2022-01-01 00:47:57		2022-01-01 00:54:09	N	1.0	150	
2	2022-01-01 00:13:38		2022-01-01 00:33:50	N	1.0	66	
2	2022-01-01 00:43:00		2022-01-01 00:49:20	N	1.0	40	
2	2022-01-01 00:41:04		2022-01-01 00:47:04	N	1.0	112	
2	2022-01-01 00:51:07		2022-01-01 01:09:31	N	1.0	256	

FIGURE 2-7 Results from reading the Parquet file with the Spark pool

Architecture of Synapse SQL

Before diving into the two flavors of Azure Synapse SQL, let's review the overall architecture of this part of Azure Synapse Analytics. Figure 2-8 represents the internal architecture of Azure Synapse SQL.

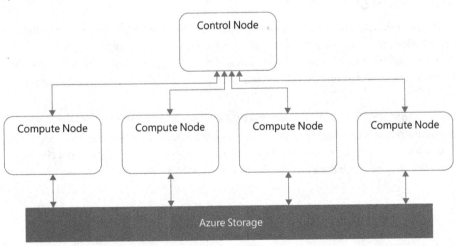

FIGURE 2-8 The internal architecture of Azure Synapse SQL

The control node is going to be the entry point of Azure Synapse SQL and the orchestrator of the distributed query to the compute node, similar to the driver node in a Spark pool. And as their name indicates, the compute nodes will do the computation.

It is important to note the decoupling of compute and storage, which will also be reflected in the pricing. You can scale your compute without affecting your storage, and vice versa.

The difference between serverless and dedicated is primarily in the number of nodes available. With serverless, the number of nodes is not predetermined and will scale automatically based on the computation needs. With dedicated, the number of nodes is preallocated.

A dedicated SQL pool also, beyond querying the data, allows ingestion of data, whereas serverless only allows querying the data. The ingestion of data will allow you to create tables in your SQL pool. Those tables will be distributed. There are three possible distributions: hash, round-robin, and replicate.

The hash distribution is typically used for large tables, such as fact tables. The round-robin is used for staging tables. And the replicate is used for small tables, such as dimensions.

EXAM TIP

You will often find questions about the optimal distribution for a use case. So it's important that you thoroughly understand each of the three distributions and when they would be appropriate to use.

NEED MORE REVIEW?   DEEP DIVE INTO DISTRIBUTIONS

If you want to review the intricacies of the distributions in Azure Synapse SQL, see the following documentation: *https://learn.microsoft.com/en-us/azure/synapse-analytics/sql/ overview-architecture#distributions.*

SQL serverless pool

Because a SQL serverless pool is serverless, that doesn't mean there is no server behind the scene, but it does mean that for you there is no infrastructure to set up or maintain. A SQL serverless pool will be automatically provisioned and ready to go when you create a Synapse Analytics workspace, and it will scale as needed. You will be charged by how much data you process.

Because of that, a SQL serverless pool is particularly suited for unpredictable workloads, such as exploratory analysis. Another perfect use case for SQL serverless pools is to create a logical data warehouse, to be queried by Power BI. Indeed, instead of provisioning a cluster so that Power BI can query your data lake, a SQL serverless pool is available whenever you need it.

EXAMPLE OF HOW TO USE IT

To see how to use SQL serverless pools, let's open our Synapse Studio:

1. Go to the **Develop** menu, as shown in Figure 2-9.

FIGURE 2-9 Develop menu in Synapse Studio

2. Select **+** > **SQL script**, as shown in Figure 2-10.

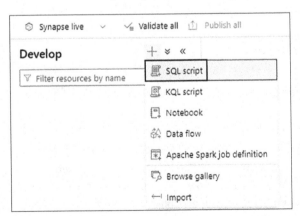

FIGURE 2-10 The Develop menu with its various capabilities

3. In the menu above the first line of the script, verify that you are connected to the **Built-in** compute. **Built-in** is the name of the SQL serverless pool automatically created for you when you create an Azure Synapse Analytics resource.

4. Using the OPENROWSET function, query the previously loaded taxi dataset, and display the top 10 rows:

```
SELECT TOP 10 *
FROM OPENROWSET(
        BULK 'https://yoursynapseresource.dfs.core.windows.net/yourfilestore/
synapse/workspaces/green_tripdata_2022-01.parquet',
FORMAT = 'PARQUET' ) AS [result]
```

5. Select **Run**.

After a few seconds—the start-up time is much less than for the Apache Spark pool—you should see a table with the first 10 rows of the dataset, as shown in Figure 2-11.

VendorID	lpep_pickup_d...	lpep_dropoff_...	store_and_fwd...	RatecodeID	PULocationID	DOLocationID	passenger_count	trip_distance	fare_amount
2	164099606100...	164099613300...	N	1	42	42	1	0.44	3.5
1	164099643500...	164099697800...	N	1	116	41	1	2.1	9.5
1	164099862200...	164099959400...	N	1	41 ·	140	1	3.7	14.5
2	164099566200...	164099615700...	N	1	181	181	1	1.69	8
2	164099567000...	164099693200...	N	1	33	170	1	6.26	22
1	164099807700...	164099844900...	N	1	150	210	1	1.3	7
2	164099601800...	164099723000...	N	1	66	67	1	6.47	22.5
2	164099778000...	164099816000...	N	1	40	195	1	1.15	6
2	164099766400...	164099802400...	N	1	112	80	1	1.3	6
2	164099826700...	164099937100...	N	1	256	186	1	4.75	17

FIGURE 2-11 Results from querying the dataset with a SQL serverless pool

EXAM TIP

It is important to understand how the function OPENROWSET works and how to use it. If you need more review, please consult the documentation here: *https://learn.microsoft.com/en-us/sql/t-sql/functions/openrowset-transact-sql?view=sql-server-ver16.*

Concepts about SQL dedicated pools

Synapse SQL dedicated pools differ from serverless in two major ways: first, because of its dedicated nature it needs to be provisioned, and second, data can be ingested in a SQL dedicated pool.

When provisioning the pool, you will have to define its size in DWUs (data warehousing units). A DWU is an abstraction representing a unit that combines CPU, memory, and I/O.

To ingest data into the dedicated pool, you can use T-SQL to query data from external sources. This is possible thanks to PolyBase, a virtualization feature that allows you to query data from various sources without the need to install a client connection software.

Table partitioning is an important topic to review for SQL dedicated pools.

ROUND-ROBIN DISTRIBUTION

Round-robin will favor data writes, not reads, so it is suitable for rapidly loading data and therefore suitable for staging tables. It randomly distributes table rows evenly across all nodes.

Querying data distributed in a round-robin fashion, particularly with joins, will yield poor performance. To accomplish that, it's better to use hash distribution.

HASH DISTRIBUTION

Hash distribution won't distribute rows randomly, but rather it will use a deterministic hash function to assign each value to a node. If two values are the same, they will be assigned to the same node. This is important to remember when choosing the column used for partitioning. If a column has skew—that is, many times the same value—one node will be a hot spot (overused) and the other nodes will barely have any data on them. So it's important to choose a column evenly distributed. The hash distribution is typical for large fact tables. For smaller tables, like dimensions, there is a third option.

REPLICATED DISTRIBUTION

As its name indicates, replicated distribution will copy the table in each node. That could be seen as a waste of space, but in a distributed workload that's a huge performance boost, since data doesn't need to move around if each node already has it. This is only possible if the table is small, so typically this distribution is used for dimension tables. The general guidance is to use replicated for tables smaller than 2 GB.

Recommend appropriate file types for querying serverless SQL pools

Synapse serverless SQL pool scales automatically and doesn't need you to provision anything. That's why it's great for unpredictable workloads and logical data warehousing. You pay depending on how much data you query. Moreover, it's important to remember that Synapse is catering for your analytics needs, not your operational needs. This affects the access patterns appropriate for Synapse serverless SQL pools. For example, an online transaction processing (OLTP) workload, updating or reading all columns of a single row, is not the appropriate use case. Analytics needs mean online analytical processing (OLAP), in other words, querying a large number of rows, on a limited number of columns, often with some aggregations performed. The ideal access pattern will be important in your choice of file to query for Synapse Analytics.

Typically three different file types can be queried with SQL serverless pools: CSV, JSON, and Parquet. CSV (comma-separated values) files are common in many businesses. JSON (JavaScript Object Notation) files are common in web applications. And Parquet files are common for analytics applications.

The syntax is the same to query them, making use of the OPENROWSET function:

```
SELECT *FROM OPENROWSET(
    BULK 'https://mydatalake.blob.core.windows.net/data/files/*.csv',
    FORMAT = 'csv') AS rows
```

Why is Parquet recommended for analytics? It comes down to the access pattern. Parquet files store the data in a columnar format, whereas JSON and CSV store files in a row format. This has two implications. First, accessing the data for OLAP queries is faster with columnar format, because the data we want to query (the whole column) is physically stored next to each other. With a CSV or JSON file, the data of the same column would be physically scattered. Second, the data is generally more homogenous in a column than in a row. Indeed, usually a row contains multiple data types, so there will be a mix of data. In a column the data has the same type and can be similar or even identical sometimes. This leads to greater potential for compression. That is why Parquet files are recommended for analytics workloads.

> **NOTE DELTA**
>
> In 2020, a new file format named Delta was released open source. It extends Parquet and includes ACID transactions. It is compatible with Synapse Analytics and is the recommended file format if you work with Spark pools.

How to query Parquet files

To review how to query a Parquet file, let's go back to our Synapse Studio:

1. Navigate to **Develop > + > SQL script**.

2. Make sure it is attached to **Built-in**, as a reminder, this is your serverless pool.

3. Using OPENROWSET, select the top 10 rows of your taxi dataset in a Parquet format:

```
SELECT
  TOP 10 *
FROM
OPENROWSET(
BULK 'https:// your-storage.dfs.core.windows.net/ your-filestore /synapse/
workspaces/green_tripdata_2022-01.parquet',
FORMAT = 'PARQUET'
) AS [result]
```

4. Select **Run**.

You should get the same results as before, as shown earlier in Figure 2-11.

Query relational data sources in dedicated or serverless SQL pools, including querying partitioned data sources

SQL pools, whether dedicated or serverless, will test your knowledge of T-SQL. Here you will learn how to query data, both with dedicated and serverless, and we will also consider partitioned data.

To review how to use SQL dedicated pools, let's go back to our Synapse Studio and:

1. Go to the **Manage** menu.

2. Under **Analytics pools** select **SQL pools > + New**.

3. Set **Dedicated SQL Pool Name** to a name of your choice

4.   Change the **Performance** level to DW100c; the default is DW1000c.

5.   Select **Review + create > Create**.

The deployment of the dedicated SQL pool will take a few minutes. Next let's look at how to ingest the data into the dedicated pool:

6.   Go to **Develop > + > SQL script**.

7.   Set the **Connect to** option to your dedicated SQL pool, not to **Built-in**.

8.   You can ingest from the data lake to your SQL dedicated pool with the COPY statement. You will need to replace the file address with your own address:

```
COPY INTO dbo.TaxiTrips
FROM 'https://your-storage.dfs.core.windows.net/your-filestore/synapse/workspaces/
green_tripdata_2022-01.parquet'
WITH
(
FILE_TYPE = 'PARQUET',
MAXERRORS = 0,
IDENTITY_INSERT = 'OFF',
AUTO_CREATE_TABLE = 'ON'
)
```

9.   You can now run a SELECT on the newly created table in your dedicated pool. You will see that the table has been populated with the data from the Parquet file.

```
SELECT TOP 10 * FROM dbo.TaxiTrips
```

10.   Select **Run**.

You should now see the first 10 rows of the table, as shown in Figure 2-12.

VendorID	lpep_pickup_d...	lpep_dropoff_...	store_and_fwd...	RatecodeID	PULocationID	DOLocationID	passenger_count	trip_distance	fare_amount
2	164150222400...	164150244400...	N	1	42	42	2	0.86	5
1	164155400300...	164155446500...	N	1	75	239	1	1.4	7.5
2	164157484400...	164157512400...	N	1	74	41	2	0.84	5
2	164158892200...	164158921000...	N	1	255	255	1	0.58	5
1	164163993800...	164164217000...	N	1	55	181	1	0	35.88
2	164165803000...	164165957600...	N	4	16	265	2	22.99	109.5
2	164167201000...	164167252000...	N	1	74	42	1	1	7
2	164172666000...	164172695300...	N	1	7	7	1	0.56	5
1	164175019800...	164175177100...	N	1	7	17	1	0	24.38
2	164180474500...	164180525200...	N	1	74	132	1	1.2	7.5

FIGURE 2-12 Results from querying the populated table with Synapse Dedicated Pool

11.   Don't forget to pause your dedicated SQL pool to limit the cost of this exercise.

Oftentimes, though, Parquet files are partitioned. To review and reproduce this use case, we'll use the SQL serverless pool. So follow these steps:

1.   Navigate to https://www.nyc.gov/site/tlc/about/tlc-trip-record-data.page and download the February and March 2022 Green Taxi Trip Records.

2.   In Synapse Studio, select **Data > Linked > Azure Data Lake Storage Gen2**.

3.   Open your primary data store.

4. With the **+ New folder** command, create a folder structure in your data store representing YEAR/MONTH, as shown in Figure 2-13.

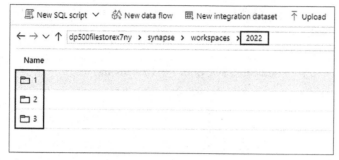

FIGURE 2-13 The file store hierarchy in Synapse Studio

5. Upload the datasets in their corresponding folders; you should have one Parquet file per month.

6. To leverage the partitioning in your query, try to count how many records are in each partition, using the OPENROWSET function, the Parquet format, and the * wildcard.

7. Run the query for Partitions 1 and 2:

```
SELECT
COUNT(*)
FROM
OPENROWSET(
BULK 'https:// your-storage.dfs.core.windows.net/ your-filestore /synapse/
workspaces/2022/*/*.parquet',
FORMAT = 'PARQUET'
) AS TaxiTrips
WHERE TaxiTrips.filepath(1) IN ('1', '2')
```

8. Run the query for Partition 1:

```
SELECT
COUNT(*)
FROM
OPENROWSET(
BULK 'https://your-storage.dfs.core.windows.net/your-filestore/synapse/
workspaces/2022/*/*.parquet',
FORMAT = 'PARQUET'
) AS TaxiTrips
WHERE TaxiTrips.filepath(1) IN ('1')
```

9. Check that the results are different.

You now know how to query a Parquet file containing partitions.

Use a machine learning PREDICT function in a query

Finally, Synapse SQL dedicated pools can be used to consume a machine learning model. For example, with our taxi dataset, we could have a model to predict the duration of the trip, based on the pickup location and the time of day. Having the ability to score, or consume, the model directly in Synapse Analytics is useful because we don't need to move the data outside of our data analytics platform. To score our model, we will use the PREDICT function.

However, a Synapse SQL dedicated pool doesn't have the ability to train a machine learning model. So to use the PREDICT function, we will need to have the model trained outside of Synapse SQL. We could, for example, train the model in a Synapse Spark pool or in another product like Azure Machine Learning.

The trained model will need to be converted to the ONNX (Open Neural Network Exchange) format. ONNX is an open source standard format, with the very purpose of enabling exchange of models between platforms.

Load a model in a Synapse SQL dedicated pool table

The model has to be stored in a dedicated SQL pool table, as a hexadecimal string in a varbinary(max) column. For instance, such a table could be created with this:

```
CREATE TABLE [dbo].[Models]
(
[Id] [int] IDENTITY(1,1) NOT NULL,
[Model] [varbinary](max) NULL,
[Description] [varchar](200) NULL
)
WITH
(
DISTRIBUTION = ROUND_ROBIN,
HEAP
)
GO
```

where **Model** is the varbinary(max) column storing our model, or models, as hexadecimal strings.

Once the table is created, we can load it with the COPY statement:

```
COPY INTO [Models] (Model)
FROM '<enter your storage location>'
WITH (
FILE_TYPE = 'CSV',
CREDENTIAL=(IDENTITY= 'Shared Access Signature', SECRET='<enter your storage key here>')
)
```

We now have a model ready to be used for scoring.

Scoring the model

Finally, the PREDICT function will come into play to score the model. Like any machine learning scoring, you will need the input data to have the same format as the training data.

The following query shows how to use the PREDICT function. It takes the model and the data as parameters.

```
DECLARE @model varbinary(max) = (SELECT Model FROM Models WHERE Id = 1);
SELECT d.*, p.Score
```

```
FROM PREDICT(MODEL = @model,
DATA = dbo.mytable AS d, RUNTIME = ONNX)
WITH (Score float) AS p;
```

> **NEED MORE REVIEW?** **THE** PREDICT **FUNCTION**
>
> The full documentation for the PREDICT function can be found here: *https://learn.microsoft. com/en-us/sql/t-sql/queries/predict-transact-sql?view=sql-server-ver15.*

Skill 2.2: Ingest and transform data by using Power BI

Power BI includes Power Query, which is an extract-transform-load (ETL) tool that uses the M language. M is a functional, case-sensitive language that, unlike DAX, does not resemble Excel formula language in any way, and differs from DAX in important ways, too. In this section, we'll look at the problems you may need to solve when working with large amounts of data in Power Query.

When the volume or number of data sources is significant, you may face performance degradation. There are tools within Power Query that will help you identify the performance problems, and later we'll review the techniques you can use to improve performance.

In addition to Power BI Desktop, Power Query is available in Power BI dataflows, and we'll review when you'd want to use dataflows and what you'd need to consider when using them.

Combining data from different data sources will lead to data privacy issues, which we'll also discuss later in this chapter.

Finally, we'll discuss how you can use Advanced Editor to write your own queries and functions, and how you can query some of the more complex data sources by using Power Query.

> **NOTE** **COMPANION FILE**
>
> Most of the Power Query queries shown in this chapter are available in the companion PBIX file.

This skill covers how to:
- Identify data loading performance bottlenecks in Power Query or data sources
- Implement performance improvements in Power Query and data sources
- Create and manage scalable Power BI dataflows
- Identify and manage privacy settings on data sources
- Create queries, functions, and parameters by using the Power Query Advanced Editor
- Query advanced data sources, including JSON, Parquet, APIs, and Azure Machine Learning models

Identify data loading performance bottlenecks in Power Query or data sources

Several reasons could be responsible for poor performance when connecting to data in Power BI. Power BI Desktop has a few features that can help identify those issues.

View native query

When you get data in Power BI from some data sources, like databases, Power Query will do its best to translate the transformations you perform into the native language of the data source—for example, SQL. This feature of Power Query is known as *query folding*. Most of the time, this will make getting data more efficient. For instance, if you connect to a database and get a subset of columns from a table, Power Query may only retrieve those columns from the data source instead of loading all columns and then locally removing the ones you don't want.

In some cases, it may be possible to view the query that Power Query sent to the data source to retrieve the data you wanted. For this, you need to right-click a query step in Power Query Editor and select **View Native Query**. The window that opens looks like Figure 2-14.

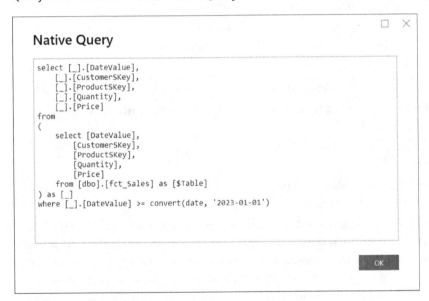

FIGURE 2-14 Native Query window

In the query shown in Figure 2-14, we connected to a SQL Server database, applied a filter, and selected a few columns. Because these operations can be translated to SQL, Power Query decided to do the transformations in the source instead of performing them after loading the whole table, which led to better performance.

You cannot edit the native query; it is provided for your information only. If you want Power BI to issue a specific query, you must provide a SQL statement when connecting to a database.

If the **View Native Query** option is grayed out, it means that the data source does not support query folding or that some query step could not be translated into the data source's native language. For example, if we applied the *Clean* transformation to a text column, the query would not fold, because there is no direct equivalent in SQL yet.

> **IMPORTANT** **POWER QUERY STEPS ORDER**
>
> The order of steps in Power Query matters. If you must have a transformation that cannot be folded, it's best to reorder your steps to fold as many steps as possible.

Query diagnostics

Power BI contains the query diagnostics toolset, which can help you identify performance bottlenecks. Query diagnostics allow you to see the queries that you emit while authoring or refreshing a dataset. They are especially useful for working with data sources that support query folding. By using query diagnostics, you can look at all queries that happen during data refreshes or while you author queries, or you can analyze a single step in detail.

To learn how to use query diagnostics, you'll connect to an OData feed first. It's a feed from Microsoft based on their fictitious AdventureWorks company.

1. Create a new Power BI Desktop file.

2. Select **Get data** (or **New Source** if you're already in Power Query Editor) > **OData feed**.

3. Enter **https://services.odata.org/AdventureWorksV3/AdventureWorks.svc** in the **URL** box and select **OK**.

4. If prompted, in the credentials window, ensure **Anonymous** is selected and select **Connect**.

5. Select the **CompanySales** check box in the Navigator window and select **Transform Data** or **OK** if you're already in Power Query Editor.

Now that you are connected to an OData feed, you can apply some transformations and see the effect on our query. To start recording traces in Power Query, select **Start Diagnostics** on the **Tools** ribbon; when finished, select **Stop Diagnostics**. Alternatively, you can analyze a single step—for this, you must select the **Diagnose Step** button on the **Tools** ribbon, or you can right-click a step and select **Diagnose**. We are going to analyze a single step in the following way:

1. Filter the **ProductCategory** column to **Bikes** by using the filter button on the column header.

2. Right-click the **ProductCategory** column header and select **Remove**.

3. In the **Query Settings** pane, right-click the last step and select **Diagnose**.

After Power Query finishes recording the traces, it creates a new query group called Diagnostics (as in Figure 2-15, which contains several queries whose names start with *CompanySales_Removed Columns*, all ending with the current date and time). The queries are sources from JSON files stored locally on your computer. The *Detailed* query contains more rows and columns than the *Aggregated* query, which is a summary query.

Among other information available in the recorded traces, you will see the time it took for a query to run and whether a native query was sent to a data source, which can help you understand if query folding took place. In Aggregated and Detailed queries, you can find the **Data Source Query** column, which contains the query sent to the data source, if available.

Occasionally, you won't be able to see the native query by using the **View Native Query** feature discussed earlier in this chapter, but you will see a native query sent to a data source when using query diagnostics. We can check whether query folding took place by following these steps:

1. In the *Aggregated* diagnostics query, filter the **Operation** column to only include **CreateResult**.

2. Go to the **Data Source Query** column and select the only column cell. You should see the result shown in Figure 2-15.

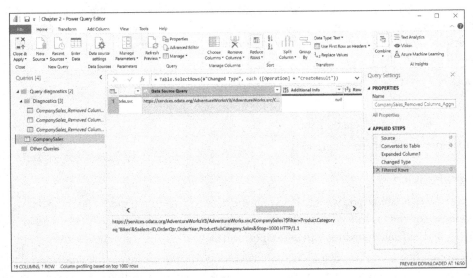

FIGURE 2-15 Native query sent to OData feed

The full query is as follows:

```
https://services.odata.org/AdventureWorksV3/AdventureWorks.svc/CompanySales?$filter=
ProductCategory eq
'Bikes'&$select=ID,OrderQtr,OrderYear,ProductSubCategory,Sales&$top=1000 HTTP/1.1
```

Note that query folding occurs; the filter we placed on the **ProductCategory** column is included in the query and the **ProductCategory** column is not included in the query result. If you only relied on the **View Native Query** feature, you would not see the query because the option would be grayed out.

Some query diagnostics may require that you run Power BI Desktop as administrator. If you are unable to record some traces, like full data refreshes, due to IT policies, you can still record traces when previewing and authoring queries in Power Query Editor. For this, go to **File** > **Options and settings** > **Options** > **Global** > **Diagnostics** > **Query diagnostics** and select **Enable in Query Editor**.

> *NEED MORE REVIEW?* **USING QUERY DIAGNOSTICS**
>
> For advanced information on how you can use the feature, including details on how to understand and visualize the recorded traces, see "Query Diagnostics" at *https://learn.microsoft.com/en-us/power-query/QueryDiagnostics*.

Implement performance improvements in Power Query and data sources

If your Power Query queries need to be improved in terms of performance, the techniques you'll use will highly depend on the data sources you're using and how you're using them. In this section, we'll explore a few methods of improving the data loading performance, divided into four parts:

- General advice
- Working with files
- Working with foldable data sources
- Improving the merge operations

General advice

In almost every situation, you want to load only the data you need. You should filter the data and remove columns as early as possible. Many operations in Power Query are performed in memory, and less data translates into better performance.

If you can choose, in many cases you should use table functions instead of operating on lists and records because Power Query includes some built-in optimizations that can make use of table functions.

When working with tables or lists that are referenced multiple times, you may improve performance by using `Table.Buffer` or `List.Buffer`, respectively. Buffering functions store data in memory and ensure that data isn't read multiple times from the source. When buffering data, you should note two things: first, buffering prevents query folding, so if you're working with foldable data source and buffer a table, then further transformations won't be folded even if they could be folded without buffering. Second, only scalar values are buffered; if your table or list includes nested structures such as records or other lists or tables, then those values won't be buffered, and if you need them later, then your data source will be read again.

Depending on the nature of your data sources and how you're using them, you may want to edit the **Parallel loading of tables** parameter in the current file data load settings

(**File** > **Options and settings** > **Options** > **Current File** > **Data Load**), where the default value is 6, meaning six tables are going to be loaded in parallel at most. If your data model contains more than six tables, which take a long time to refresh, you can try to set a custom parameter value higher than 6, allowing more tables to load in parallel, and your data model may refresh more quickly as a result. On the other hand, if you're getting some data from a web API and then reference the data a few times, you may want to disable parallel loading, because that way the API may be called fewer times, resulting in better data refresh performance.

In case you've got a slow data source that's updated less frequently than you refresh your dataset, you may benefit from loading data to a dataflow first and then loading it to your dataset. Dataflows are discussed in the next section.

Working with files

If you work with Excel files, then you should ensure the third parameter of Excel.Workbook is set to true to leave the column types untyped, which can make reading the files quicker.

If you can choose the file types you work with, then instead of Excel you may want to choose CSVs. While sometimes Excel files may be smaller than the equivalent CSV files, the latter are simpler in structure and therefore faster to read.

While Parquet and CSV files offer approximately the same performance, Parquet files are smaller, which may be relevant when you're using a gateway to access files from your company's network.

Working with foldable data sources

If you can make use of incremental refresh, then it may decrease the data refresh times substantially. We'll discuss incremental refresh in Chapter 3, "Implement and Manage Data Models."

In general, you should push as many transformations as you can as close to the data source as possible, because in many cases data sources may perform data operations more efficiently than Power Query. Some transformations may still fold, even if the *View native query* option of the step is grayed out, as discussed earlier in this chapter in the "Query diagnostics" section. For example, if you need to filter some SQL data based on a data source of a different type, like Excel, then instead of merging tables, you should use a native query and make use of the WHERE clause in SQL. For example, the following query applies a filter on the pbi.Product table from a SQL database based on a list of items from a different Power Query query, ProductSubCategories:

```
let
    FilterItems = "'" & Text.Combine(List.Buffer(ProductSubCategories), "', '") &
"'",
    Source = Sql.Databases("mydatabase.database.windows.net"),
    sakes = Source{[Name="sales"]}[Data],
    Result = Value.NativeQuery(sales, "SELECT * FROM pbi.Product WHERE [Product
Type] IN (@Items)", [Items = FilterItems])
in
    Result
```

Improving the merge operations

When you merge two tables and one table has a unique key, you should add a key to it. While it's possible to use the `Table.AddKey` function in Power Query, doing so won't guarantee uniqueness; it's preferable to remove duplicates from the key column or columns, which will add a key automatically and improve the merge performance.

While you should not keep data you don't need in general, it's especially important in case of merges; since merges take place in memory, fewer columns mean quicker merges. You can remove columns before the merge or immediately after, and the performance gains are going to be similar.

If you work with data that has its keys pre-sorted, then instead of `Table.NestedJoin`, you can use `Table.Join` with `JoinAlgorithm.SortMerge` as the last parameter. Note that if your data isn't sorted, then you're going to get unexpected results without any error message.

Create and manage scalable Power BI dataflows

In addition to Power BI Desktop, Power Query can be found in the Power BI service: you can prep, clean, and transform data in dataflows. Dataflows can be useful when you want your Power Query queries to be reused across your organization without necessarily being in the same dataset. For this reason, you cannot create a dataflow in your own workspace, because only you have access to it.

To create a dataflow in a workspace, select **New > Dataflow**. From there, you have several choices:

- **Add new tables**—Define new tables from scratch by using Power Query.
- **Add linked tables**—Linked entities are tables in other dataflows that you can reuse to reduce duplication of data and improve consistency across your organization.
- **Import model**—If you have a previously exported dataflow model file, you can import it.
- **Create and attach**—Attach a Common Data Model folder from your Azure Data Lake Storage Gen2 account and use it in Power BI.

The Power Query Online interface looks similar to Power Query Editor in Power BI Desktop and is shown in Figure 2-16.

Once you finish authoring your queries, you can select **Save & close** and enter the name of the new dataflow. After saving, you'll need to refresh it by selecting **Refresh now** from the dataflow options in the workspace—otherwise it won't contain any data. When a dataflow finishes refreshing, you can connect to it from Power BI Desktop and get data from it.

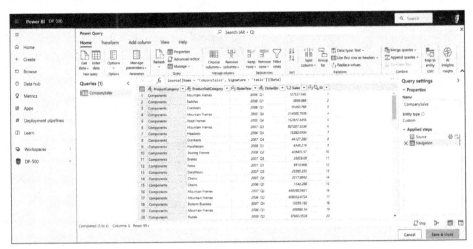

FIGURE 2-16 Power Query interface when editing a dataflow

If you transform data in dataflows, for best performance you may want to separate data extraction and transformation into different dataflows, which is especially helpful in case of slow data sources. If you then enable the enhanced compute engine in the dataflow settings, the transformations will be performed in a more efficient way.

When you used linked tables, the dataflow that depends on a linked table will be automatically refreshed when you refresh the dataflow that contains the original table.

Similar to datasets, you can configure incremental refresh in dataflows. We'll review incremental refresh in the next chapter.

Identify and manage privacy settings on data sources

When you combine data from different data sources, it is important to set the privacy levels correctly. Privacy levels determine the rules according to which data will be combined. These rules may affect the performance of queries, and in some cases, queries will not be executed at all if it is not permitted by privacy levels. To illustrate what happens in an example, we are going to filter an OData table by using data from a CSV file by performing the following steps:

1. Get the data from **https://raw.githubusercontent.com/DaniilMaslyuk/DP-500/main/ProductSubcategory.csv**.

2. Right-click the **Column1** column header and select **Drill Down**.

3. Create a new parameter by selecting **Manage Parameters** > **New Parameter**, as shown in Figure 2-17.

FIGURE 2-17 New parameter

4. Get the **ProductCatalog** table from the following OData feed: **https://services.odata.
    org/AdventureWorksV3/AdventureWorks.svc.**

5. Select the filter button of the **ProductSubcategory** column and select **Text Filters >
    Equals**.

6. Apply the filter criteria as shown in Figure 2-18:

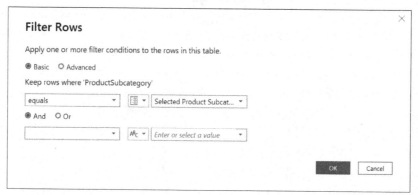

FIGURE 2-18 Filter rows

7. Select **OK**.

After following the steps above, you should be prompted to set privacy levels, as shown in Figure 2-19.

⚠ Information is required about data privacy. | Continue |

FIGURE 2-19 Data privacy prompt

If you do not see the prompt from Figure 2-17, it means you have already combined data from GitHub and the OData feed; the permissions you set can be cleared in **Home** > **Data Sources** > **Data Source Settings**. You will see a list of data sources used in the current file, as shown in Figure 2-20.

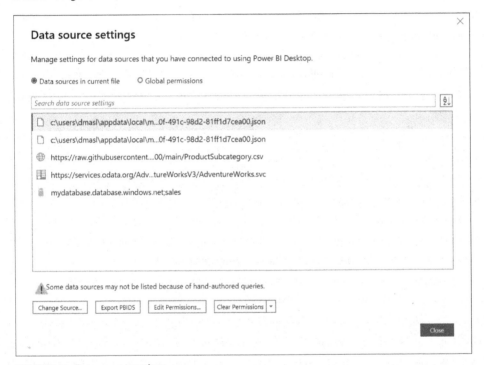

FIGURE 2-20 Data source settings

To clear the permissions for all data sources in the current file, below the list select the dopdown arrow next to **Clear Permissions** and select **Clear All Permissions**, then confirm by selecting **Delete** in the Clear All Permissions dialog box.

When you select **Continue** in the data privacy prompt from Figure 2-19, the **Privacy Levels** dialog box opens, where you are prompted to select privacy levels. The dialog box can be seen in Figure 2-21.

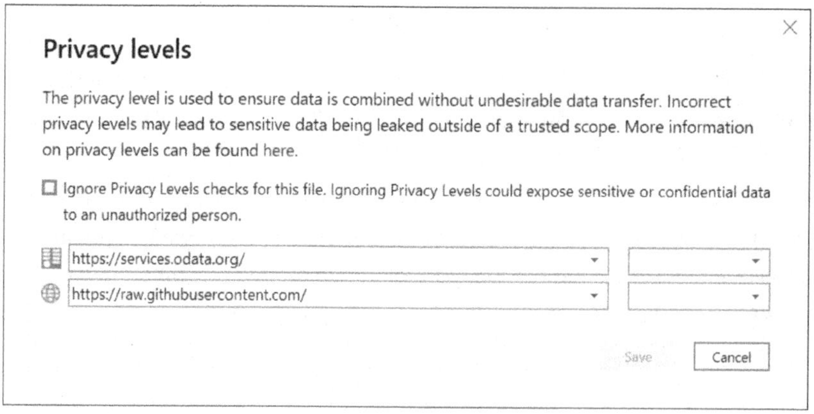

FIGURE 2-21 Privacy Levels dialog box

In the drop-down lists on the right, you can select one of the following privacy levels:

- **Public**—This option should be used for publicly accessible sources, such as Wikipedia pages.
- **Organizational**—This can be used for data sources accessible to others within your network, such as a corporate database. This privacy level is isolated from the Public data sources, but it is visible to other Organizational data sources.
- **Private**—Should be used for confidential or sensitive information, such as payroll information. This privacy level is completely isolated from all data sources, including other data sources marked as Private.

For now, select **Public** for both OData and GitHub. If you previously cleared data source settings, you might need to specify credentials for your data sources.

After selecting the right privacy levels, you will see the filtered table. If we diagnose the last step, you'll see the following native source query:

```
https://services.odata.org/AdventureWorksV3/AdventureWorks.svc/ProductCatalog?$filter=Pr
oductSubcategory eq 'Shorts'&$top=1000 HTTP/1.1
```

We can now review what happens when we change the privacy level of one of the data sources to Private:

1. Select **Home** > **Data Sources** > **Data Source Settings**.
2. Select the GitHub data source.
3. Select **Edit Permissions**.
4. From the **Privacy Level** drop-down list, select **Private**.
5. Select **OK** > **Close**.
6. Ensure the ProductCatalog query is selected.
7. Select **Home** > **Query** > **Refresh Preview**.

At this stage, you will see that the query still executes, and if you diagnose the **Filtered Rows** step, no query folding takes place. What this means is that no data from the GitHub is sent to OData; instead, the whole ProductCatalog table is downloaded from OData, then filtering is done inside Power Query. As a result, performance is degraded, but data is not leaked outside of Power Query. Even if the OData owners checked the logs, they would not be able to check which values are contained in your files.

While this is an artificial example, it illustrates how privacy levels work. If you are confident that privacy is not an issue with your data, you can disable privacy settings in **File** > **Options and Settings** > **Options**. You can set privacy settings either globally—for every file—or for this file only in the **Global** and **Current File** sections, respectively.

Create queries, functions, and parameters by using the Power Query Advanced Editor

Power Query Editor uses a strongly typed, case-sensitive functional language called M, and it's rich in features with which you can perform basic and advanced transformations. Each transformation you apply from the user interface is recorded in a step, and each step has an identifier (name) and expression (formula). The full query code can be edited in the Advanced Editor. To learn how you can use Advanced Editor, we'll examine the building blocks of M first.

The let/in expressions

Most queries will be in the form of let/in expressions like these:

```
let
    FirstWord = "Hello",
    SecondWord = "World",
    Result = FirstWord & ", " & SecondWord
in
    Result
```

The let part contains one or more expressions, and the in part contains the expression that you want the query to return, and there can be only one. The expression you return does not have to be one of the expressions defined in the let sections; the following query returns the same result as the previous one:

```
let
    FirstWord = "Hello",
    SecondWord = "World"
in
    FirstWord & ", " & SecondWord
```

While the result is the same, you should note that the second query won't show the steps in the Applied Steps pane like the first one does, so in most cases you'll be better off returning the last expression defined in the let section.

You can also nest let/in expressions like so:

```
let
    FirstPart = "Hello",
    SecondPart =
        let
```

```
            Punctuation = ", ",
            Word = "World",
            FullPart = Punctuation & Word
        in
            FullPart,
    Result = FirstPart & SecondPart
in
    Result
```

In case there's a conflict between identifier names, then the identifier within the current scope will be used. To avoid any confusion, it's best to ensure that identifier names are unique in your queries.

Data types

Unlike Excel, Power Query is strongly typed, and it won't implicitly convert values. Broadly, Power Query has the following basic data types:

- Number
- Date/Time
- Duration
- Text
- Logical

The Number and Date/Time data types have several variations, like whole numbers and decimal numbers. There's also a special value—*null*—which does not have a data type.

In addition to the basic data types, there are the following complex data types:

- List
- Record
- Table

Any of these three complex data types may have other data types nested into them.

LIST

A list is an ordered list of values, which can be of any data type. You can create a list by using braces like so:

```
{"a", "b", "c"}
```

This list contains three values. If the values are sequential, you can use the double dot notation to generate a list like so:

```
{"a".."z"}
```

This list contains 26 values: lowercase English alphabet.

Additionally, there are several functions that can generate lists. For example, you can create a list of five odd numbers, starting with 1:

```
List.Numbers(1, 5, 2)
```

You can use the following operators on lists:

- & to combine two lists into one
- = to check the equality of two lists
- <> to check if two lists are different

Note that if two lists have the same elements but in different order, they're not considered to be the same.

You can access list elements by using zero-based index and braces. For example, the following expression returns **b**:

```
{"a".."c"}{1}
```

Lists are commonly used in table transformation functions, like when you rename columns or change data types. The following formula is an example of a step that changes column types:

```
Table.TransformColumnTypes(Source,{{"Sales", Currency.Type}, {"OrderYear",
type text}})
```

Notice that the second parameter in `Table.TransformColumnTypes` is a list of lists.

There are many useful list functions, which can be broadly divided into the following categories:

- **Arithmetic**—Functions like `List.Sum` and `List.Average` will perform arithmetic operations on a list.
- **Transformation**—An example is `List.Transform`, which allows you to operate on each member of a list. `List.Accumulate` allows you to perform transformations on list values while saving the results of the previous transformation.
- **Selection**—`List.Select` can select list items based on your criteria, and `List.Skip` can skip a few list values.
- **Membership**—A very useful function is `List.Contains`, which can check whether a value belongs to a list.
- **Set**—You can operate on sets with `List.Difference`, `List.Union`, `List.Intersect`, and `List.Zip`.
- **Generation**—Like `List.Numbers` mentioned earlier, other list functions can generate values: `List.Times` and `List.Generate`, to name a couple.
- **Other**—Not all functions fall into these categories; a useful example is `List.IsEmpty`, which can tell you if a list has no items. `List.Buffer` will buffer a list in memory.

NEED MORE REVIEW? **LIST FUNCTIONS**

The full list of list functions in Power Query is available at *https://learn.microsoft.com/en-us/powerquery-m/list-functions*.

RECORD

Records are key-value pairs, where each key must be unique. To create a record, you can enclose key-value pairs in brackets like so:

```
[Letter = "A", Number = 1]
```

If you want to get a record value, you can either use the `Record.Field` function or add the field name wrapped in brackets. Both of these expressions return 1:

```
[Letter = "A", Number = 1][Number]
Record.Field([Letter = "A", Number = 1], "Number")
```

You can use the & operator to combine records. If two records have the same fields, the value from the last record will be kept to preserve the uniqueness of fields.

Compared to the list functions, there are fewer commonly used record functions; you can use `Record.HasFields` to check if a record has certain fields, and you can use functions like `Record.SelectFields`, `Record.RemoveFields`, and `Record.AddField` to create a new copy of a record with a different set of fields.

> **NEED MORE REVIEW?** **RECORD FUNCTIONS**
>
> The full list of table functions in Power Query is available at *https://learn.microsoft.com/en-us/powerquery-m/record-functions*.

TABLE

Table is probably the most common data type, not least because you can only load tables in Power BI, with other data types being converted to tables if you leave them as other types.

You can create a table directly in the code by using `#table` like so:

```
#table({"Letter", "Number"}, {{"A", 1}, {"B", 2}})
```

To access a table column, which will be a list, you can append the column name to a table name like so:

```
TableName[ColumnName]
```

You can also access individual rows by using a zero-based index enclosed in braces, which will return a record:

```
TableName{0}
```

Power Query includes many table functions, which can be broadly grouped into the following categories, each with a few examples:

- **Construction**—Functions like `Table.FromRecords` and `Table.FromList` will create tables from records and lists, respectively.

- **Transformation**—This is one of the biggest function categories. One of the most used functions is `Table.AddColumn`, which adds a new column to a table; another example is

`Table.FillDown`, which fills null values in a column below with the non-null value from above.

- **Selection**—`Table.SelectRows` will filter a table, while `Table.FirstN` will keep the first N rows.
- **Other**—An example is `Table.Buffer`, which will buffer a table in memory.

NEED MORE REVIEW? **TABLE FUNCTIONS**

The full list of table functions in Power Query is available at *https://learn.microsoft.com/en-us/ powerquery-m/table-functions.*

Functions

Functions mostly look like other expressions, except they've got the parameter declaration in the beginning. For example, the following function multiplies two numbers:

```
(a as number, b as number) as number =>
let
    Result = a * b
in
    Result
```

You can also define functions within larger queries and call them later like so:

```
let
    Function = (a as number, b as number) as number => a * b,
    Result = Function(2, 3)
in
    Result
```

Parameters

Parameters are special kinds of queries that are usually created by using the user interface. Parameters are especially useful for Power BI templates and for deployment pipelines. In case you wish to create a parameter by using Advanced Editor, you'll need to skip using the let/in expression and define the parameter value, followed by metadata like so:

```
5 meta [IsParameterQuery=true, Type="Number", IsParameterQueryRequired=true]
```

Query advanced data sources, including JSON, Parquet, APIs, and Azure Machine Learning models

Power Query has scores of connectors, and you can use Power Query to get data from complex data sources, such as Parquet and JSON files, as well as from APIs. Power Query also has built-in support for Azure machine learning (ML) APIs, including text analytics and ML models.

Complex files

Power Query has several connectors to extract data from non-flat files such as JSON or Parquet, as discussed next.

JSON

To connect to a JSON file, you need to select **Get Data** > **JSON** (or **Web** if it's on the web). After selecting the file and clicking **Open**, you will be taken directly to Power Query Editor. To extract the data from your JSON file, you will likely need to perform various transformations, depending on the structure of your file. Figure 2-22 shows an imported JSON file that contains a record inside, which in turn contains another record.

FIGURE 2-22 Power Query Editor after opening a JSON file

If you want to extract the data from your JSON file, you can either transform the starting list to a table by clicking the **Transform** tab and selecting **To Table** in the **Convert** group, or you can drill down into a specific record by selecting a specific **Record** link. If you would like to see a preview of data in a record, you can select its cell without clicking on the link, which will open a data preview pane at the bottom of Power Query Editor.

Selecting the cog wheel next to the **Source** step in Query Settings opens a window where you can specify advanced settings. Among other things, you can specify file encoding in the **File Origin** drop-down list. Once you are done with transformations, you can click **Close & Apply** to load data into Power BI data model.

> **NOTE** **JSON FILE SAMPLE**
>
> If you want to try to connect to a JSON file, you can get one at *https://raw.githubusercontent. com/DaniilMaslyuk/DP-500/main/ConsolidatedPurchaseOrders.json*.

XML

To connect to an XML file, select **Get Data** > **XML**. Unlike JSON files, XML files have a structure that can be parsed and shown by Power Query. Once you select the file you want in the Open window, you are taken to a Navigator window, as shown in Figure 2-23, where you see the structure of the file.

After selecting the items that you want to import to your data model, you can apply transformations to your data. In Power Query Editor, you can select the cog wheel next to the **Source** step to open the advanced file settings, where you can specify file encoding if need be. Selecting the **Home** tab and then selecting **Close & Apply** in the **Close** group will load the data to the data model.

> **NOTE** **XML FILE SAMPLE**
>
> If you want to try to connect to an XML file, you can get one at *https://raw.githubusercontent.com/DaniilMaslyuk/DP-500/main/ConsolidatedPurchaseOrders.xml.*

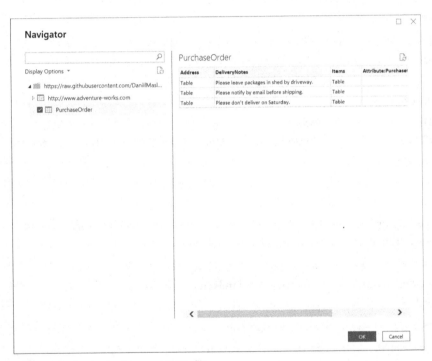

FIGURE 2-23 Contents of a sample XML file

PARQUET

Apache Parquet is a column-oriented data storage format, and Power BI can read Parquet files natively. Unlike JSON and XML files, Parquet files work especially well for flat tables, and usually Parquet files are smaller and more performant than CSV files.

To get data from a Parquet file, select **Get Data** > **Parquet** and enter the URL of the file; if your file is stored locally, you can enter the full file path. Figure 2-24 shows the Wide World Importers sales data from a Parquet file.

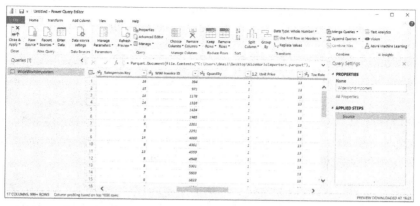

FIGURE 2-24 Contents of a sample Parquet file

As you can see, a loaded Parquet file looks similar to a CSV file, except the column headers and data types are already defined in the file.

> **NOTE PARQUET FILE SAMPLE**
>
> If you want to try to connect to a Parquet file, you can get one at *https://github.com/Daniil-Maslyuk/DP-500/raw/91bbb117da46a46e5e6756439888c2222d1b6c82/WideWorldImporters.parquet*.

APIs

Power BI supports connections to APIs by using the `Web.Contents` function in Power Query. As an example, we can connect to the openFDA Tobacco API endpoint in the following way:

1. Select **Get Data > Web**.

2. Enter **https://api.fda.gov/tobacco/problem.json** in the **URL** text box.

3. Select **OK**.

4. If prompted for credentials, select **Anonymous > Connect**.

    Once you perform these steps, you'll see a result like the one in Figure 2-25.

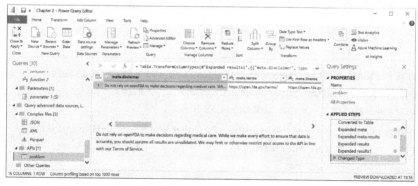

FIGURE 2-25 The result of an API call in Power Query

As you can see, Power BI applies some automatic transformations that it deems appropriate. You should always review the transformations for validity. You can remove all automatically created steps by right-clicking the **Converted to Table** step and selecting **Delete Until End**.

You can also notice that if the API data comes in some complex format, such as JSON in this case, then you'll likely see some nested structures within the response—in our example there are some records and lists.

Since there are many different formats that APIs return data in, covering all possible scenarios is outside the scope of this book. However, we'll review a common scenario that you need to deal with when working with APIs: paging.

REST APIs usually divide data into pages to avoid transmitting too much data in a single call. The indicator of a next page varies from API to API, and before you can solve the problem of paging, you'll likely need to answer the following questions:

- Does the API provide the URL for the next page in the response? If not, do you need to calculate the next page value?
- How do you know when to stop calling the API? Some APIs return empty responses, while some will have an indicator that there's no data.
- What are the parameters associated with paging, such as page size and start/skip?

In the openFDA example, after exploring the API documentation and API responses, we can note the following:

- The meta record contains the total number of records.
- We can use the limit parameter to define the page size.
- We can use the skip parameter to tell the API where to start.

For example, the following API call will return five records, skipping 10 records:

```
https://api.fda.gov/tobacco/problem.json?limit=5&skip=10
```

In this case, we'll need to fix the limit parameter and increment the skip parameter with each successive call until we get all data. Since the total number of records is usually unknown in advance, we'll need to know when to stop. There are several ways to get all data in the openFDA example, and we'll explore the following two:

- Rely on the meta record to know when to stop calling the API.
- Use the List.Generate function in Power Query to page through the results.

Either way, before we get all data, we should create a custom function that will make use of the skip parameter because we'll be changing the value of the parameter with each call. While the value of the limit parameter will be the same in each call, we'll make it a parameter too.

CREATE AN OPENFDA TOBACCO CUSTOM FUNCTION

If you want to create a function with no intention of using it in the Power BI service, you can create a blank query called **fCallApi** and replace its formula in the Advanced Editor with the following code:

```
(Limit, Skip) =>
let
```

```
    SafeLimit = Text.From(Limit ?? ""),
    SafeSkip = Text.From(Skip ?? ""),
    CallApi = Web.Contents("https://api.fda.gov/tobacco/problem.json?limit=" & SafeLimit
& "&skip=" & SafeSkip),
    AsJson = Json.Document(CallApi)
in
    AsJson
```

In this formula, you can note the following:

- The function uses two parameters, Limit and Skip.

- SafeLimit and SafeSkip transform the Limit and Skip parameters, respectively, into text, because we construct a URL in CallApi, and we can only construct text from text parts.

- In SafeLimit and SafeSkip, the ?? (coalesce) operator ensures we don't use null values when constructing our URL. While the openFDA API allows empty strings as parameter values, adding a null value to a URL will result in an error like in Figure 2-26.

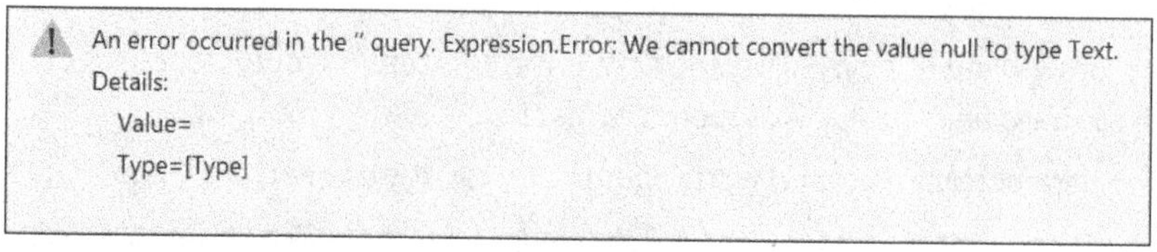

> ⚠ An error occurred in the '' query. Expression.Error: We cannot convert the value null to type Text.
>   Details:
>   Value=
>   Type=[Type]

FIGURE 2-26 Error when combining text and nulls

- In the last step, we're converting the API response into JSON. If we were certain of which part of the response we needed, we could include extra steps to drill into the specific records or lists within the response.

As a test, we can invoke the function with no parameter values and note that it works in Power BI Desktop. If you publish your report to the Power BI service and attempt to refresh, you'll see the error message shown in Figure 2-27.

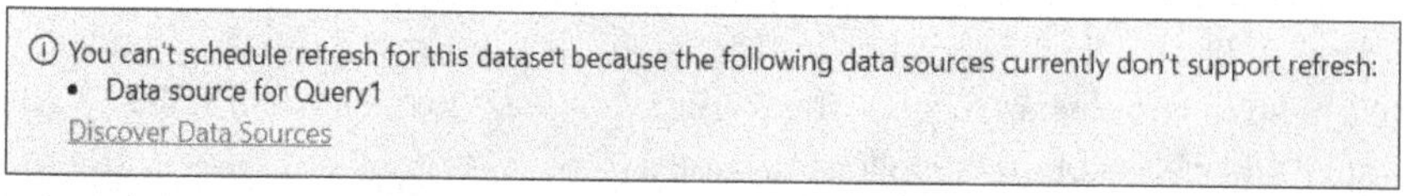

> ⓘ You can't schedule refresh for this dataset because the following data sources currently don't support refresh:
>   • Data source for Query1
>   Discover Data Sources

FIGURE 2-27 Power BI service dataset refresh error

To ensure our function refreshes in the Power BI service, we'll need to use query options in the Web.Contents function. We can use the following code:

```
(Limit, Skip) =>
let
    SafeLimit = Text.From(Limit ?? ""),
    SafeSkip = Text.From(Skip ?? ""),
    CallApi  = Web.Contents(
        "https://api.fda.gov",
        [
            RelativePath = "tobacco/problem.json",
            Query = [limit = SafeLimit, skip = SafeSkip]
```

```
      ]
   ),
   AsJson = Json.Document(CallApi )
in
   AsJson
```

Compared to the previous version of the formula, the `CallApi` step now uses query options:

- `RelativePath` specifies the API endpoint. `RelativePath` can be especially useful if you want to parameterize the relative path to make your function useful for more than one endpoint.

- `Query` is a record that contains parameter values.

After making the change to the function, you'll be able to refresh your dataset in the Power BI service. Note that when editing credentials in dataset settings, you'll need to select the **Skip test connection** option, as shown in Figure 2-28.

FIGURE 2-28 Web Contents data source configuration

If you don't check the **Skip test connection** option, you'll get the 404 error in this example, since the base URL isn't a valid API endpoint for openFDA.

USE TOTAL NUMBER OF RECORDS

If you call the openFDA API without using the `limit` and `skip` parameters, you'll get one record, while there can be many more records. Increasing the `limit` parameter may not always work, since the maximum number of records returned may still be less than the total number of records. Therefore, we'll need to call the API multiple times to get all records, increasing the `skip` parameter value with every call. One way of getting all records is by relying on the total number of records that is returned within the API response. To get the total number of records, perform the following steps:

1. Invoke the **fCallApi** function with no parameters, which will create a new query.

2. Rename the new query to **All records 1**.

3. Select the **Record** link in the **meta** record value.

4. Select the **Record** link in the **results** record value.

5. Right-click the number in the **total** record value and select **Drill Down**.

The result should be one number, and if you inspect the code in the Advanced Editor, you should see the following:

```
let
    Source = fCallApi(null, null),
    #"meta" = Source[meta],
    results = #"meta"[results],
    total = results[total]
in
    total
```

Now that we have the total number of records, we can generate the `skip` parameter values in the following way:

1. Ensure the *total* step is selected, and in the formula bar, select **Add Step** (*fx*), which will add a new step called Custom1 with the following formula:

```
= total
```

2. Replace the formula in the new step with the following one:

```
= 500
```

3. Rename the Custom1 step to **Limit**. In this step, we'll keep the `limit` parameter value (set to 500 in our example, although it could be a different number if needed).

4. Add another step and rename it to **Skips**. This step will contain the `skip` parameter values that we're going to iterate over. To create the values, we'll generate a list of numbers from 0, incrementing by using the `Limit` value (the previous step), and the last value in the list will be less than or equal to the total number of records thanks to the `Number.IntegerDivide` function.

5. Replace the formula in the **Skips** step with the following one:

```
= List.Numbers(0, Number.IntegerDivide(total, Limit) + 1, Limit)
```

6. Create a new step and rename it to **Calls**. This step will contain all API calls to get all the available records from the endpoint. Again, we'll make use of the `Limit` step, and we'll iterate over the `Skips` list by using the `List.Transform` function.

7. Replace the formula of the **Calls** step with the following one:

```
= List.Transform(Skips, each fCallApi(Limit, _))
```

At this point, we've got all the records the API endpoint can return. The full query formula should be as follows:

```
let
    Source = fCallApi(null, null),
    #"meta" = Source[meta],
```

```
    results = #"meta"[results],
    total = results[total],
    Limit = 500,
    Skips = List.Numbers(0, Number.IntegerDivide(total, Limit) + 1, Limit),
    Calls = List.Transform(Skips, each fCallApi(Limit, _))
in
    Calls
```

We'll still need to process the results further to make it a table. If you want to complete the example and create a table that you can load, there are several ways of doing it. For example, you can perform the following steps:

1. On the **List Tools** > **Transform** ribbon, select **To Table** > **OK**.

2. Select the double-arrow button on the **Column1** column header, deselect **meta**, ensure **Use original column name as prefix** is not selected, and select **OK**.

3. Select the double-arrow button on the **results** column header and select **Expand to New Rows**.

4. Select the double-arrow button on the **results** column header, ensure **Use original column name as prefix** is not selected, and select **OK**.

5. Remove the columns that have *List* values:

   - reported_health_problems

   - reported_product_problems

   - tobacco_products

6. Rename columns and change the column data types as you desire, and you can load the data.

Next time you refresh data, the query will load all the available records.

USE LIST.GENERATE

While in the openFDA example the API response includes the total number of records, different APIs may not always include the number in their responses. If you want to keep calling the API until there's no data returned, you can use the List.Generate function in Power Query. If you want to follow along, ensure you've got the fCallApi function as a separate query, as described earlier, and follow these steps:

1. Create a blank query called **All records 2**.

2. Open Advanced Editor and replace all code with the following:

```
let
    Limit = 500,
    Calls = List.Generate(
        () => 0,
        each not (try fCallApi(Limit, _))[HasError],
        each _ + Limit,
        each fCallApi(Limit, _)
    )
in
    Calls
```

3. Select **Done** to close Advanced Editor.

By now you should have a list of records, which collectively contain all data returned by the API. You can now convert it to a table that can be loaded, in the same way as in the previous method when we relied on the total number of records.

Here are the things to note in this query:

1. In Limit, we set the value we'll use for the `limit` parameter later in the `Calls` step. The limit value will stay the same for all calls.

2. The first parameter of `List.Generate` is the initial seed. We're using 0 because that's the value we'll start with for the `skip` parameter.

3. The second parameter of `List.Generate` is the condition that must be satisfied for the next call to be made. In the openFDA example, we want the API not to return an error. If you call the openFDA API and the sum of `limit` and `skip` parameters is greater than the total number of records, you'll get an error, so this condition is specific to openFDA, and for other APIs you may need to use a different condition.

4. The third parameter of `List.Generate` is how to increment the current parameter value. In the openFDA example, we're adding the `limit` value to the `skip` value to get the next `skip` value.

5. The fourth and last parameter of `List.Generate` is the selection, or what you want `List.Generate` to return for each call. In the openFDA example, we want `List.Generate` to call the API with the current `skip` value.

Again, there are multiple ways in which we could've retrieved all data from the API endpoint, including using the total number of records together with `List.Generate`. The specific way to call an API highly depends on the API, and we've covered two of the most popular ways.

AI insights

In Power BI, you can leverage AI to enhance your data during the data preparation stage by connecting to certain pretrained machine learning models. You can find the following AI Insights on the **Home** or **Add column** ribbon in Power Query Editor:

- **Text Analytics**—Can detect the language, extract key phrases, or score sentiment in a text column

- **Vision**—Analyzes images to generate tags based on what they contain

- **Azure Machine Learning**—Applies an Azure Machine Learning model to your data

> **NOTE AI INSIGHTS REQUIREMENTS**
>
> The Text Analytics and Vision options require access to a Power BI Premium capacity. For Azure Machine Learning, you need to have access to an Azure ML model. Details on how to grant access to an Azure ML model are outside the scope of this book. For more details, see "Use AI Insights in Power BI Desktop" at *https://learn.microsoft.com/en-us/power-bi/ transform-model/desktop-ai-insights*.

For example, you can extract key phrases from the Stock Item names in the following way:

1. In Power Query Editor, get the **ProductCatalog** table from the OData feed: **https://services.odata.org/AdventureWorksV3/AdventureWorks.svc**.

2. Right-click the **Description** column and select **Remove other columns**.

3. Select **Keep Rows** > **Keep Top Rows**, enter **20**, and select **OK**.

4. On the Home ribbon, select **AI Insights** > **Text Analytics**. You may be prompted to sign in with your organizational account.

5. At the left, select **Detect language**. The configuration is shown in Figure 2-29.

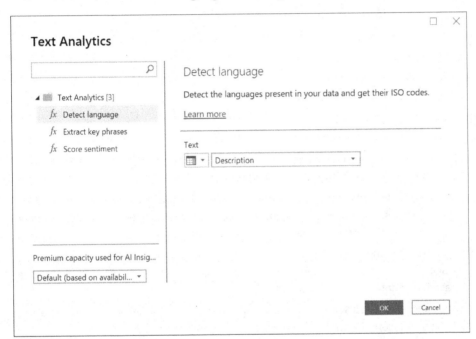

FIGURE 2-29 Text Analytics

6. Select **OK**.

Once the process finishes running, you should see the results in Figure 2-30.

The function adds two new columns: *Detect language.Detected Language Name* and *Detect language.Detected Language ISO Code*. Other AI insights functions work in a similar way.

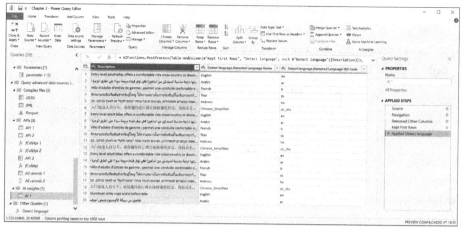

FIGURE 2-30 Key phrases

Chapter summary

- Synapse Analytics includes three types of pools: Spark, Dedicated SQL, and Serverless SQL. They work differently and are suited for different use cases.

- Different file formats have different use cases. Synapse Analytics can work with CSV, JSON, Parquet, and Delta files. For analytics purposes and its access patterns, columnar files make the most sense, so Parquet and Delta are recommended.

- Synapse SQL, whether dedicated or serverless, can query relational data sources with T-SQL. The OPENROWSET function allows you to connect to external data sources, and even partitioned data can be handled natively.

- A Synapse dedicated SQL pool can also support machine learning workflows. In particular, you can score a model with the PREDICT function after loading it in a table.

- Power Query allows you to perform query diagnostics, which can help identify performance issues in your queries. It can also show whether Power BI tries to translate its transformations into the data source's native language.

- You'll apply different techniques to improve performance in Power Query depending on your data source. Many techniques focus on reducing the data size either by pushing transformations to the source or limiting the amount of data that Power Query needs to process in memory.

- Power BI dataflows can be a useful addition to a business intelligence solution by providing a central repository of transformed data in a similar way to a data warehouse.

- Every data source has its own privacy level, which can be one of the following: Private, Organizational, and Public. Each Private data source is completely isolated from all other data sources. Organizational data sources are visible to each other and are isolated from Public data sources. By default, Power BI combines data from different sources according to each; this behavior can be disabled in Power BI settings, though privacy is not guaranteed in this case.

- In addition to using the user interface, you can use the Advanced Editor to write your own M code. Writing your own code allows you to do more than what's available in the user interface.
- Power Query can query complex files, such as JSON and Parquet, as well as APIs and use the AI insights functions such as text analytics.

Thought experiment

In this thought experiment, demonstrate your skills and knowledge of the topics covered in this chapter. You can find the answers in the section that follows.

Situation setup

1. You need to create staging tables in a Synapse SQL dedicated pool. The tables are more than 2 GB. What distribution strategy do you recommend? Your solution must optimize for writes.

   A. Round Robin

   B. Hash

   C. Distributed

   D. Broadcast

2. Your organization is going to migrate from Azure Databricks to Azure Synapse Analytics. Which Azure Synapse pool do you recommend for your organization? The solution must minimize the learning curve.

   A. SQL Serverless pool

   B. SQL Dedicated pool

   C. Spark pool

   D. Synapse Pathway

3. You get data from a data source used across the whole organization by various people and tools. One of the tables you get has all column names with a "sys_" prefix, which you'd like to remove. How should you rename columns? Your solution must ensure that others can continue using the data source and you won't need to update your script in case there's a new column.

   A. Rename columns manually.

   B. Use the following formula step:

   ```
   Table.TransformColumnNames(Source, each Text.Replace(_, "sys_", ""))
   ```

   C. Request the data source to be modified.

   D. Use the following formula step:

   ```
   Table.TransformColumnNames(Source, each Text.Range(_, 4))
   ```

4. You're merging two tables in Power Query, which come from two different CSV files. One of the files is a lookup table with a unique key. How can you improve the merge performance? Your solution must minimize effort.

    A. Configure incremental refresh.

    B. Add a key to the lookup table by removing duplicates from the key column.

    C. Request the producers of files to provide another file.

    D. Convert CSV files to Excel files before connecting to them.

5. You need to apply a series of the same transformations to several tables before loading. At the moment you've got five tables, and you expect to add three more soon. How should you apply the transformations? Your solution must minimize effort.

    A. Create a custom function in Power Query.

    B. Copy and paste transformations from query to query.

    C. Combine all tables, apply the transformations, then split tables.

Thought experiment answers

1. The answer is **A** because round-robin distribution is ideal for writes and so is typically used for staging tables. Option B is wrong because hash distribution is used for large fact tables. Option C is also wrong because replicated distribution is used for small dimensions (>2 GB). Option D is wrong because broadcasting is an option in Spark pools, similar to replicated, and is not available in SQL dedicated pools.

2. The answer is **C** because both Azure Databricks and Spark pools use Spark under the hood. The options A and B are wrong because they use the Synapse SQL engine. The option D is wrong because Synapse Pathway is a migration tool, not a compute engine.

3. The answer is **D** because Text.Range will skip four characters, removing the "sys_" suffix in every column. If you rename a column manually, then new columns will still have the prefix, making option A incorrect. If you use Text.Replace, then you may also replace "sys_" in the middle of a column name, where it may be legitimate, so option B is wrong. Option C won't work because it may break other people's solutions.

4. The answer is **B** because adding a key improves the merge performance. Option A is wrong because incremental refresh isn't possible for CSV files. Option C could only be correct if the data source owner was capable of changing the output; some files are produced by legacy systems and cannot have a different format. Option D is wrong because Excel files are less performant than CSV files, in general.

5. The answer is **A** because a custom function will apply the same transformations consistently, and if you need to change logic in the future, you'll only need to change it in one place, as opposed to in every table. Option B is not right because if there are changes in logic later, you'll expend more effort compared to using a custom function. Option C is wrong because tables may not be of the same shape, and combining then splitting will surely add a performance overhead.

CHAPTER 3

Implement and manage data models

The previous chapter reviewed the skills necessary to connect to data sources and transform data using Power Query Editor—the process also known as data shaping.

This chapter covers data modeling skills. In Power BI, a data model is a collection of one or more tables connected by relationships. Apart from the M language, which is used for data shaping, Power BI uses DAX, which is its native formula and query language. Power BI possesses rich data modeling capabilities, which includes creating relationships as well as enriching a data model with hierarchies, measures, calculated columns, calculated tables, and calculation groups.

Skills covered in this chapter:

- 3.1: Design and build tabular models
- 3.2: Optimize enterprise-scale data models

Skill 3.1: Design and build tabular models

In this skill, we'll cover the different ways of building an enterprise-scale data model, including composite models, row- and object-level security, DAX, and external tools.

This skill covers how to:

- Choose when to use DirectQuery for Power BI datasets
- Choose when to use external tools, including DAX Studio and Tabular Editor 2
- Create calculation groups
- Write calculations that use DAX variables and functions, for example, handling blanks or errors, creating virtual relationships, and working with iterators
- Design and build a large format dataset
- Design and build composite models, including aggregations
- Design and implement enterprise-scale row-level security and object-level security

Choose when to use DirectQuery for Power BI datasets

The most common way to consume data in Power BI is to import it into the data model. When you import data in Power BI, you create a copy of it that is kept static until you refresh your dataset. Data from files and folders can only be imported in Power BI. When it comes to databases, you can create data connections in one of two ways.

First, you can import your data, which makes the Power BI data model cache it. This method offers you the greatest flexibility when you model your data because you can use all the available modeling features in Power BI.

Second, you can connect to your data directly in its original source. This method is known as *DirectQuery*. With DirectQuery, data is not cached in Power BI. Instead, the original data source is queried every time you interact with Power BI visuals. Not all data sources support DirectQuery.

When you use the DirectQuery connectivity mode, you are not caching any data in Power BI. All data remains in the data source, except for metadata, which Power BI caches. Metadata includes column and table names, data types, and relationships.

For most data sources supporting DirectQuery, when connecting to a data source, you select the entities you want to connect to, such as tables or views. Each entity becomes a table in your data model. Data from DirectQuery tables cannot be seen in the **Data** view of Power BI Desktop; if all tables in a data model are in DirectQuery mode, the **Data** view button will not be visible, though you can still use the **Model** view.

Advantages

The main advantage of this method is that you are not limited by the hardware of your development machine or the capacity of the server to which you will publish your report. All data is kept in the data source, and all the calculations are done in the source as well.

Another advantage of using DirectQuery is that your reports will always use the latest available data, which means you won't have to worry about the discrepancy between the data in the database and the figures that your report is showing.

If you only use DirectQuery in your data model, the Power BI file size will be negligible compared to a file with imported data, so you won't be affected by the file size limits when publishing to the Power BI service.

Disadvantages

When you're working in DirectQuery mode, it's unlikely that your visuals will be displayed as quickly as if you were using the import mode. Data sources that are too slow may result in unacceptable user experience.

There's a limit on the number of rows that a single query in DirectQuery mode can return. The default is one million rows, which is relevant when you're trying to display data that hasn't been summarized.

Not all data transformations are supported in DirectQuery mode. In case your data needs to be transformed, it's best to create the necessary views in the database and connect to the new views in Power BI.

Choose when to use external tools, including DAX Studio and Tabular Editor 2

Some Power BI features aren't available in Power BI Desktop, and you may want to use an external tool to perform some operations. External tools connect to the underlying data model and allow you to query and make changes to your model. In this section, we'll discuss some of the reasons to use DAX Studio and Tabular Editor 2.

DAX Studio

DAX Studio is an open source tool for querying tabular data models, including Power BI and Analysis Services.

> **NOTE**   **DOWNLOADING DAX STUDIO**
>
> You can download DAX Studio from *https://daxstudio.org*.

After you install DAX Studio, you can launch it from Power BI Desktop by selecting **External tools > DAX Studio**. You can see the DAX Studio interface in Figure 3-1.

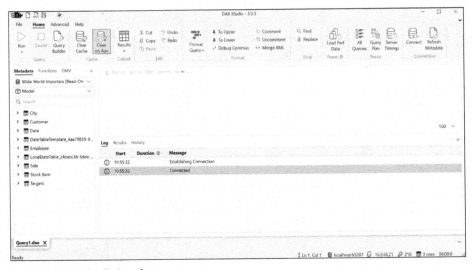

FIGURE 3-1 DAX Studio interface

While the full functionality of DAX Studio is outside the scope of this book, here are some features that can be useful to many users of Power BI:

- **Writing and analyzing queries**—The primary function of DAX Studio is to query data models. We review DAX queries in detail in Skill 4.2: Visualize data by using Power BI. If you don't want to write your own queries, you can use **Query Builder**, which will write DAX queries for you.

- **Clearing cache**—In many cases, Power BI caches the query results to improve the report viewing experience. When analyzing queries, you'll find it useful to clear cache to ensure that your timings aren't tainted by caching. You can clear cache in DAX Studio by selecting **Clear Cache**.

- **Viewing model metrics**—You can see the relative size of tables and columns in your data model, which we'll review in Skill 3.2: Optimize enterprise-scale data models.

Tabular Editor 2

Tabular Editor 2 is an open source tool for development of tabular data models. Tabular Editor is available as an open source version called Tabular Editor 2 and as a paid version called Tabular Editor 3. We only cover Tabular Editor 2 in this book.

> **NOTE   DOWNLOADING TABULAR EDITOR 2**
>
> You can download Tabular Editor 2 from *https://github.com/TabularEditor/TabularEditor/releases/latest*.

Figure 3-2 shows Tabular Editor 2 connected to a local Power BI data model.

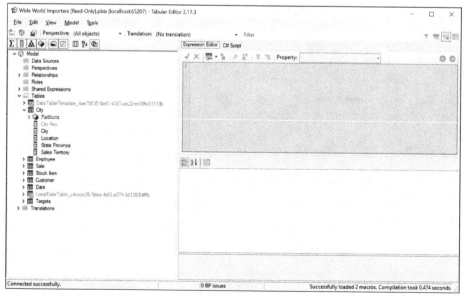

FIGURE 3-2 Tabular Editor 2

As mentioned in Skill 1.3: Manage the analytics development lifecycle, Tabular Editor 2 can be used in your source control setup. Additionally, you can edit the data model metadata, including but not limited to adding or editing measures. Most actions in Tabular Editor 2 can be scripted and automated. For example, the following C# script will format the selected measures:

```
Selected.Measures.FormatDax();
```

To execute the script, select some measures in Tabular Editor, select **C# Script**, enter the script, and select **Run script**.

> **NOTE USEFUL SCRIPT SNIPPETS**
>
> For more examples of scripts you can run in Tabular Editor 2, see "Useful script snippets" at *https://docs.tabulareditor.com/te2/Useful-script-snippets.html.*

One of the standout features of Tabular Editor 2 is Best Practice Analyzer (BPA), which we'll review in Skill 3.2: Optimize enterprise-scale data models. You can also create calculation groups in Tabular Editor 2, which we'll cover next.

Create calculation groups

Calculation groups are a feature of tabular models; the main use of calculation groups is to reduce the amount of code you need to write. For example, if you need to apply the same filters, such as month-to-date, year-to-date, and so on, to a set of measures, you can create a time intelligence calculation group instead of creating a separate measure for each calculation.

There are other reasons you may want to use calculation groups; for instance, you can create a calculation group to switch between different measures in a visual. A calculation group can apply measure formatting dynamically, unlike a solution based on the SWITCH function in DAX, and a calculation group will work when connecting from Excel, unlike a field parameter.

While it's possible to create calculation groups by using several tools, the best way is to use Tabular Editor 2, which we'll use in this book.

> **IMPORTANT CALCULATION GROUPS AND IMPLICIT MEASURES**
>
> You should be aware that if you choose to use calculation groups in your data model, you won't be able to use implicit measures anymore. Power BI creates implicit measures when you add a summarized field to a visual. The implicit measures you created before creating a calculation group will continue to work, except they won't be affected by calculation groups.

To create a calculation group in Tabular Editor, select **Model > New Calculation Group**. You'll be prompted to enter a name for the new calculation group, and you'll see the calculation group properties, as shown in Figure 3-3.

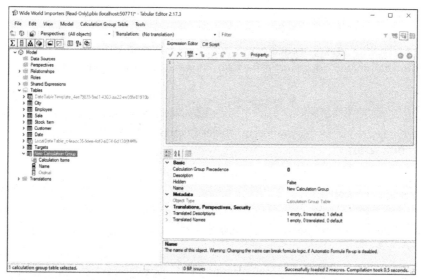

FIGURE 3-3 New calculation group created

An important property of a calculation group is the precedence, which becomes relevant when your data model contains more than one calculation group. The precedence determines the order in which calculation groups are applied: the higher the number, the earlier it will be applied.

A calculation group contains one or more calculation items, which become rows in a calculation group table. To create a calculation item, right-click a calculation group and select **Create New > Calculation Item**. You'll be prompted to enter a new calculation item name, and you'll see the calculation item properties, as shown in Figure 3-4.

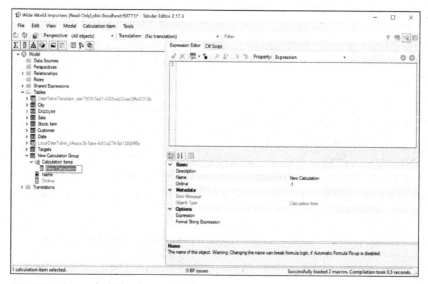

FIGURE 3-4 New calculation item created

Apart from Name, the following are the most important calculation item properties:

- **Ordinal**—Because calculation items appear as rows in a calculation group, the Ordinal property determines the order of calculation items. You can edit this property manually, or you can drag and drop calculation items within a calculation group to adjust the order.

- **Expression**—The expression determines which calculation applies to measures when you select a calculation item. While you see and can edit the calculation item expression in the properties section, it's easier to work in the Expression Editor section. Later in this section, we'll review the kinds of expressions you can apply.

- **Format String Expression**—This property determines the format that'll be applied to measures when you select a calculation item. You can use a DAX formula to specify a format dynamically. Again, you can edit the property in the Expression Editor after you select Format String Expression from the Property drop-down list.

Calculation groups can make use of the following special DAX functions:

- **SELECTEDMEASURE**—Returns the currently used measure. Used as a placeholder in calculation item expressions.

- **SELECTEDMEASURENAME**—Returns the name of the currently used measure. Can be useful in case you want to apply different calculations to different measures, depending on the measure names.

- **SELECTEDMEASUREFORMATSTRING**—Returns the format string of the currently used measure. Can be useful when you want to dynamically change the format string of measures.

- **ISSELECTEDMEASURE**—Logical function that checks whether the currently used measure is contained in a list of measures you specify.

For example, you can create a calculation item with the following expression to calculate the month-to-date value of the currently selected measure:

```
CALCULATE(
    SELECTEDMEASURE(),
    DATESMTD('Date'[Date])
)
```

Note that you're not forced to use the SELECTEDMEASURE function in calculation items; for instance, the following expression will substitute the currently used measure with the Total Quantity measure, regardless of the measure used:

```
[Total Quantity]
```

After you create one or more calculation items in your calculation group, you'll need to save changes to your model by selecting **Save** in the upper-left corner or by pressing **Ctrl+S**. You may also need to refresh the calculation group table in Power BI Desktop.

To use a calculation group, you need to add the visible calculation group column to a slicer or filter and select a calculation item. By default, the visible column's name will be *Name*, which you can change in Tabular Editor or Power BI Desktop; the *Ordinal* column contains the Ordinal property values of each calculation item.

You can also use calculation groups in DAX. In the following example, we're applying the logic of the *MTD* calculation item from the calculation group called *Time Intelligence*:

```
Quantity MTD =
CALCULATE(
    [Total Quantity],
    'Time Intelligence'[Period] = "MTD"
)
```

Note that you can only use calculation groups with measures; therefore, the following measure will not apply the MTD calculation item logic:

```
Quantity MTD Wrong =
CALCULATE(
    SUM(Sale[Quantity]),
    'Time Intelligence'[Period] = "MTD"
)
```

Calculation groups can be especially useful when you need to apply the same filters consistently, particularly when filters come from different tables and creating a column to filter is difficult.

Write calculations that use DAX variables and functions, for example, handling blanks or errors, creating virtual relationships, and working with iterators

While in some cases you can create insightful visuals without writing DAX, for more sophisticated analysis, you might need to enrich your model with calculated columns, calculated tables, and measures.

With DAX, you can derive many more insights from your data compared to using just the existing fields. For example, DAX allows you to dynamically calculate period-over-period figures, as well as percentages, such as weighted averages. In this section, we are going to explore the skills needed to perform calculations and query with DAX.

DAX is a functional language that resembles the Excel formula language, and there are many functions that appear in both. Unlike the M language, DAX is not case-sensitive in most cases. At the same time, there are some important differences:

- In DAX, there is no concept of a cell in a data table. If you need to get a value from a table, you will need to filter a specific column down to that value.

- DAX is strongly typed; it is not possible to mix values of different data types in the same column.

DAX data types

Every column in a Power BI data model has exactly one data type. Currently, DAX supports the following eight data types:

- **Decimal Number**—This is the most popular numeric data type. It is designed to hold fractional numbers, and it can handle whole numbers as well.
- **Fixed Decimal Number**—This data type is similar to Decimal Number, but the number of decimal places is fixed at four. Internally, numbers of this type are stored as integers divided by 10,000.
- **Whole Number**—This data type stores integers.
- **Date/Time**—This data type stores dates and times together. Internally, values are stored as decimal numbers.
- **Date**—Allows you to store dates without time. If you convert a Date/Time value to date, the time portion is truncated, not rounded.
- **Time**—This data type stores time only, without dates.
- **Text**—Stores text strings in Unicode format.
- **True/False**—Also known as Boolean, this data type stores True and False values, which, if converted to a number, will be 1 and 0, respectively.

DAX can perform implicit type conversions if needed. For example, you can add TRUE to a text string, "2", and the result will be 3:

```
3 = "2" + TRUE
```

On the other hand, if you concatenate two numbers, you will get a text string as a result:

```
23 = 2 & 3
```

You can perform explicit type conversion with functions such as INT and VALUE, which convert values to integers. For example, the following expression results in 45069:

```
45069 = INT("2018-05-23")
```

Dates in the form of text strings can be converted to dates using the DATEVALUE function:

```
23 May 2023 = DATEVALUE("2023-05-23")
```

Alternatively, you can prefix date strings with dt like so:

```
23 May 2023 = dt"2023-05-23"
```

You can convert numeric and datetime values to text using the FORMAT function, which takes two arguments: an expression to convert and a format string. FORMAT is an example of a function that is case-sensitive. The following two expressions provide different results:

```
// AM or PM, depending on time of the day
Upper = FORMAT(NOW (), "AM/PM")
```

```
// am or pm, depending on time of the day
Lower = FORMAT(NOW (), "am/pm")
```

NEED MORE REVIEW? **DAX FORMAT FUNCTION**

To learn more about the FORMAT function in DAX, including information on which format strings it accepts, see "FORMAT Function (DAX)" at *https://learn.microsoft.com/en-us/dax/format-function-dax.*

Blank or null values in DAX act like zeros in many cases; this behavior is very different from SQL nulls and Excel empty cells. For example, a sum of two blanks is blank, whereas in Excel you would get 0; the sum of 1 and blank is 1, whereas in SQL, the sum is NULL. You can generate a blank value using the BLANK function. You can check whether an expression is blank with the ISBLANK function.

NEED MORE REVIEW? **DATA TYPES IN POWER BI**

For a more detailed overview of data types supported in Power BI, including a table of implicit type conversions and BLANK behavior, see "Data types in Power BI Desktop" at *https://learn.microsoft.com/en-us/power-bi/connect-data/desktop-data-types.*

DAX operators

In DAX, you can use the following operators, as shown in Table 3-1.

TABLE 3-1 DAX operators

Type	Operator	Meaning	Example	Result
Arithmetic	+	Addition	2 + 3	5
	–	Subtraction or sign	2 – 3	–1
	*	Multiplication	2 * 3	6
	/	Division	3 / 2	1.5
	^	Exponentiation	2 ^ 3	8
Comparison	=	Equal to	0 = BLANK()	TRUE
	==	Strictly equal to	0 == BLANK()	FALSE
	>	Greater than	2 > 3	FALSE
	<	Less than	2 < 3	TRUE
	>=	Greater than or equal to	2 >= 3	FALSE
	<=	Less than or equal to	2 <= 3	TRUE

Type	Operator	Meaning	Example	Result
	<>	Not equal to	2 <> 3	TRUE
Text concatenation	&	Concatenates two text values	"2" & "3"	23
Logical	&&	AND condition between two Boolean expressions	(2 = 3) && (1 = 1)	FALSE
	||	OR condition between two Boolean expressions	(2 = 3) || (1 = 1)	TRUE
	IN	Belongness in a list	2 IN { 1, 2, 3 }	TRUE
	NOT	Negation	NOT 2 = 3	TRUE

Some logical operators are also available as functions. Instead of the double ampersand, you can use the AND function:

```
AND(2 = 3, 1 = 1)
```

Instead of a double pipe, you can use the OR function:

```
OR(2 = 3, 1 = 1)
```

Both functions, AND and OR, take exactly two arguments. If you need to evaluate more than two conditions, you can nest your functions:

```
AND(2 = 3, AND(1 = 1, 5 = 5))
```

The NOT operator can be used as a function as well:

```
NOT(2 = 3)
```

NEED MORE REVIEW?   **DAX OPERATOR REFERENCE**

For more examples and details on DAX operators, including operator precedence, see "DAX operators" at *https://learn.microsoft.com/en-us/dax/dax-operator-reference*.

Create DAX formulas for calculated columns

A calculated column is an additional column in a table that you define with a DAX formula. The difference between a custom column created with M and a calculated column created with DAX is that the latter is based on data that has already been loaded into your model. Furthermore, calculated columns do not appear in Power Query Editor.

You can create a calculated column in several ways, for example, by selecting **Modeling > Calculations > New column** in the Report view. This will create a calculated column in the table that is selected in the Data pane. Alternatively, you can right-click a table in the Data pane and select New Column. Power BI will then open a formula bar (Figure 3-5) where you can write your DAX formula, then select the check mark or press Enter to validate the formula. Power BI will also create a new field in the Data pane, and this new field will have a column icon next to it.

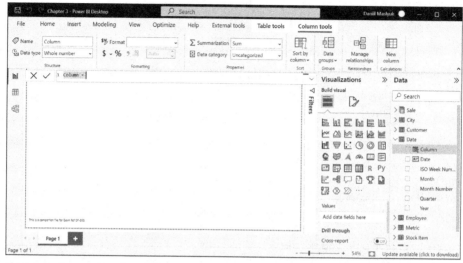

FIGURE 3-5 Formula bar after clicking New Column

The formula that you write is automatically applied to each row in the new column. You can reference another column in the following way:

```
'Table name'[Column name]
```

For example, calculate Unit Price Including Tax by creating a calculated column in the Sale table with the following formula:

```
Unit Price Including Tax = Sale[Unit Price] *(1 + Sale[Tax Rate] / 100)
```

Note that the formula includes both the column name—it precedes the equals operator—and the column formula itself, which follows the equals operator.

The Power BI Desktop formula bar has IntelliSense enabled, and it helps you with selecting tables, columns, and functions after you type a few characters, and it also highlights syntax. Instead of copying the previous formula, you can start by specifying the column name, followed by the equals operator, then start typing **uni**. At this stage, IntelliSense will give you a list of all column and functions that have "uni" appear as part of their names (Figure 3-6). If you select a function from the list, it will also display the function's description.

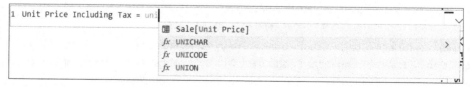

FIGURE 3-6 IntelliSense suggested values

You can navigate in this list with arrow keys on your keyboard and press Tab to autocomplete the statement. Alternatively, you can select a value by using your mouse, which has the same effect as pressing the Tab key.

In general, columns should always be referenced using a fully qualified syntax, which is a table name in single quotation marks followed by a column name in square brackets. If a table name does not contain spaces, does not start with a number, and is not a reserved keyword such as Calendar, then you can safely omit the single quotation marks. If IntelliSense highlights a word, then it is likely a reserved keyword.

When you are referencing a column in the same table, you can use just a column name in square brackets. Although this is syntactically correct, it might be difficult to read, especially because it is best practice to reference measures without table names. Measures are discussed in more detail later in this chapter.

If you want to reference a column from a table that is on the one side of a one-to-many relationship with the current table, you need to use the RELATED function. For example, you could add a Customer column to the Sale table with the following formula:

```
Customer = RELATED(Customer[Customer])
```

RELATED has a companion function, RELATEDTABLE, which can work in the opposite direction. For example, you could add a calculated column to the Date table that counts the number of rows in the Sale table. Because it is not possible to store a multi-row table in one row, you would also need to apply an aggregation function to RELATEDTABLE. In this case, we can use COUNTROWS, which counts the number of rows in a table:

```
Sales # = COUNTROWS(RELATEDTABLE(Sale))
```

Note that RELATEDTABLE only works in one direction by default. If you have not enabled bidirectional relationships, the following calculated column in the Date table will contain the same value for each row of the column, which is the same as the number of rows in the City table:

```
Cities # = COUNTROWS(RELATEDTABLE(City))
```

If this column is defined in the Date table, changing cross-filter direction between the Sale and City tables from Single to Both ensures that each row shows the number of cities to which we sold on a particular date.

USING DAX FUNCTIONS IN CALCULATED COLUMNS

DAX has hundreds of functions. Some functions return scalar values, whereas others return tables. If a function results in a one-column, one-row table, it can be implicitly converted to a scalar value.

There are many functions that perform the same tasks as some M functions. For example, the LOWER, UPPER, LEN, and TRIM functions transform text values in the same way as the M Text. Lower, Text.Upper, Text.Length, and Text.Trim functions, respectively.

Unlike M functions, DAX functions can perform implicit type conversion. For instance, in M, the following expression results in the error shown in Figure 3-7:

```
Text.Length(100)
```

 Expression.Error: We cannot convert the value 100 to type Text.
Details:
    Value=100
    Type=[Type]

FIGURE 3-7 Error message

In DAX, on the other hand, LEN(100) returns 3. Using LEN on non-text values, however, is somewhat unpredictable, and it should be combined with the FORMAT function. For example, if the 'Date'[Date] column contains a date value of 1 January 2018, then a corresponding value in the following calculated column will result in 9:

```
DAX Length = LEN('Date'[Date])
```

However, if you format values explicitly inside the LEN function, then it is possible to control the results. The following calculated column returns 10:

```
DAX Formatted Length = LEN(FORMAT('Date'[Date], "dd-MM-yyyy"))
```

The LEN function, as well as FIND or SEARCH, can be useful when you want to extract substrings of a variable length. For instance, in the Customer table, there is a column called Buying Group, which has three distinct values:

- N/A
- Tailspin Toys
- Wingtip Toys

Let's say you want to extract the first word only, so you are looking to create a column with the following three values:

- N/A
- Tailspin
- Wingtip

Note that each word has a different length. If the number of characters you wanted to extract were fixed, you could use the LEFT function, which gives you the first N characters. This function, along with RIGHT, MID, and LEN, also exists in Excel. To create a calculated column with the first three characters from Buying Group, you would write the following formula:

```
Buying Group First Three Characters = LEFT(Customer[Buying Group], 3)
```

To extract the first word, first calculate the length of the first word. For this, you need to find the position of the space symbol in a string. In this case, use the FIND or SEARCH function. Both functions have two required arguments: the text to find and where to search. The only difference between them is that FIND is case-sensitive, whereas SEARCH is not. Because we are looking for a space symbol, we can use either function. We can first try the following formula:

```
Buying Group First Space Position = FIND(" ", Customer[Buying Group])
```

Because there is no space in "N/A," we get an error that propagates to the entire column, even though there is only one row in which the space was not found. You can see the error in Figure 3-8.

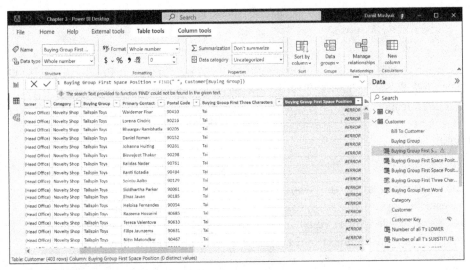

FIGURE 3-8 DAX error message in the whole column

This behavior is typical for DAX calculated columns. One way to solve this problem is to use the optional parameters in FIND. The third parameter specifies the number of character to start the search from; if omitted, it is 1. The fourth parameter specifies the value to return in case nothing is found. For example, return 0 if nothing is found:

```
Buying Group First Space Position No Error = FIND(" ", Customer[Buying Group], , 0)
```

In this case, you get no error. An alternative way to solve the same problem is to use the IFERROR function, which takes two arguments: an expression to evaluate and a value to return in case of an error. The following calculated column returns the same result as the previous one:

```
Buying Group First Space Position No Error = IFERROR(FIND(" ", Customer[Buying
Group]), 0)
```

To extract the first word from Buying Group, use the following formula:

```
Buying Group First Word = IFERROR(LEFT(Customer[Buying Group], FIND(" ",
Customer[Buying
Group]) - 1), Customer[Buying Group])
```

There are two things to note about this formula. First, subtract 1 from the result of FIND, because DAX starts counting from 1, which is different from M. Second, this formula is quite long and could benefit from formatting to make the code easier to read. There is a tool by SQLBI called DAX Formatter (http://daxformatter.com), which helps you make your code cleaner and easier to read. DAX Formatter can also be called from DAX Studio and Tabular Editor.

The following code has been formatted with DAX Formatter:

```
Buying Group First Word =
IFERROR (
LEFT ( Customer[Buying Group], FIND ( " ", Customer[Buying Group] ) - 1 ),
    Customer[Buying Group]
)
```

The LEN function can also be useful when you want to calculate how many times a text string appears in another text string. For this, use the SUBSTITUTE function.

The SUBSTITUTE function, which is case-sensitive, has three required parameters: text, old text, and new text. For instance, replace all a's with o's in "Alabama." As a result, you get "Alobomo":

```
Alobomo = SUBSTITUTE("Alabama", "a", "o")
```

Because SUBSTITUTE is case-sensitive, the first A is not affected. To count the number of times a character appears in a string, substitute the character with an empty string and calculate the difference in lengths of the old and the new strings. The following expression counts the number of times the capital letter T appears in the Buying Group column values:

```
Number of T's = LEN(Customer[Buying Group]) - LEN(SUBSTITUTE(Customer[Buying Group],
    "T", ""))
```

To count the number of times the letter T appeared regardless of case, you can either use another SUBSTITUTE function or use LOWER or UPPER. The following three formulas provide identical results, and it shows that in DAX there is often more than one way to solve the same problem:

// Using second SUBSTITUTE

```
Number of all T's SUBSTITUTE =
LEN(Customer[Buying Group]) - LEN(SUBSTITUTE(SUBSTITUTE(Customer[Buying Group], "t",
    ""), "T", ""))
```

// Using LOWER

```
Number of all T's LOWER =
LEN(Customer[Buying Group]) - LEN(SUBSTITUTE(LOWER(Customer[Buying Group]), "t", ""))
```

// Using UPPER

```
Number of all T's UPPER =
LEN(Customer[Buying Group]) - LEN(SUBSTITUTE(UPPER(Customer[Buying Group]), "T", ""))
```

The Number of T's and Number of all T's columns provide the following results, shown in Table 3-2.

TABLE 3-2 Comparison of the Number of T's and Number of all T's columns

Buying Group	Number of T's	Number of all T's LOWER
N/A	0	0
Tailspin Toys	2	2
Wingtip Toys	1	2

> ***NEED MORE REVIEW?*** **TEXT DAX FUNCTIONS**
>
> **For more information on the available text functions in DAX, see "Text Functions (DAX)" at**
> ***https://learn.microsoft.com/en-us/dax/text-functions-dax.***

DAX has several mathematical functions available, many of which are similar to the Excel functions with which they share their names. In the following list, you can see how some of the most common mathematical DAX functions work:

- **ABS(Number)**—Returns the absolute value of a number.
- **DIVIDE(Numerator, Denominator, AlternateResult)**—Safe division function that can handle division by 0.
- **EXP(Number)**—Returns e raised to the power of a number.
- **EVEN(Number)**—Returns a number rounded up to the nearest even number. You can check if a number is even using the ISEVEN function.
- **ODD(Number)**—Returns a number rounded up to the nearest odd number. You can check if a number is odd using the ISODD function.
- **FACT(Number)**—Returns the factorial of a number.
- **LN(Number)**—Returns the natural logarithm of a number.
- **LOG(Number, Base)**—Returns the logarithm of a number to the base you specify.
- **MOD(Number, Divisor)**—Returns the remainder of a number divided by a divisor.
- **PI()**—Returns the number Pi, accurate to 15 digits.
- **POWER(Number, Power)**—Returns the result of a number raised to a power. This is the function equivalent of the exponentiation (^) operator.
- **QUOTIENT(Numerator, Denominator)**—Returns the integer portion of a division.
- **SIGN(Number)**—Returns –1 if a number is negative, 1 if it is positive, and 0 if it is zero.
- **ROUNDDOWN(Number, NumberOfDigits)**—Rounds a number toward 0 to a specified number of decimal places.
- **FLOOR(Number, Significance)**—Rounds a number toward 0 to the nearest multiple of significance.

- **TRUNC(Number, NumberOfDigits)**—Truncates a number, keeping the specified number of decimal places.

- **ROUND(Number, NumberOfDigits)**—Rounds a number to a specified number of decimal places.

- **MROUND(Number, Multiple)**—Rounds a number to the nearest multiple.

- **ROUNDUP(Number, NumberOfDigits)**—Rounds a number away from 0 to a specified number of decimal places.

- **CEILING(Number, Significance)**—Rounds a number up to the nearest multiple of significance.

- **INT(Number)**—Rounds a number down to the nearest integer.

- **RAND()**—Returns a random number greater than or equal to 0 and less than 1.

- **RANDBETWEEN(Bottom, Top)**—Returns a random integer between two specified numbers.

- **SQRT(Number)**—Returns the square root of a number.

NEED MORE REVIEW? **MATHEMATICAL DAX FUNCTIONS**

For more information on the available mathematical and trigonometric functions in DAX, see "Math and Trig Functions (DAX)" at *https://learn.microsoft.com/en-us/dax/math-and-trig-functions-dax*.

The date and time functions in DAX help you create calculations based on dates and time. The following list shows some of the most common date and time functions:

- **TODAY()**—Returns the current system date in datetime format.

- **NOW()**—Returns the current system date and time in datetime format.

- **DATE(Year, Month, Day)**—Returns the specified date in datetime format.

- **DATEVALUE(TextDate)**—Converts a text date to a date in datetime format.

- **YEAR(Date)**—Returns the year portion of a date.

- **MONTH(Date)**—Returns the month number of a date.

- **DAY(Date)**—Returns the day number of a date.

- **TIME(Hour, Minute, Second)**—Returns the specified time in datetime format.

- **TIMEVALUE(TextTime)**—Converts a text time to time in datetime format.

- **HOUR(Datetime)**—Returns the hour of a datetime.

- **MINUTE(Datetime)**—Returns the minute of a datetime.

- **SECOND(Datetime)**—Returns the second of a datetime.

- **DATEDIFF(StartDate, EndDate, Interval)**—Returns the number of intervals between two dates. The interval can be any of the following: SECOND, MINUTE, HOUR, DAY, WEEK, MONTH, QUARTER, YEAR.

- **EDATE(Date, Months)**—Shifts a date back or forward by a specified number of months.

- **EOMONTH(Date, Months)**—Returns the end of month date of a specified date, shifted by a specified number of months.

- **WEEKDAY(Date, ReturnType)**—Returns the number of the day of the week according to the specified `ReturnType`.

- **WEEKNUM(Date, ReturnType)**—Returns the week number in the year according to the specified `ReturnType`.

NEED MORE REVIEW? **DATE AND TIME DAX FUNCTIONS**

For more information on the available date and time functions in DAX, see "Date and Time Functions (DAX)" at *https://learn.microsoft.com/en-us/dax/date-and-time-functions-dax.*

USING LOOKUPVALUE

If there is a many-to-one relationship between two tables, you can bring a related value from the one side to the many side with RELATED, as discussed earlier in the chapter. With LOOK-UPVALUE, it is possible to look up values from another table based on one or more conditions. This is especially useful when there are two or more conditions to look up by because DAX allows creating physical relationships based on one column only.

LOOKUPVALUE uses the following syntax: the column to retrieve values from, followed by pairs of arguments, in which the first item is a column to search and the second item is a scalar expression to look for. If there is no match, a blank value is returned. If there are multiple values that match the same condition, an error is returned.

For review purposes, use the following example. In the Sale table, you can insert values from the Targets table using the following formula:

```
Target Target Excluding Tax =
LOOKUPVALUE (
    Targets[Target Excluding Tax],
    Targets[Month], EOMONTH(Sale[Invoice Date Key], -1) + 1,
    Targets[Buying Group], RELATED(Customer[Buying Group])
)
```

Note that this particular calculated column does not provide useful results because the granularity of the Sale and Targets tables is different, but LOOKUPVALUE can nonetheless be useful in situations where the granularity of tables is the same or does not matter. Also note that the following formula, which is not specific enough, does not work and results in an error, as shown in Figure 3-9.

```
Target Target Excluding Tax Wrong =
LOOKUPVALUE (
    Targets[Target Excluding Tax],
```

```
    Targets[Buying Group], RELATED(Customer[Buying Group])
)
```

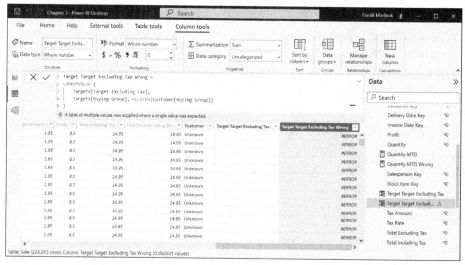

FIGURE 3-9 LOOKUPVALUE that results in an error

GROUPING VALUES

Calculated columns can be very useful for grouping values. For instance, if you have a column with unit prices, such as 'Stock Item'[Unit Price], you may want to put them into Low, Medium, and High categories based on business requirements. The column contains 58 distinct values. Let's say that items under $100 can be placed in the Low category, items from $100 to $1,000 can be placed into the Medium category, and the rest can be placed into the High category.

One way to do it would be by using the IF function. IF, like many other DAX functions, can be nested. The following calculated column produces the necessary grouping:

```
Price Category =
IF (
    'Stock Item'[Unit Price] < 100,
    "Low",
    IF (
        'Stock Item'[Unit Price] < 1000,
        "Medium",
        "High"
    )
)
```

If you use this calculated column in a visual, you will notice that the values are sorted in alphabetic order: High, Low, Medium. To solve this problem, try the following code:

```
Price Category Number =
IF (
```

```
        'Stock Item'[Price Category] = "Low",
    1,
    IF (
        'Stock Item'[Price Category] = "Medium",
        2,
        3
    )
)
```

An alternative way to produce the same column is to use the SWITCH function. The first parameter in this function is an expression to be evaluated multiple times. The other parameters come in pairs: a value to evaluate against the expression, and a result to return in case the value and the expression match. The last argument, which is optional, is the result to return if no value matched the expression.

The following formula returns the same results as the previous formula:

```
Price Category Number SWITCH = SWITCH('Stock Item'[Price Category], "Low", 1, "Medium",
2, 3)
```

Once you create the column using either approach and try to sort the Price Category column by Price Category Number, you will get the error shown in Figure 3-10.

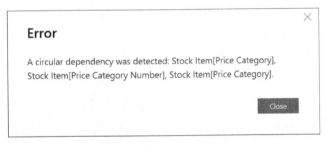

FIGURE 3-10 Sort by another column error

This error message appears because you are trying to sort the Price Category column by a column that derives its values from Price Category. Note that you can sort Price Category Number by Price Category. This problem can be fixed in at least two ways. One way is to create the two calculated columns in reverse order:

// First, create Price Category Number

```
Price Category Number =
IF (
    'Stock Item'[Unit Price] < 100,
    1,
    IF (
        'Stock Item'[Unit Price] < 1000,
        2,
        3
    )
)
```

// Second, create Price Category

```
Price Category = SWITCH('Stock Item'[Price Category Number], 1, "Low", 2, "Medium",
"High")
```

Now the Price Category column can be sorted by the Price Category Number column without any errors. An alternative approach is to write the two calculated columns in the same way so that both of them reference the Unit Price column without referencing each other:

// The order of creation does not matter in this case

```
Price Category =
IF (
    'Stock Item'[Unit Price] < 100,
    "Low",
    IF (
        'Stock Item'[Unit Price] < 1000,
        "Medium",
        "High"
    )
)
Price Category Number =
IF (
    'Stock Item'[Unit Price] < 100,
    1,
    IF (
        'Stock Item'[Unit Price] < 1000,
        2,
        3
    )
)
```

In this way, you can also sort the Price Category column by the Price Category Number column without any problem.

The SWITCH function is especially useful when you have many conditions you want to check. For instance, if you decide to group unit prices into five categories, use four IF statements:

```
Five Price Categories =
IF (
    'Stock Item'[Unit Price] < 10,
    "Very Low",
    IF (
        'Stock Item'[Unit Price] < 100,
        "Low",
        IF (
            'Stock Item'[Unit Price] < 200,
            "Medium",
```

```
        IF (
            'Stock Item'[Unit Price] < 1000,
            "High",
            "Very High"
        )
      )
    )
  )
)
```

With SWITCH, you can use the SWITCH TRUE pattern to check Boolean statements:

```
Five Price Categories SWITCH =
SWITCH (
    TRUE (),
    'Stock Item'[Unit Price] < 10, "Very Low",
    'Stock Item'[Unit Price] < 100, "Low",
    'Stock Item'[Unit Price] < 200, "Medium",
    'Stock Item'[Unit Price] < 1000, "High",
    "Very High"
)
```

You can also group values with the user interface. To group the Unit Price values, right-click the column in the **Data** pane, then select **New Group**. The Groups window, shown in Figure 3-11, will then open, where you can specify the settings for grouping, also called *binning*.

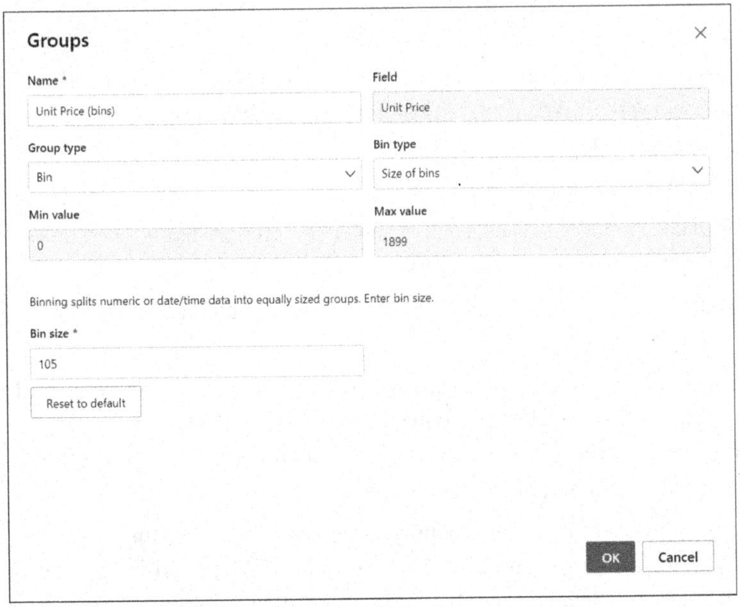

FIGURE 3-11 The Groups window with Bin selected as group type

Power BI analyzes the values in the column and chooses the group type that it deems best for the selected column. Because we have numeric values in Unit Price, Power BI decided that it's best to group the values into bins. Power BI gave the new column a default name, Unit Price (bins), which can be changed.

Two bin types are available: Size of Bins and Number of Bins. For Size of Bins, Power BI determines the best bin size, which can be adjusted. In our case, Power BI deemed 105 to be the best bin size. If necessary, you can reset the bin size to its default. If you select OK with default settings, Power BI will create a calculated column in which unit prices are rounded down to the nearest multiple of 105.

In this specific case, the new column will contain five distinct values:

- 0
- 105
- 210
- 315
- 1890

Internally, Power BI uses the following formula:

```
Unit Price (bins) =
IF(
ISBLANK('Stock Item'[Unit Price]),
BLANK(),
INT('Stock Item'[Unit Price] / 105) * 105
)
```

Note that this calculated column has a special icon next to it: squares inside squares. This is different from the icons shown with other calculated columns that we have created so far. You can see the Unit Price (bins) icon in Figure 3-12.

The other calculated columns have one of two icons:

- When a column is of a numeric data type, such as the Price Category Number column, it has a calculated column icon with a capital sigma.
- When a column is of other data type text, like the Price Category column, it has a calculated column icon with *fx* written on it.

Even though technically Unit Price (bins) is a calculated column, it is not possible to see and modify its formula with Power BI Desktop. Instead, you can edit the group by right-clicking the column and selecting **Edit groups**. The Groups window will then open where you make changes, but you will not be able to change the group type.

If you choose to change Bin Type to Number of Bins, you will need to specify the number of bins, which, for the Unit Price column, Power BI set to 18 by default. When you edit the Bin Count field, Power BI will show you the approximate bin size; for the default 18 bins, the bin size is 105.5. You can see the Groups dialog box in Figure 3-13.

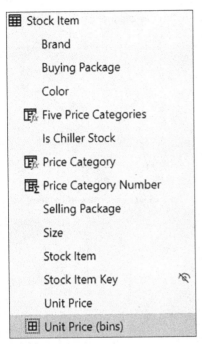

FIGURE 3-12 The Unit Price (bins) column in the fields list

FIGURE 3-13 Groups window with Number of Bins selected as Bin Type

Grouping Unit Price by number of bins results in the following five distinct values, which are different from groups based on bin size:

- 0
- 105.50
- 211
- 316.50
- 1793.50

When you create a new group, you can also choose the List group type. If you choose List in the **Group type** drop-down list, the Groups window interface will change, allowing you to pick values and group them. The Groups dialog box with List selected as Group type can be seen in Figure 3-14.

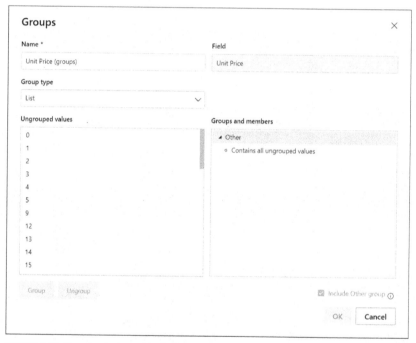

FIGURE 3-14 Groups window with List group type

In this dialog box, you can either group items individually, resulting in single-item groups, or you can select multiple values at once by holding the Ctrl key. Holding the Shift key allows you to select a range of values. Once you select some values and select the **Group** button, the values are transferred to the list on the right, **Groups and members**, and you can specify a new name for each group. By default, every group is given a name that is the list of values separated by ampersands. Below the **Groups and members** list, the **Include Other group** check box enables you to create the Other group, which contains all ungrouped values. If you choose not to include the Other group, ungrouped values will be left as is.

USING VARIABLES IN CALCULATED COLUMNS

By using variables in DAX, you can write more readable and concise code. For example, let's say you want to define a discounted unit price that includes tax, but if the new price is less than $20, then you keep the old price, including tax. The discount rate is 20 percent. One way to write this formula is as follows:

```
New Price =
IF (
    Sale[Unit Price]
        *(1 + Sale[Tax Rate] / 100)
        * 0.8
        < 20,
    Sale[Unit Price]
        *(1 + Sale[Tax Rate] / 100),
    Sale[Unit Price]
        *(1 + Sale[Tax Rate] / 100)
        * 0.8
)
```

Note that the formula contains repeated code. If we rewrite the formula with variables, it will become easier to read. The general pattern for using variables is as follows:

```
Measure name =
VAR FirstVariable = … // DAX expression
VAR NthVariable = … // DAX expression
RETURN = … // DAX expression
```

The names of variables cannot include spaces or be reserved keywords, such as Measure. You can reference previously declared variables inside variables. The variables can only be accessed in the expression they are defined in; you cannot access variables defined in column A from column B, for example.

If we rewrite the New Price formula with variables, it may look as follows:

```
New Price =
VAR TaxPct = Sale[Tax Rate] / 100
VAR PriceInclTax = Sale[Unit Price] *(1 + TaxPct)
VAR DiscountedPriceInclTax = PriceInclTax * 0.8
RETURN
    IF (
        DiscountedPriceInclTax < 20,
        PriceInclTax,
        DiscountedPriceInclTax
    )
```

Another way to solve the problem of repetitive code in calculated columns is to split inter-mediate calculations in different columns. For instance, you can instead create four calculated columns as follows:

```
TaxPct = Sale[Tax Rate] / 100
PriceInclTax = Sale[Unit Price] *(1 + Sale[TaxPct])
DiscountedPriceInclTax = Sale[PriceInclTax] * 0.8
New Price =
IF (
    Sale[DiscountedPriceInclTax] < 20,
    Sale[PriceInclTax],
    Sale[DiscountedPriceInclTax]
)
```

While this approach results in the same values as the previous New Price formulas, it has an important drawback: increased data model size. Every calculated column is materialized, resulting in greater file size. Because Power BI uses VertiPaq, an in-memory engine, calculated columns also occupy RAM space. The size of a calculated column depends on the number of its distinct values, so some columns may take more space than others.

EVALUATION CONTEXT

Most functions that we have reviewed so far were executed in so-called row context. Row con-text can be thought of as the current row. When you define a calculated column, its formula is evaluated for each row of a table to which the column is added. Some table and aggregation functions, such as FILTER and SUMX, iterate over tables and, as a result, also use row context.

Some functions ignore row context, and they use filter context instead. Filter context can be thought of as all the filters that are applied to a calculation. Filters can come from several places: visual-, page-, and report-level filters; axes in a visual; slicers; rows and columns in the Matrix visual; and more. For example, when you create a bar chart with Calendar Year Label on the axis and Profit in values, then each Calendar Year Label provides filter context for its Profit values, and as a result, each bar is different. Filters can also be applied programmatically with DAX.

> **IMPORTANT SORT BY COLUMN AND FILTER CONTEXT**
>
> Columns used for sorting are part of filter context. For example, if you show Profit by Month, and you sort Month by Month Number, then Month Number is also part of filter context.

The two contexts always coexist at the same time, though either of them can be empty at certain times. For instance, when you define a calculated column in a physical table with a formula that uses no functions, the filter context is empty.

Functions that ignore row context include, but are not limited to, SUM, AVERAGE, and COUNTROWS. To see the effect of using a formula that ignores the row context, let's say we've got a table called Scale with the following values:

- 1
- 1000
- 1000000

We can create a calculated column in the Scale table with the following formula:

```
Sum of Scale = SUM(Scale[Scale])
```

The resulting column can be seen in Figure 3-15.

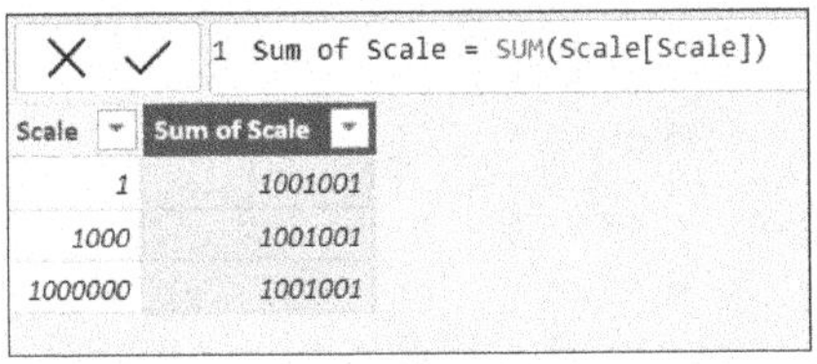

Scale	Sum of Scale
1	1001001
1000	1001001
1000000	1001001

1 Sum of Scale = SUM(Scale[Scale])

FIGURE 3-15 Sum of Scale calculated column

Note that the new column has the same value for each row because SUM works in filter context and ignores row context. In other words, SUM calculates its values irrespective of what the current row's value in the Scale[Scale] column is.

By default, row context ignores any relationships that are in place unless you use the RELATED or RELATEDTABLE function. You can only leverage the effect of relationships between tables using filter context. It is possible to transform row context into equivalent filter context. For this purpose, we can use the CALCULATE function, which has one required parameter: an expression that works in filter context. This function can also take optional filter arguments, which we are going to discuss later in this chapter. At this time, we are going to focus on the context transition capability of CALCULATE. To see the effect of context transition, create the following calculated column:

```
Sum of Scale Calculate = CALCULATE(SUM(Scale[Scale]))
```

Note that writing CALCULATE(Scale[Scale]) results in an error because Scale[Scale] can only work in row context. The reason why you cannot use Scale[Scale] in filter context is that DAX does not know what you want to do with values in the column. Do you want to sum the values, take an average of them, or something else? The Sum of Scale Calculate column is shown in Figure 3-16.

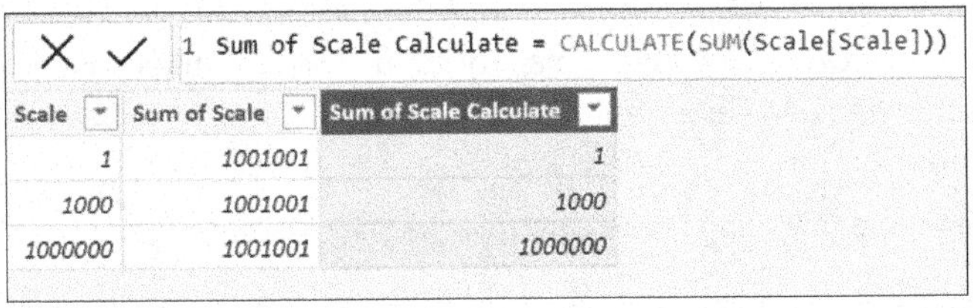

Scale	Sum of Scale	Sum of Scale Calculate
1	1001001	1
1000	1001001	1000
1000000	1001001	1000000

1 Sum of Scale Calculate = CALCULATE(SUM(Scale[Scale]))

FIGURE 3-16 Sum of Scale Calculate column

When context transition happens, the row context is transformed into equivalent filter context. This means that for each row, a table is filtered to contain only those rows where the values are the same as in the current row. For example, when we define the Sum of Scale Calculate calculated column with CALCULATE and context transition happens, in the first row the following filter context is applied: Scale[Scale] = 1 and Scale[Sum of Scale] = 1001001. For the Scale rows that remain after filtering, SUM(Scale[Scale]) is performed. Therefore, every row contains a different value in the Sum of Scale Calculate column.

It's important to remember that the current row and the equivalent filter context are not the same thing. For an example that highlights the difference, add a duplicate row to the Scale table. To do that, follow these steps:

1. In the **Model** view, select the **Scale** table.

2. In **Properties**, ensure no column is selected as **Key column**.

3. Right-click the **Scale** table in the **Data** pane and select **Edit query**.

4. In Power Query Editor, click the gear icon next to the **Source** step.

5. Type **1** in the fourth row and select **OK**.

6. Select **Close & Apply**.

You can see the results in Figure 3-17.

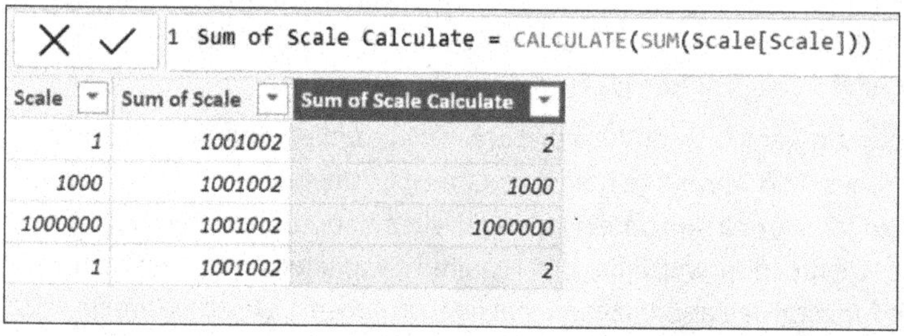

Scale	Sum of Scale	Sum of Scale Calculate
1	1001002	2
1000	1001002	1000
1000000	1001002	1000000
1	1001002	2

1 Sum of Scale Calculate = CALCULATE(SUM(Scale[Scale]))

FIGURE 3-17 Resulting Sum of Scale Calculate values with duplicate rows

Note that the rows in which Scale = 1 has the Sum of Scale Calculate value of 2. For these rows, here are the steps that DAX followed to arrive at these figures:

1. Identify the row context: Scale = 1, Sum of Scale = 1001002.

2. Convert the row context into the equivalent filter context: filter the Scale table and keep only those rows where Scale = 1 and Sum of Scale = 1001002.

3. For the two rows that remain, sum the values in the Scale column: 1 + 1 = 2.

4. Return the result of the summation, which is 2.

Because there are two identical rows, DAX follows the same procedure twice. The filter context cannot distinguish between identical rows, and as a result, the Sum of Scale Calculate values are not the same as the Scale column values.

Earlier in this chapter, we defined the following two columns in the Date table:

```
// Returns different values for each row
Sales # = COUNTROWS(RELATEDTABLE(Sale))
```

```
// Returns different values only with bidirectional filtering enabled
    Cities # = COUNTROWS(RELATEDTABLE(City))
```

The reason why these calculated columns returned different values is that RELATEDTABLE is an alias for CALCULATETABLE, a sister function of CALCULATE, which works similarly, but receives a table expression as the first parameter instead of a scalar expression. Therefore, for each row in the Date table, context transition occurred, which filtered the Sale and City tables to only those rows that were related to the current row.

CIRCULAR DEPENDENCIES IN CALCULATED COLUMNS

DAX evaluates every expression and does so in the order that respects every dependency of one expression on another. To understand circular dependencies, first review with the following calculated column in the Stock Item table:

```
    Profit $ = 'Stock Item'[Recommended Retail Price] - 'Stock Item'[Unit Price]
    Profit % = DIVIDE('Stock Item'[Profit $], 'Stock Item'[Unit Price])
```

Note that the Profit % column references and depends on the Profit $ column. At this point, we can attempt to change the Profit $ column formula to the following one:

```
    Profit $ = 'Stock Item'[Profit %] * 'Stock Item'[Unit Price]
```

Using this formula results in a circular dependency error: "A circular dependency was detected: Stock Item[Profit %], Stock Item[Profit $], Stock Item[Profit %]." This is because Profit % depends on Profit $, which also depends on Profit % to calculate its value. As a result, neither column can be calculated.

You can now remove both columns and go to the Scale table, where you have previously added the following column:

```
    Sum of Scale Calculate = CALCULATE(SUM(Scale[Scale]))
```

For clarity purposes, rename it to Calculate1 and remove the Sum of Scale column, keeping only the Scale and Calculate1 columns. Now, try to add the following column to the Scale table:

```
    Calculate2 = CALCULATE(SUM(Scale[Scale]))
```

Note that this formula is the same as the Calculate1 column formula, and neither column references the other. At the same time, we get the circular dependency error: "A circular dependency was detected: Scale[Column], Scale[Calculate1], Scale[Column]."

The reason this happens lies in context transition. When DAX evaluates Calculate1, it converts the row context into equivalent filter context: it filters the Scale table to those rows where Scale and Calculate2 column values are the same as the values of the current row. For Calculate2, it keeps those Scale rows where Scale and Calculate1 column values are the same as current row values. Therefore, Calculate1 implicitly depends on Calculate2, and vice versa.

This situation happens in tables in which there is no column that is used as a primary key. In our case, the Scale column can be used as a primary key, because it contains unique values only. When a column is used as a primary key, DAX performs context transition differently: because it knows it can rely on the column having unique values, it uses this column to filter the table during context transition, without using values from other columns. For the Scale table, it means that during context transition DAX will only look at the Scale column values to filter the table. To fix the error, follow these steps:

1. Go to the **Model view**.
2. Select the **Scale** table.
3. In the **Properties** pane, select **Scale** from the **Key column** drop-down list.
4. If prompted to refresh a calculated column, select **Refresh now**.
5. If necessary, go to the Calculate2 formula and press Enter, prompting Power BI to reevaluate the column.

At this stage, you can see that the Calculate2 column can be evaluated with no errors.

Calculated tables

As previously mentioned, some DAX functions return tables. Table expressions can be used inside formulas of calculated columns and measures, as well as by themselves to materialize calculated tables. There are a few ways to create a calculated table; for example, you can create a calculated table by selecting **Modeling > Calculations > New table** in the Report view. You will then need to write a DAX formula for a table in the formula bar.

One way to create a calculated table is to duplicate an existing one. For example, you can duplicate the Date table:

```
Date Duplicate = 'Date'
```

Because Date is a reserved keyword, you need to enclose it in single quotation marks.

The technique of duplicating tables can be useful if you want to separate multiple relationships between two tables—for example, between Sale and Date.

FILTER

By using FILTER, you can filter a table based on specified condition. The FILTER function takes two arguments: a table expression and a filter condition. The filter condition is evaluated in row context for each row of the table. For example, create a calculated table for stock items in which unit price is greater than $300. Use the following formula:

```
Expensive Stock Items =
FILTER (
    'Stock Item',
    'Stock Item'[Unit Price] > 300
)
```

This formula creates a table with six rows. Note that if you had calculated columns in the Stock Item table, those columns would appear as native columns in the Expensive Stock Items table.

Although FILTER takes only one condition, you can combine the conditions into a single Boolean condition with AND or OR logic. For instance, if you want to select only those stock items that are more expensive than $300 or are gray, you can write the following formula:

```
Expensive or Gray Stock Items =
FILTER (
    'Stock Item',
    OR (
        'Stock Item'[Unit Price] > 300,
        'Stock Item'[Color] = "Gray"
    )
)
```

You would get 15 rows in this case.

Unlike CALCULATETABLE, FILTER does not trigger context transition. The following two calculated columns, created in the Date table, produce different results:

// Different value for each row
```
Countrows Calculatetable = COUNTROWS(CALCULATETABLE(Sale))
```

// Same number for each row
```
Countrows Filter = COUNTROWS(FILTER(Sale, TRUE))
```

Note that while CALCULATETABLE has only one mandatory parameter, FILTER always uses two parameters.

When you use FILTER in context transition—for example, in a calculated column—it generates new row context. This means that in each row of the table where you create a calculated column, DAX iterates over each row in the table used inside FILTER. It is possible to access the original row context from the new one with the EARLIER function. Doing so allows you to perform calculations in a way similar to SUMIF in Excel. For instance, you can count the number of rows in the Date table for each year in the following calculated column formula:

```
Days in Year EARLIER =
COUNTROWS (
    FILTER (
        'Date',
        'Date'[Year] = EARLIER('Date'[Year])
    )
)
```

The same effect can be achieved by using a variable instead of EARLIER. Because variables always stay constant after being evaluated, they are not affected by the new context. In a way, variables behave like constants. This behavior will be reviewed again later in this chapter. You can see an example of using a variable in the following formula:

```
Days in Year VAR =
VAR CurrentMonth = 'Date'[Year]
```

```
    RETURN
        COUNTROWS (
            FILTER (
                'Date',
                'Date'[Year] = CurrentMonth
            )
        )
```

If needed, you can perform context transition inside FILTER. For example, you can create a calculated table for salespeople who have made over 5,000 sales:

```
Productive Salespeople =
FILTER (
    Employee,
    CALCULATE(COUNTROWS(Sale)) > 5000
)
```

> **IMPORTANT   CONTEXT TRANSITION AND FILTERING**
>
> Remember that when you perform context transition in large tables, the operation is much slower than filtering column values. Therefore, instead of filtering a table and doing context transition, it is advisable to precalculate the results in a calculated column and then filter by the column.

ALL

The ALL function removes any filters that were placed on a table or columns. This function can also be used to create calculated tables. When used to create a calculated table, the function can accept one or more columns from a table, or a whole table as a parameter. The ALL function cannot accept another function as an argument. When you use a table as an argument for ALL, every row, including duplicated rows, is returned in the new table. When you use one column in ALL, a one-column table containing distinct values from the column is returned. When you use multiple columns from the same table in ALL, a table containing all existing combinations of the column values is returned. It is not possible to use columns from different tables inside one ALL statement. Note that if a table contains duplicate rows, then ALL with a table as the only argument and ALL with all columns listed will return tables with a different number of rows.

For examples of using ALL to create calculated tables, create the following three tables:

```
All Stock Item = ALL('Stock Item')
All Color = ALL('Stock Item'[Color])
All Color, Buying Package = ALL('Stock Item'[Color], 'Stock Item'[Buying Package])
```

- The first table, All Stock Item, is a duplicate of the Stock Item table.
- The second table, All Color, contains distinct values from the Color column from the Stock Item table.
- The third table, All Color, Buying Package, contains all existing distinct combinations of the Color and Buying Package columns from the Stock Item table. This table is shown in Figure 3-18.

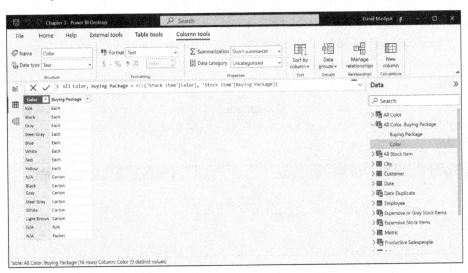

FIGURE 3-18 All Color, Buying Package

To see the difference that ALL makes in filter context, create the following calculated columns in the Customer table:

```
Customer Rows = COUNTROWS(Customer)
Customer Rows Calculate = CALCULATE(COUNTROWS(Customer))
Customer Rows Calculate All = CALCULATE(COUNTROWS(ALL(Customer)))
```

- The first calculated column, Customer Rows, returns the total number of rows in the Customer table. Because there is no context transition, you get the same value, the total number of rows, for every row in the calculated column.

- The second calculated column, Customer Rows Calculate, includes CALCULATE, which triggers context transition. This means that for every row of the table, DAX counts only those rows that have the same column values as the current row. Because there is a primary key in this table, the result is always 1.

- The third calculated column, Customer Rows Calculate All, also includes CALCULATE, but it has Customer wrapped in ALL. Here's what happens: First, context transition transforms the row context into equivalent filter context. Because we have a primary key in the table, the Customer table for each row is filtered to include that row only. Next, the changes produced by filter placed on the Customer table are undone with ALL.

Note that the calculated columns, Customer Rows and Customer Rows Calculate All, return the same value, 403, which is the total number of rows in the Customer table. These two values are not always equivalent. As discussed earlier in this chapter, when a table on the many side of a relationship includes some values that are not present in the table on the one side of a relationship, DAX adds a virtual row to the table on the one side. This row is blank and not visible by default. To review this effect on our formulas, follow these steps:

1. In the **Data** pane, right-click the **Customer** table and select **Edit query**.

2. Select the **AutoFilter** button of the Customer Key column.

3. If necessary, click **Load More** in the bottom-right corner of the filter list.

4. Deselect values 1, 2, and 3, and click **OK**.

5. Click **Close & Apply**.

Once the Customer table is updated, you can see different values in the Customer Rows and Customer Rows Calculate All calculated columns: 400 and 401, respectively, as shown in Figure 3-19.

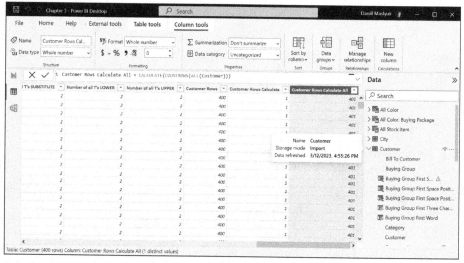

FIGURE 3-19 Customer Rows calculated columns

Note that the total number of rows in the Customer table is now 400, which can be seen at the bottom of the screen. The Customer Rows Calculate All, however, displays 401, which includes the virtual row that DAX included for those Customer Key values in the Sale table that do not have a corresponding value in the Customer table.

You can see this row materialized if you create the following calculated table:

```
All Customer = ALL(Customer)
```

Note that this table has 401 rows, which includes the special blank row. Create a duplicate of the Customer table without the blank row in at least three ways. First, reference the original table without using any functions:

```
Duplicate Customer = Customer
```

Second, filter out the blank row:

```
Filter All Customer =
FILTER (
    ALL(Customer),
    NOT ISBLANK(Customer[Customer Key])
)
```

Third, use a variation of ALL–ALLNOBLANKROW:

```
AllNoBlankRow Customer = ALLNOBLANKROW(Customer)
```

The ALLNOBLANKROW function returns a table without the virtual blank row that is added in cases in which a table on the many side contains values that are not in the table on the one side. Note that if a table or a column contains a genuine blank row or value, the ALLNOBLANKROW function will not filter it out. This function, like ALL, also removes any filters on a specified table or column.

At this stage, go back to Power Query Editor and remove the Filtered Rows step from the Customer query.

The third variation of the ALL function, ALLEXCEPT, has a different syntax from ALL and ALL-NOBLANKROW: it receives a table as the first argument, followed by at least one column to exclude. ALLEXCEPT returns all columns from a specified table except the excluded columns. This function can be useful when you want to include more columns than you want to exclude.

Another application of the ALLEXCEPT function can be inside calculated columns to calculate subtotals without using the combination of FILTER and EARLIER or VAR. Earlier in this chapter, we created two calculated columns that calculated the number of rows in the Date table for each year. The following formula returns the equivalent results:

```
Days in Year ALLEXCEPT =
CALCULATE(
    COUNTROWS('Date'),
    ALLEXCEPT('Date', 'Date'[Year])
)
```

CALCULATETABLE

Earlier in the chapter, we encountered CALCULATETABLE when discussing the RELATEDTABLE function. The latter is an alias for the former when only one argument is used. In CALCULATETABLE, you can specify optional conditions, which are combined with AND logic. CALCULATETABLE accepts either tables or Boolean statements as filter conditions. Any table expression can be used in place of filters, including functions that return tables. The following is an example of a Boolean filter condition:

```
'Stock Item'[Color] = "Black"
```

In the following example, we are reducing the number of rows in the Stock Item table, keeping only those in which Unit Price is greater than $300:

```
Expensive Stock Items =
CALCULATETABLE (
    'Stock Item',
    'Stock Item'[Unit Price] > 300
)
```

Same as when using FILTER before, we receive a table with six rows. Unlike FILTER, CALCU-LATETABLE can accept more than one filter parameter. The following calculated table contains stock items that are both black and priced higher than 300:

```
Expensive and Black Stock Items =
CALCULATETABLE (
    'Stock Item',
    'Stock Item'[Unit Price] > 300,
    'Stock Item'[Color] = "Black"
)
```

It is possible to combine filter conditions with OR logic instead of AND logic using either the OR function or the double pipe operator. For example, the following calculated table will filter the Stock Item table to contain only those items that are priced either below 1 or above 1000, but not at 0:

```
Stock Items below $1 or above $1000 =
CALCULATETABLE (
    'Stock Item',
    OR (
        'Stock Item'[Unit Price] < 1,
        'Stock Item'[Unit Price] > 1000
    ),
    'Stock Item'[Unit Price] <> 0
)
```

When you combine filters using the OR logic, the filters that you specify must be applied to columns from one table only.

VALUES AND DISTINCT

The VALUES and DISTINCT functions work similarly; they return tables that contain only distinct rows. Both functions can receive a column reference as a parameter. For example, the following table returns 12 month names from the Date table:

```
Months = DISTINCT('Date'[Month])
```

Both functions can also receive a table as a parameter. While the VALUES function can only receive a physical table as a parameter, the DISTINCT function can also work with table expressions, which means that the table can be either a physical table or a table returned by another function.

Unlike the ALL function, which also returns a table with distinct rows, the VALUES and DISTINCT functions do not remove filters from their tables. In practice, this means that these two calculated columns in the Employee table return the same results:

```
Sale Rows Calculate = CALCULATE(COUNTROWS(Sale))
Sale Rows Calculate VALUES = CALCULATE(COUNTROWS(VALUES(Sale)))
```

As previously mentioned, if a table expression returns a table with one row and one column, it can be converted to a scalar value. The following calculated column in the Employee table works, too; it contains the same values as the Employee column:

```
Employee Calculate = CALCULATE(VALUES(Employee[Employee]))
```

Another major difference between the VALUES and DISTINCT functions is that the former might include a special blank row that is added when some values on the many side of a relationship do not have a matching value on the one side. The DISTINCT function never includes a blank row unless a blank row physically exists in the data. To illustrate this difference, use the Date table, which has an active relationship with the Sale table using the Delivery Date Key column. There are null values in the column, which causes a special blank row to be added. The following two tables return a different number of rows:

// 13 rows

```
Month Values = VALUES('Date'[Month])
```

// 12 rows

```
Month Distinct = DISTINCT('Date'[Month])
```

In this regard, the behavior of VALUES corresponds to ALL, while the behavior of DISTINCT corresponds to ALLNOBLANKROW.

SUMMARIZE AND SUMMARIZECOLUMNS

The SUMMARIZE function allows you to group a table by one or more columns and add new columns, if necessary. The general syntax is as follows:

```
SUMMARIZE(Table, OldColumns, NewColumns)
```

The new columns are defined by specifying a name and formula for each column. SUMMARIZE expects at least two arguments: a table to summarize and a column to group by.

The following formula produces a table with month names and numbers:

```
Month = SUMMARIZE('Date', 'Date'[Month], 'Date'[Month Number])
```

In this case, the table does not include the special blank row that results from null values being present in the Delivery Date Key column of the Sale table. If we decide to add a column that contains the number of rows in the Sale table for each month, the blank row will still not be included. The summarized table can be seen in Figure 3-20.

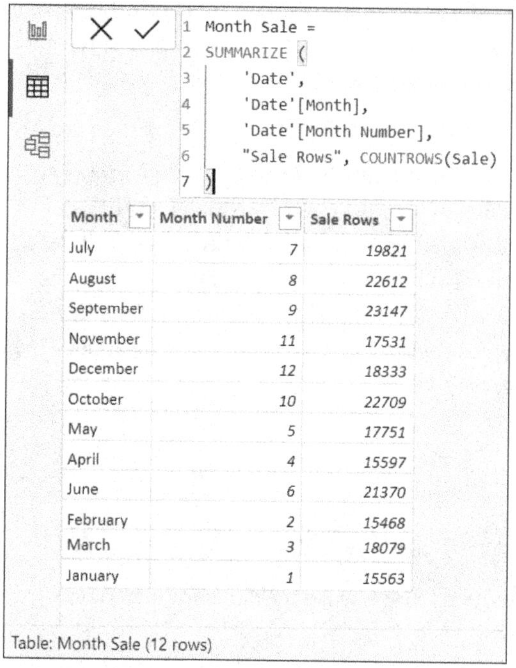

```
Month Sale =
SUMMARIZE (
    'Date',
    'Date'[Month],
    'Date'[Month Number],
    "Sale Rows", COUNTROWS(Sale)
)
```

FIGURE 3-20 Date table summarized

Note that we summarized the Date table. If instead we summarize the Sale table with the same columns, the blank row will appear, and it does not matter whether we include the Sale Rows column. The table can be seen in Figure 3-21.

```
Month Sale from Sale =
SUMMARIZE (
    Sale,
    'Date'[Month],
    'Date'[Month Number],
    "Sale Rows", COUNTROWS(Sale)
)
```

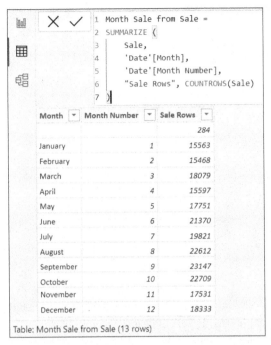

```
1  Month Sale from Sale =
2  SUMMARIZE (
3      Sale,
4      'Date'[Month],
5      'Date'[Month Number],
6      "Sale Rows", COUNTROWS(Sale)
7  )
```

Month	Month Number	Sale Rows
		284
January	1	15563
February	2	15468
March	3	18079
April	4	15597
May	5	17751
June	6	21370
July	7	19821
August	8	22612
September	9	23147
October	10	22709
November	11	17531
December	12	18333

Table: Month Sale from Sale (13 rows)

FIGURE 3-21 Sale table summarized

The columns to group by are optional. You can specify a table to summarize, new column names, and expressions. If you specify only one new column name and expression, it will result in a one-row and one-column table with a single value. As in the previous examples, the table you summarize can make a difference.

// Returns 198043439.45

```
Summarize Sale Single =
SUMMARIZE (
    Sale,
    "Total Sales", SUM(Sale[Total Including Tax])
)
```

// Returns 197776428.01

```
Summarize Date Single =
SUMMARIZE (
    'Date',
    "Total Sales", SUM(Sale[Total Including Tax])
)
```

An example of such a table can be seen in Figure 3-22.

FIGURE 3-22 Sale table summarized to one row

SUMMARIZE only returns rows that have data. For example, if you summarize the Date table by Year and Month, you will get 72 rows. If you summarize the Sale table instead, you will get 43 rows: 42 Year and Month combinations when sales happened plus the special blank row.

// Returns 72 rows

```
Date Year Month =
SUMMARIZE (
    'Date',
    'Date'[Year],
    'Date'[Month],
    'Date'[Month Number]
)
```

// Returns 43 rows

```
Sale Year Month =
SUMMARIZE (
    Sale,
    'Date'[Year],
    'Date'[Month],
    'Date'[Month Number]
)
```

In SUMMARIZE, you do not have access to row context of the table you are summarizing. Instead, SUMMARIZE divides the table into parts, grouping them by the columns you select, with each part of the original table having its own filter context. This is why you don't need to wrap COUNTROWS(Sales) in CALCULATE to trigger context transition, as no context transition is necessary.

There is a function similar to SUMMARIZE: SUMMARIZECOLUMNS. It performs similar operations, except you do not need to specify the table you want to summarize. It also works in a slightly different way from SUMMARIZE. For instance, if you use the function to create a table with Calendar Year and Month combinations, you will get a table with 73 rows: 72 existing Calendar Year and Month combinations, plus the special blank row. If you add a count of Sale rows, the table will have 43 rows, which is the same as using SUMMARIZE with the Sale table:

// 73 rows

```
Month Year = SUMMARIZECOLUMNS('Date'[Year], 'Date'[Month])
```

// 43 rows

```
Month Year =
SUMMARIZECOLUMNS (
    'Date'[Year],
    'Date'[Month],
    "Sale Rows", COUNTROWS(Sale)
)
```

ADDCOLUMNS AND SELECTCOLUMNS

The ADDCOLUMNS function adds new columns to a table, generating row context in the process. The new columns are also known as extension columns. The function expects at least three arguments: a table to add columns to, a new column name, and a new column expression. For example, the following calculated table is equivalent to the *Month Sale from Sale* table we created before:

```
AddColumns Month Sale =
ADDCOLUMNS (
    ALL('Date'[Month], 'Date'[Month Number]),
    "Sale Rows", CALCULATE(COUNTROWS(Sale))
)
```

The row context in ADDCOLUMNS makes this function different from SUMMARIZE in two ways:

- First, you need to perform context transition to get different values for each row (you can see it in the preceding formula). Without CALCULATE, we would get the same value for each row, which would be the total number of rows in the Sale table.

- Second, you can reference columns in the table to which you add columns. For instance, you can take all the Year and Month Number combinations from the Date table and create a column that puts them in a sequential order:

```
AddColumns YearMonthSequential =
ADDCOLUMNS (
    ALL (
        'Date'[Year],
        'Date'[Month Number]
    ),
```

```
        "Year Month Sequential",
        'Date'[Year] * 12 + 'Date'[Month Number]
)
```

To achieve the same effect using SUMMARIZE or SUMMARIZECOLUMNS, which use filter context, you must use VALUES to convert multiple column values into scalar values:

```
SummarizeColumns YearMonthSequential =
SUMMARIZECOLUMNS (
    'Date'[Year],
    'Date'[Month Number],
    "Year Month Sequential",
    VALUES('Date'[Year]) * 12
        + VALUES('Date'[Month Number])
)
```

The SELECTCOLUMNS function works like ADDCOLUMNS, except it does not keep the original columns. If you want to keep some of them using this function, you will have to create new columns that reference them. For example, you can take a table that contains all Calendar Year and Month combinations and keep only the Calendar Year column:

```
SelectColumns Calendar Year =
SELECTCOLUMNS (
    ALL('Date'[Year], 'Date'[Month]),
    "Year", 'Date'[Year]
)
```

The first few rows of the resulting table can be seen in Figure 3-23. Note that SELECTCOLUMNS does not produce distinct values in its columns.

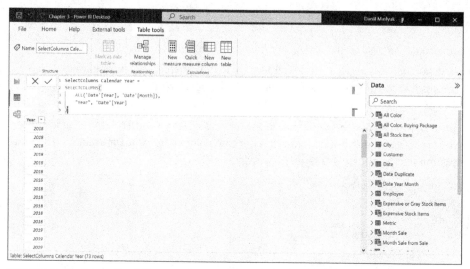

FIGURE 3-23 Partial results of the SelectColumns Calendar Year calculated table

It is possible to group the results by extension columns using SUMMARIZE. For example, you can create an extension column that returns a quarter label for each date and then get the distinct values of this column. The results can be seen in Figure 3-24.

```
Summarize SelectColumns Quarter =
SUMMARIZE (
    SELECTCOLUMNS (
        'Date',
        "Quarter", FORMAT('Date'[Date], "\QQ")
    ),
    [Quarter]
)
```

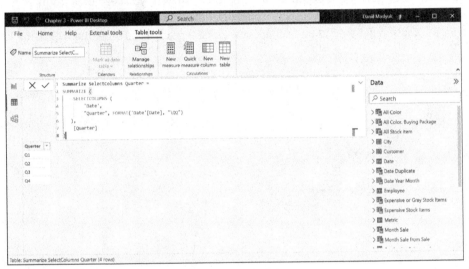

FIGURE 3-24 Date summarized by extension column, Quarter

Note that you must reference the extension column without a table name because it is not a physical column.

TOPN

The TOPN function ranks table rows by specified criteria and takes the top N rows. There are three arguments, the first two of which are required: N number, table expression, and expression to order rows by. The fourth argument, which is optional, defines the order: ASC for ascending and DESC for descending. If omitted, the default value is DESC. The order of rows is not guaranteed.

For example, you can rank salespeople by sales amount and take the top three. The result is a subset of the original table and does not include the values you are ranking by.

```
Top 3 Employees by Sales =
TOPN (
```

```
    3,
    VALUES(Employee[Employee]),
    CALCULATE(SUM(Sale[Total Excluding Tax]))
)
```

Employee
Hudson Hollinworth
Anthony Grosse
Archer Lamble

Note that TOPN uses row context, so to rank employees properly you need to perform context transition. Without CALCULATE, you would get incorrect results. Because we can use row context, you can also get the first three employees alphabetically if you order them by name:

```
Top 3 Employees by Name =
TOPN (
    3,
    VALUES(Employee[Employee]),
    Employee[Employee],
    ASC
)
```

Employee
Archer Lamble
Anthony Grosse
Amy Trefl

In case of ties, you get more rows than expected. For instance, if you order Wide World Importers employees by sales in ascending order and take the top three, you end up with five rows because five employees did not sell anything. As a result, they all tie for the first place with zero (more precisely, blank) sales.

```
Bottom 3 Employees by Sales =
TOPN (
    3,
    VALUES(Employee[Employee]),
    CALCULATE(SUM(Sale[Total Excluding Tax])),
    ASC
)
```

Employee
Henry Forlonge
Unknown
Isabella Rupp
Jai Shand
Jack Potter

CROSSJOIN, GENERATE, AND GENERATEALL

The CROSSJOIN function allows you to create a Cartesian product between two or more tables. For example, you can create a table with all possible Brand and Buying Package combinations, not just those that exist in your data:

```
Buying Package, Brand =
CROSSJOIN (
    VALUES('Stock Item'[Buying Package]),
    VALUES('Stock Item'[Brand])
)
```

The resulting table has eight rows: four Buying Package values multiplied by two Brand values. If you wrote ALL('Stock Item'[Buying Package], 'Stock Item'[Brand]), you would get only five rows. All columns in the resulting tables must be unique. This means that if you want to create a Cartesian product of a table with itself, you must rename the columns of one of the tables in advance. For example, you could rename one of the columns using SELECTCOLUMNS:

```
Buying Package CrossJoin =
CROSSJOIN (
    VALUES('Stock Item'[Buying Package]),
    SELECTCOLUMNS (
        VALUES('Stock Item'[Buying Package]),
        "Buying Package 2", 'Stock Item'[Buying Package]
    )
)
```

With CROSSJOIN, there is no row context that you can use when writing the expression of the second and subsequent tables. The GENERATE function, which always receives two table expressions as parameters, allows you to reference the current row in the first table when writing the second table expression. For instance, create a table with calendar years and top three employees in each year:

```
Top 3 Employees per Year =
GENERATE (
    SUMMARIZE(Sale, 'Date'[Year]),
    TOPN (
```

```
        3,
        VALUES(Employee[Employee]),
        CALCULATE(SUM(Sale[Total Excluding Tax]))
    )
)
```

Year	Employee
	Archer Lamble
	Taj Shand
	Anthony Grosse
2019	Hudson Hollinworth
2019	Anthony Grosse
2019	Archer Lamble
2020	Hudson Hollinworth
2020	Anthony Grosse
2020	Archer Lamble
2021	Hudson Hollinworth
2021	Anthony Grosse
2021	Archer Lamble
2022	Sophia Hinton
2022	Anthony Grosse
2022	Archer Lamble

The resulting table includes only those years and employees that actually had sales, including the blank year. If you want to include all years and employees that meet our criteria, even those that did not make any sales, use the GENERATEALL function. It works in the same way as GENERATE, except it includes all possible combinations:

// Returns 126 rows

```
Top 3 Employees per Calendar Year Month =
GENERATE (
    ALLNOBLANKROW('Date'[Year], 'Date'[Month]),
    TOPN (
        3,
        SUMMARIZE(RELATEDTABLE(Sale), Employee[Employee]),
```

```
                CALCULATE(SUM(Sale[Total Excluding Tax]))
        )
    )
```

// Returns 156 rows

```
    Top 3 Employees per Calendar Year Month =
    GENERATEALL (
        ALLNOBLANKROW('Date'[Year], 'Date'[Month]),
        TOPN (
            3,
            SUMMARIZE(RELATEDTABLE(Sale), Employee[Employee]),
            CALCULATE(SUM(Sale[Total Excluding Tax]))
        )
    )
```

In these expressions, the 30-row difference comes from months that have no deliveries, yet we have these combinations in our Date table.

GENERATESERIES

With GENERATESERIES, you can generate a table with one column, called Value, containing a list of numbers with predefined increment. These values need not exist in the data model. The function expects at least two arguments: the start value and the end value. If the start value is greater than the end value, the result will be a table with no rows. The optional third parameter specifies the increment; if omitted, it is 1 by default. The following expression outputs a list of numbers from 1 to 5:

```
    1 to 5 = GENERATESERIES(1, 5)
```

Value
1
2
3
4
5

Using the optional third parameter, you can create consecutive lists that increment by a number other than 1. For example, generate a list of odd numbers from 1 to 9 inclusive:

```
    Odd 1 to 9 = GENERATESERIES(1, 10, 2)
```

Value
1
3

Value
5
7
9

Note that even though we specified 10 as the end value, the table only goes up to 9 because the next value in the sequence, 11, falls outside of the specified range.

The GENERATESERIES function automatically detects the data type. The only column in the previous table has the Whole Number data type. In the following expression, the data type is set as Decimal Number:

```
0.1 to 0.5 Decimal = GENERATESERIES(0.1, 0.5, 0.1)
```

Value
0.1
0.2
0.3
0.4
0.5

It is also possible to specify data types explicitly. For instance, you can use the CURRENCY function to convert values to the Fixed Decimal Number type:

```
1 to 5 Fixed Decimal = GENERATESERIES(CURRENCY(1), CURRENCY(5))
```

GENERATESERIES can be used to generate lists of datetime values as well. The following table expression creates a one-column table of Date/Time data type that starts at 12 a.m. on May 1, 2023 and finishes at 12 a.m. on May 3, 2023, incrementing by 12 hours:

```
1 to 3 May 2023 at 12-hour intervals =
GENERATESERIES (
    DATE(2023, 5, 1),
    DATE(2023, 5, 3),
    TIME(12, 0, 0)
)
```

Value
1/05/2023 12:00:00 AM
1/05/2023 12:00:00 PM

Value
2/05/2023 12:00:00 AM
2/05/2023 12:00:00 PM
3/05/2023 12:00:00 AM

Though GENERATESERIES can only generate numeric or datetime value lists, it is possible to generate lists of letters by combining SELECTCOLUMNS and UNICHAR:

```
Uppercase Latin alphabet: =
SELECTCOLUMNS (
    GENERATESERIES(65, 90),
    "Letter", UNICHAR([Value])
)
```

Letter
A
B
C
...
Z

CALENDAR AND CALENDARAUTO

The CALENDAR function works like GENERATESERIES when you work with dates only: it generates a one-column table of datetime data type called Date. This function can be especially useful when your data model does not have a Date table and you want to create your own calendar.

CALENDAR has two required parameters: the start date and the end date. By default, the values increment by one day. The following expression generates a table with 365 rows, starting with January 1, 2023 and ending with December 31, 2023:

```
Year 2023 = CALENDAR(DATE(2023, 1, 1), DATE(2023, 12, 31))
```

Date
1/01/2023 12:00:00 AM
2/01/2023 12:00:00 AM
3/01/2023 12:00:00 AM
...
29/12/2023 12:00:00 AM

Date
30/12/2023 12:00:00 AM
31/12/2023 12:00:00 AM

The CALENDARAUTO function generates a list of dates, taking into account all date and date-time type columns in the data model; it takes the minimum and maximum of all dates found and extracts years and then generates a list of dates starting with January 1 of the minimum year and ending with December 31 of the maximum year.

CALENDARAUTO has one optional parameter, which is the fiscal year end month. If omitted, the default value is 12, which corresponds to the year ending on December 31. If your data model contains only dates from January 1, 2023 to December 31, 2023, then the following calculated table returns all dates from July 1, 2022 to June 30, 2024:

```
Fiscal Date = CALENDARAUTO(6)
```

Because CALENDARAUTO considers all the date and datetime columns in a data model, some-times this can lead to tables having more rows than necessary. For example, data warehouses often use the date December 31, 9999 to denote the currently valid value. If your Power BI data model contains such a date, then creating the following calculated table will result in a table with close to 3 million rows:

```
All Dates = CALENDARAUTO ()
```

Unless your data model contains many meaningful date or datetime columns, it is prefer-able to use the CALENDAR function, referencing the relevant date columns. If we did not have the Date table in our data model, and the only date column we had was the Invoice Date Key column in the Sale table, we could create the following date table:

```
Calendar = CALENDAR(MIN(Sale[Invoice Date Key]), MAX(Sale[Invoice Date Key]))
```

Because we also have the Delivery Date Key column in our data model, you can use the alternative MIN and MAX syntax, which allows the comparison of two scalar values:

```
Calendar =
CALENDAR (
    MIN (
        MIN(Sale[Delivery Date Key]),
        MIN(Sale[Invoice Date Key])
    ),
    MAX (
        MAX(Sale[Delivery Date Key]),
        MAX(Sale[Invoice Date Key])
    )
)
```

If you prefer having complete years in your calendar table, you can use the DATE/YEAR combination:

```
Calendar =
CALENDAR (
    DATE (
        YEAR (
            MIN (
                MIN(Sale[Delivery Date Key]),
                MIN(Sale[Invoice Date Key])
            )
        ),
        1,
        1
    ),
    DATE (
        YEAR (
            MAX (
                MAX(Sale[Delivery Date Key]),
                MAX(Sale[Invoice Date Key])
            )
        ),
        12,
        31
    )
)
```

You can then add calculated columns, such as month name and calendar year number, to the newly created table to make it a proper calendar table.

ROW

With the ROW function, you can create one-row tables with several columns at once. The arguments come in pairs: a column name goes first, then an expression. Only one pair of arguments is required. For example, you can create a one-row table with two columns: the number of rows in the Sale table and the number of rows in the Date table:

```
One Row =
ROW (
    "Sale Rows", COUNTROWS(Sale),
    "Date Rows", COUNTROWS('Date')
)
```

Sale Rows	Date Rows
228265	2191

The ROW function can be useful when you want to add a row to another table using the UNION function, covered next.

UNION

The UNION function works similarly to the Append feature in Power Query Editor: it combines two or more tables vertically. If the tables you are combining have the same rows among them, duplicate rows will be retained. The names of the columns do not have to match, but the number of columns in tables must be the same because tables are combined by the position of columns, not the names. The output table will have the same column names as the first table. If tables have different data types, they will be combined in accordance with DAX data type coercion. The following is an example of using UNION:

```
Table1 =
UNION (
    ROW("Color", "Red", "Value 1", 1),
    ROW("Color", "Red", "Value 1", 2),
    ROW("Color", "Green", "Value 1", 3),
    ROW("Color", "Blue", "Value 1", CURRENCY(1))
)
```

Color	Value 1
Red	1.00
Red	2.00
Green	3.00
Blue	1.00

Note that in this case, the second column will have the Fixed Decimal Number data type.

UNION can be used to create common dimensions from several different tables. For instance, we have the Buying Group column in both the Targets and Customer tables. To create a bridging table to pass filters from the Customer table to the Targets table, we can create the following calculated table:

// Bridging table between Customer and Targets

```
Buying Group =
DISTINCT (
    UNION (
        ALLNOBLANKROW(Targets[Buying Group]),
```

```
        ALLNOBLANKROW(Customer[Buying Group])
    )
  )
```

We can then hide the bridging table and create the following relationships:

- From 'Targets'[Buying Group] to 'Buying Group'[Buying Group]
- Bidirectional from 'Customer'[Buying Group] to 'Buying Group'[Buying Group]

At this point, if you go to the relationships view, your data model, excluding tables created for illustration purposes, should look similar to Figure 3-25.

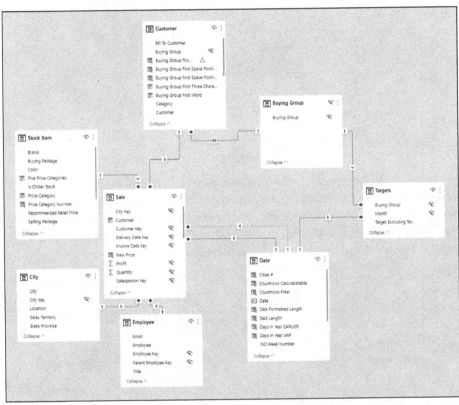

FIGURE 3-25 Relationships view after adding and relating bridging tables

INTERSECT

The INTERSECT function creates a table that consists of rows that are present in both tables that are used as arguments in INTERSECT. In the following examples, we are going to use the function on these two tables, called TableOne and TableTwo, as shown in Table 3-3 and Table 3-4, respectively.

TABLE 3-3 TableOne

Color	Value 1
Red	1
Red	2
Green	3
Blue	1

TABLE 3-4 TableTwo

Color	Value 2
Green	3
Blue	1
Blue	1
Yellow	2

Note that there is a common column name, Color, which differs from the name of the second column. Also, these tables have common rows. INTERSECT has the same requirements for tables as UNION: both tables must have the same number of columns, and the tables are combined based on the position of columns. The result of the following expression is a two-row table that has the same column names as TableOne:

```
IntersectOneTwo =
INTERSECT (
    UNION (
        ROW("Color", "Red", "Value 1", 1),
        ROW("Color", "Red", "Value 1", 2),
        ROW("Color", "Green", "Value 1", 3),
        ROW("Color", "Blue", "Value 1", 1)
    ),
    UNION (
        ROW("Color", "Green", "Value 2", 3),
        ROW("Color", "Blue", "Value 2", 1),
        ROW("Color", "Blue", "Value 2", 1),
        ROW("Color", "Yellow", "Value 2", 2)
    )
)
```

Color	Value 1
Green	3
Blue	1

The order in which two tables are used in INTERSECT matters. In the following calculated table, we are also using TableOne and TableTwo, but in reverse order:

```
IntersectTwoOne =
INTERSECT (
    UNION (
        ROW("Color", "Green", "Value 2", 3),
        ROW("Color", "Blue", "Value 2", 1),
        ROW("Color", "Blue", "Value 2", 1),
        ROW("Color", "Yellow", "Value 2", 2)
    ),
    UNION (
        ROW("Color", "Red", "Value 1", 1),
        ROW("Color", "Red", "Value 1", 2),
        ROW("Color", "Green", "Value 1", 3),
        ROW("Color", "Blue", "Value 1", 1)
    )
)
```

Color	Value 2
Green	3
Blue	1
Blue	1

Note that the second column name is now Value 2 instead of Value 1. Also, the output table retains duplicate rows from the first table but not from the second table.

EXCEPT

The EXCEPT function takes two tables as arguments and outputs all rows that are in the first table but not in the second table. Columns are compared based on their positions, so the number of columns in both tables must be the same, which is the same behavior as with the UNION and INTERSECT functions.

As with INTERSECT, the order of tables used as arguments influences the results. Note the difference in the results when EXCEPT is used with TableOne and TableTwo versus TableTwo and TableOne:

```
ExceptOneTwo =
EXCEPT (
```

```
    UNION (
        ROW("Color", "Red", "Value 1", 1),
        ROW("Color", "Red", "Value 1", 2),
        ROW("Color", "Green", "Value 1", 3),
        ROW("Color", "Blue", "Value 1", 1)
    ),
    UNION (
        ROW("Color", "Green", "Value 2", 3),
        ROW("Color", "Blue", "Value 2", 1),
        ROW("Color", "Blue", "Value 2", 1),
        ROW("Color", "Yellow", "Value 2", 2)
    )
)
```

Color	Value 1
Red	1
Red	2

```
ExceptTwoOne =
EXCEPT (
    UNION (
        ROW("Color", "Green", "Value 2", 3),
        ROW("Color", "Blue", "Value 2", 1),
        ROW("Color", "Blue", "Value 2", 1),
        ROW("Color", "Yellow", "Value 2", 2)
    ),
    UNION (
        ROW("Color", "Red", "Value 1", 1),
        ROW("Color", "Red", "Value 1", 2),
        ROW("Color", "Green", "Value 1", 3),
        ROW("Color", "Blue", "Value 1", 1)
    )
)
```

Color	Value 2
Yellow	2

Like with INTERSECT, the output table has the same column names as the first table. Duplicate rows from the first table, if any, are retained.

NATURALINNERJOIN

The NATURALINNERJOIN function works like the Merge feature in Power Query Editor: it receives two tables as arguments and joins them based on common column names. The columns that are used for joining must have the same data types. NATURALINNERJOIN joins two tables and outputs a table that has the same values present in join columns of both tables.

In the following examples, we are again using TableOne and TableTwo:

```
NaturalInnerJoinOneTwo =
NATURALINNERJOIN (
    UNION (
        ROW("Color", "Red", "Value 1", 1),
        ROW("Color", "Red", "Value 1", 2),
        ROW("Color", "Green", "Value 1", 3),
        ROW("Color", "Blue", "Value 1", 1)
    ),
    UNION (
        ROW("Color", "Green", "Value 2", 3),
        ROW("Color", "Blue", "Value 2", 1),
        ROW("Color", "Blue", "Value 2", 1),
        ROW("Color", "Yellow", "Value 2", 2)
    )
)
```

Color	Value 1	Value 2
Green	3	3
Blue	1	1
Blue	1	1

Note that in this case, the order in which you join tables only matters when considering the order of columns:

```
NaturalInnerJoinTwoOne =
NATURALINNERJOIN (
    UNION (
        ROW("Color", "Green", "Value 2", 3),
        ROW("Color", "Blue", "Value 2", 1),
        ROW("Color", "Blue", "Value 2", 1),
        ROW("Color", "Yellow", "Value 2", 2)
    ),
    UNION (
        ROW("Color", "Red", "Value 1", 1),
        ROW("Color", "Red", "Value 1", 2),
```

```
        ROW("Color", "Green", "Value 1", 3),
        ROW("Color", "Blue", "Value 1", 1)
    )
  )
```

Color	Value 2	Value 1
Green	3	3
Blue	1	1
Blue	1	1

NATURALINNERJOIN can also join physical tables that have a relationship between them. For instance, create the following two calculated tables:

// Many side of a relationship

```
ColorOne =
UNION (
    ROW("ColorOne", "Red", "Value 1", 1),
    ROW("ColorOne", "Red", "Value 1", 2),
    ROW("ColorOne", "Green", "Value 1", 3),
    ROW("ColorOne", "Blue", "Value 1", 1)
)
```

ColorOne	Value 1
Red	1
Red	2
Green	3
Blue	1

// One side of a relationship

```
ColorThree =
UNION (
    ROW("ColorThree", "Green", "Value 3", 3),
    ROW("ColorThree", "Blue", "Value 3", 1),
    ROW("ColorThree", "Yellow", "Value 3", 2)
)
```

ColorThree	Value 3
Green	3
Blue	1
Yellow	2

Once you create a relationship between ColorOne and ColorThree, you can create the following calculated table:

```
NaturalInnerJoin One Three = NATURALINNERJOIN(ColorOne, ColorThree)
```

ColorThree	Value 3	ColorOne	Value 1
Blue	1	Blue	1
Green	3	Green	3

In this case, the order of arguments makes no difference. Note that we are only able to create this calculated table because there are no columns that have the same name and there is a relationship between these tables. Without a relationship, we would get the following error: "No common join columns detected. The join function 'NATURALINNERJOIN' requires at-least one common join column."

If we were joining two related tables that had columns that shared names, we would get an error like the following one: "The Column with the name of 'ColorOne' already exists in the 'Table' Table." This limitation is not unique to NATURALINNERJOIN—in general, all column names in materialized tables must be unique in DAX. Virtual tables can have the same column names in some cases. The following calculated table works even if TableOne and TableThree have common column names:

```
Aggregated Virtual Table =
ROW (
    "NumRows",
    COUNTROWS(NATURALINNERJOIN(ColorOne, ColorThree))
)
```

NumRows
2

The ability to join tables with common names can be useful when passing filters to CALCULATE or CALCULATETABLE.

NATURALLEFTOUTERJOIN

The NATURALLEFTOUTERJOIN function is similar to NATURALINNERJOIN, but it performs the left outer join instead of the inner join. NATURALLEFTOUTERJOIN returns a table with all rows from the first table and extra columns from the second table where values in the join columns of the right table are present in the join columns of the first table:

```
NaturalLeftOuterJoinOneTwo =
NATURALLEFTOUTERJOIN (
    UNION (
        ROW("Color", "Red", "Value 1", 1),
        ROW("Color", "Red", "Value 1", 2),
```

```
            ROW("Color", "Green", "Value 1", 3),
            ROW("Color", "Blue", "Value 1", 1)
        ),
        UNION (
            ROW("Color", "Green", "Value 2", 3),
            ROW("Color", "Blue", "Value 2", 1),
            ROW("Color", "Blue", "Value 2", 1),
            ROW("Color", "Yellow", "Value 2", 2)
        )
    )
)
```

Color	Value 1	Value 2
Red	1	
Red	2	
Green	3	3
Blue	1	1
Blue	1	1

Because NATURALLEFTOUTERJOIN performs a left outer join, the order of tables used as parameters is very important. The following table not only has a different order of columns, but the rows are also different:

```
NaturalLeftOuterJoinTwoOne =
NATURALLEFTOUTERJOIN (
    UNION (
        ROW("Color", "Green", "Value 2", 3),
        ROW("Color", "Blue", "Value 2", 1),
        ROW("Color", "Blue", "Value 2", 1),
        ROW("Color", "Yellow", "Value 2", 2)
    ),
    UNION (
        ROW("Color", "Red", "Value 1", 1),
        ROW("Color", "Red", "Value 1", 2),
        ROW("Color", "Green", "Value 1", 3),
        ROW("Color", "Blue", "Value 1", 1)
    )
)
```

Color	Value 2	Value 1
Green	3	3

Color	Value 2	Value 1
Blue	1	1
Blue	1	1
Yellow	2	

Same as NATURALINNERJOIN, NATURALLEFTOUTERJOIN can be used with tables that have a relationship and no common column names.

DATATABLE

The DATATABLE function allows you to create calculated tables with data that you enter manually. Earlier in this book, you used the Enter Data feature of Power BI to enter data manually—DATATABLE provides an alternative.

At a minimum, DATATABLE takes three arguments: column name, data type, and list of values. The data types that you can choose are as follows:

- **BOOLEAN**—True/False
- **CURRENCY**—Fixed Decimal Number
- **DATETIME**—Date/Time
- **DOUBLE**—Decimal Number
- **INTEGER**—Whole Number
- **STRING**—Text

The final argument is a list of values in curly braces that resembles what you would type in M inside the #table construct. Create the Scale table using the DATATABLE function as follows:

```
Scale DataTable =
DATATABLE (
    "Scale", INTEGER,
    {
        {1},
        {1000},
        {1000000}
    }
)
```

Scale
1
1000
1000000

You can create a table with more than one column by listing all column names and data types in pairs:

```
Enriched Scale =
DATATABLE (
    "Scale", INTEGER,
    "Description", STRING,
    {
        {1, "Normal"},
        {1000, "Thousands"},
        {1000000, "Millions"}
    }
)
```

Scale	Description
1	Normal
1000	Thousands
1000000	Millions

Note that all values in curly braces must be constants—you cannot use expressions inside DATATABLE. For instance, the following calculated table cannot be created:

```
Scale Wrong =
DATATABLE (
    "Scale", INTEGER,
    {
        {1 + 0},
        {1000},
        {1000000}
    }
)
```

The error message we get in this case is as follows: "The tuple at index '1' from the table definition of the DATATABLE function does not have a constant expression in the column at index '1'."

DAX also allows you to create anonymous tables without defining column names, though the syntax is slightly different from the DATATABLE syntax. After the equation operator, you also use curly braces, but inside them, you do not use curly braces again. If you define a one-column table, you list your values separated by a comma, and DAX will call the new column Value. You can also define multicolumn tables by listing values of each row in parentheses; the parenthesis sets should be separated by commas as well. In this case, DAX will give the new columns names like Value1, Value2, and so on. Data types will also be defined automatically. For instance, we can create the following table:

```
Single-column table = {1, 2}
```

Value
1
2

The following is an example of an anonymous table with three columns:

```
Anonymous table =
{
    (1, "a", DATE(2023, 5, 1)),
    (2, "b", DATE(2023, 5, 23))
}
```

Value1	Value2	Value3
1	a	1/05/2023 12:00:00 AM
2	b	23/05/2023 12:00:00 AM

USING VARIABLES IN CALCULATED TABLES

DAX variables can store scalar values, as well as tables. For example, rewrite one of the previous table expressions as follows:

```
Tables Var =
VAR Table1 =
    UNION (
        ROW("Color", "Red", "Value 1", 1),
        ROW("Color", "Red", "Value 1", 2),
        ROW("Color", "Green", "Value 1", 3),
        ROW("Color", "Blue", "Value 1", 1)
    )
VAR Table2 =
    UNION (
        ROW("Color", "Green", "Value 2", 3),
        ROW("Color", "Blue", "Value 2", 1),
        ROW("Color", "Blue", "Value 2", 1),
        ROW("Color", "Yellow", "Value 2", 2)
    )
RETURN
    NATURALINNERJOIN(Table1, Table2)
```

While variables improve the readability of your code and potentially increase performance, it is important to understand that variables are evaluated only once in the context in which they are defined, and they become immutable. This means that using CALCULATE or CALCU-LATETABLE on a variable has no effect.

Variables in calculated tables can be used to create more readable code that is still complex. This allows you to save the time spent on creating calculated columns one by one; instead, you can define them in one calculated table expression. For instance, you can create a full calendar table in one expression using the GENERATE/ROW pattern developed by Marco Russo:

```
Calendar =
VAR Days =
    CALENDAR("2023-1-1", "2025-12-31")
RETURN
    GENERATE (
        Days,
        VAR BaseDate = [Date]
        VAR MonthName = FORMAT(BaseDate, "MMM")
        VAR MonthNumber = MONTH(BaseDate)
        VAR BaseYear = YEAR(BaseDate)
        RETURN
            ROW (
                "Month", MonthName,
                "MonthNo", MonthNumber,
                "Year", BaseYear
            )
    )
```

Date	Month	MonthNo	Year
1/01/2023 12:00:00 AM	Jan	1	2023
2/01/2023 12:00:00 AM	Jan	1	2023
3/01/2023 12:00:00 AM	Jan	1	2023
...	...	...	...
31/12/2025 12:00:00 AM	Dec	12	2025

Note that in this case, you have multiple levels of VAR/RETURN constructs. At the top level, you are defining the Days variable, which stores the table returned by the CALENDAR function. Use the Days variable in the outer RETURN expression. You have another VAR/RETURN construct, where you define more variables; this time, the variables hold scalar values, because GENERATE enables you to access the row context. The variables defined in the inner VAR/RETURN construct are not accessible in the outer construct.

Measures

An important limitation of calculated columns is that not all values can be calculated with them. For example, if you need to calculate the profit percentage, the calculated column formula might look as follows:

```
Net Profit % = DIVIDE(Example[Net Profit], Example[Gross Profit])
```

While this formula calculates the profit percentage for each row of the table, it would be incorrect to use the values from this column in a visual, because they would show an arithmetic average at best. To illustrate the problem, consider the following two-row table called Example, shown in Table 3-5.

TABLE 3-5 Sample profit values in the Example table

Product	Gross Profit	Net Profit	Net Profit %
A	3,000	300	10%
B	2,000	1,000	50%

If you use the Net Profit % column from this table in a visual, you can only show 30%, the average of 10% and 50%. This is not correct; a correct value would be (300 + 1,000) / (3,000 + 2,000) = 26%. In other words, you need to sum all Net Profit values first, then divide the result by the sum of all Gross Profit values. While displaying this value in a calculated column is possible, this value will be incorrect as soon as you filter by Product. In this case, you need to create a measure.

To create a measure, you can select **Modeling > Calculations > New measure** in the Report view. This will create a measure in the currently selected table. Alternatively, you can right-click a table in which you want to create a measure and select **New Measure**. Either option will open the formula bar where you can write your DAX formula. Once you are finished, you can either click the tick icon to the left of the formula bar or press Enter. If you create a measure in the wrong table, you can move it by selecting the correct table by selecting **Modeling > Properties > Home Table**.

Measures aggregate columns and tables, and they always work in filter context. For this reason, there is no concept of current row in measures by default. A measure with the following formula cannot be created:

```
Net Profit % = DIVIDE(Example[Net Profit], Example[Gross Profit])
```

Note that this is the same formula that works for a calculated column. This formula does not work in a measure because DAX does not know what it should do with the columns that you used. Because of this, any table or column used in a measure must be aggregated. The following functions are the most popular aggregation functions:

- SUM
- AVERAGE
- MIN
- MAX

For instance, you can create a measure that sums all Net Profit column values as follows:

```
Total Net Profit = SUM(Example[Net Profit])
```

The functions listed here always take one argument: column reference. If you want to reference two columns in an aggregation function, you need to use the iterator functions, which usually have an x suffix. These are the most commonly used ones:

- SUMX
- AVERAGEX
- MINX
- MAXX

These functions always take two arguments: a table to iterate over and an expression to evaluate for each row in row context. The aggregation functions without an x suffix are often syntactic sugar for their x-suffixed counterparts. The following two expressions are equivalent:

```
Total Net Profit = SUM(Example[Net Profit])
Total Net Profit = SUMX(Example, Example[Net Profit])
```

As mentioned earlier, the iterator functions can reference more than one column at a time. For example, in the following expression we iterate over the Sale table and, for each row, multiply Quantity by Unit Price. Finally, sum all of the resulting values:

```
Gross Sales = SUMX(Sale, Sale[Quantity] * Sale[Unit Price])
```

Because iterators generate row context, all row functions, such as RELATED, can be used:

```
Full Price Sales =
SUMX (
    Sale,
    Sale[Quantity] * RELATED('Stock Item'[Recommended Retail Price])
)
```

In the Example table, you can create the weighted profit percentage measure with the following code:

```
Net Profit % =
DIVIDE (
    SUM(Example[Net Profit]),
    SUM(Example[Gross Profit])
)
```

While this measure works and displays the correct values, you can make the code more readable and easier to maintain by splitting the calculation into three measures: Total Net Profit, Total Gross Profit, and Net Profit %. Because you can reference other measures when you create a measure, you can first create the Total Net Profit and Total Gross Profit measures, then the Net Profit % one:

```
// Create these two measures first

    Total Net Profit = SUM(Example[Net Profit])
    Total Gross Profit = SUM(Example[Gross Profit])
```

// Create this measure last

```
    Net Profit % = DIVIDE([Total Net Profit], [Total Gross Profit])
```

At this stage, the Net Profit and Gross Profit columns can be hidden. This practice is called fixing implicit measures; when you use a column in the values field well in a visual, an implicit measure is created using the default aggregation. When you write measures with DAX, you are creating explicit measures. Hiding the columns you aggregate in explicit measures is usually a good practice because it prevents user confusion over which field should be used.

MEASURES VS. CALCULATED COLUMNS

In many cases, the same values can be computed by using either a measure or a calculated column. Calculated columns are computed when they are defined and at data refresh time. Because they are materialized in a data model, they consume RAM and disk space. Measures, on the other hand, are calculated at query time, which means every time you interact with a visual, a measure recalculates its value. For this reason, measures consume CPU resources.

As you have seen, some values, such as weighted averages, cannot be computed in a calculated column, which leaves creating measures as the only option. At the same time, there are situations in which you should create a calculated column instead of a measure:

- **Slicing or filtering by values**—It is currently impossible to put a measure into a slicer. If you want to slice by newly created values, such as Price Category we created before, you must create a calculated column and not a measure.

- **Writing CPU-intensive formulas**—If your formula is very complex and it takes many seconds to compute its values, this may result in a poor user experience. In this case, it might be a good idea to precompute results in a calculated column or a calculated table, and then aggregate the results with a measure.

COUNTING VALUES IN DAX

There are several functions in DAX with which you can count values:

- COUNT
- COUNTA
- COUNTAX
- COUNTBLANK
- COUNTROWS
- COUNTX
- DISTINCTCOUNT
- DISTINCTCOUNTNOBLANK

One of the most frequently used functions is COUNTROWS, which we have already used before. The function takes one parameter: a table expression. The following measure counts the number of rows in the Sale table in the current filter context:

```
Sale Rows = COUNTROWS(Sale)
```

Because you are not limited to physical tables, you can also count rows in tables calculated dynamically. The following measure returns the number of Calendar Year and Month combinations in which we had sales:

```
Years and Months with Sales =
COUNTROWS (
    SUMMARIZE (
        Sale,
        'Date'[Year],
        'Date'[Month]
    )
)
```

The COUNT function takes a column reference as the only argument and counts the number of non-blank values in a column. For example, the following measure counts the number of non-blank Delivery Date Key values in the Sale table:

```
Count DeliveryDate = COUNT(Sale[Delivery Date Key])
```

The limitation of the COUNT function is that it cannot count Boolean values. To count the number of non-blank values regardless of data type, you can use the COUNTA function.

The COUNTX and COUNTAX functions, the behavior of which correspond to COUNT and COUNTA, respectively, allow you to count non-blank expressions when iterating over a table. Both tables take two arguments: a table to iterate over and an expression to be evaluated in row context. For instance, the following measure counts the number of rows in the Sale table where either Invoice Date Key or Delivery Date Key is not blank:

```
CountX Invoice Delivery =
COUNTX (
    Sale,
    Sale[Invoice Date Key] + Sale[Delivery Date Key]
)
```

This measure returns the same results as COUNTROWS because in our data model, either Invoice Date Key or Delivery Date Key will always be not blank for any row.

To count blank values in a column, you can use the COUNTBLANK function, which always receives a column reference as its only parameter. You can count the number of blank Delivery Date Key values with the following measure:

```
CountBlank DeliveryDate = COUNTBLANK(Sale[Delivery Date Key])
```

Note that COUNTBLANK doesn't count the special blank row. The sum of COUNT (and its equivalent COUNTA, COUNTX, and COUNTAX expressions) and COUNTBLANK will always give you the same result as COUNTROWS, unless the special blank row is involved. In Table 3-6, you can see that the sum of Count DeliveryDate and CountBlank DeliveryDate is equal to Sale Rows.

TABLE 3-6 Sale Rows, Count DeliveryDate, and CountBlank DeliveryDate sliced by Calendar Year Label

Year	Sale Rows	Count DeliveryDate	CountBlank DeliveryDate
	284		284
2019	36907	36907	
2020	63760	63760	
2021	69845	69845	
2022	57469	57469	
Total	228265	227981	284

If you want to count the number of distinct values in a column, you can either use a combination of COUNTROWS and DISTINCT, or you can use DISTINCTCOUNT, which takes a column reference as its only parameter. For instance, the following measure returns the number of Stock Item Key values that have been sold at least once:

```
Sold StockItems = DISTINCTCOUNT(Sale[Stock Item Key])
```

Note that this measure returns different results compared to a measure that counts the distinct Stock Item Key values in the Stock Item table when sliced by Calendar Year Label or Brand. Note also that when a column contains unique values only, you can safely use COUNTROWS instead. The following two measures produce equivalent results, as shown in Table 3-7:

```
Distinct StockItems = DISTINCTCOUNT( 'Stock Item'[Stock Item Key])
Distinct StockItems = COUNTROWS('Stock Item')
```

TABLE 3-7 Sold StockItems and Distinct StockItems sliced by Calendar Year Label

Calendar Year Label	Sold StockItems	Distinct StockItems
	164	672
2018		672
2019	219	672
2020	219	672
2021	219	672

Calendar Year Label	Sold StockItems	Distinct StockItems
2022	227	672
2023		672
Total	227	672

We see the same value for `Distinct StockItems` in this table because filter context from the Date table does not pass to the Stock Item table. Note that because of the nature of distinct counts, the results might not always be additive.

In Table 3-8, the difference between `Sold StockItems` and `Distinct StockItems` is that some stock items do not sell at all, even though we have them in our data model.

TABLE 3-8 `Sold StockItems` and `Distinct StockItems` sliced by Brand

Brand	Sold StockItems	Distinct StockItems
N/A	209	605
Northwind	18	67
Total	227	672

USING CALCULATE IN MEASURES

The CALCULATE function, covered earlier in the chapter, is most often used in measures. Its syntax is identical to CALCULATETABLE except it received a scalar expression as the first parameter instead of a table expression. Using CALCULATE in a measure without filters is useless because every measure has an implicit CALCULATE wrapped around it. To illustrate this effect, look at the Scale table and create the following calculated column and measure in it:

// Calculated column
```
Sum Column = SUM(Scale[Scale])
```

// Measure
```
Sum Measure = SUM(Scale[Scale])
```

Note that the formula used in two expressions is the same. As expected, `Sum Column` shows the same value for each row. Now, create the following calculated column in the Scale table:

```
Sum Measure Column = [Sum Measure]
```

In this calculated column, you are referencing `Sum Measure` only. Note the square brackets around the measure name; this is the standard way to reference measures in DAX. Now, the Scale table should look like the one in Figure 3-26.

FIGURE 3-26 The Scale table with Sum Column and Sum Measure Column created

Even though the formulas of Sum Measure and Sum Column are identical, the values in the Sum Measure Column calculated column are different because each measure has an implicit CALCULATE wrapped around it. In other words, you can rewrite the Sum Measure Column expression as follows:

```
Sum Measure Column = CALCULATE(SUM(Scale[Scale]))
```

For this reason, CALCULATE becomes useful inside measures when you want to change the filter context. As with CALCULATETABLE, you can pass Boolean expressions or tables as filter parameters in CALCULATE. For example, you can create the All-time Profit measure, which displays the all-time profit made, regardless of the selections made in the Date table:

// Create the Total Profit measure first

```
Total Profit = SUM(Sale[Profit])
```

// Create the All-time Profit measure that references Total Profit

```
All-time Profit = CALCULATE([Total Profit], ALL('Date'))
```

If you use this measure in a table visual alongside Total Profit, you will see results similar to Figure 3-27.

As expected, the measure shows the same value for each row, which is the same as the grand total of Total Profit. While ALL removes the filter, we can also set the new filter context at the same time. For example, here we show profit made in January regardless of the selected Month. Figure 3-28 shows the desired result.

Month	Total Profit	All-time Profit
	119,456.90	85,729,180.90
January	5,833,234.25	85,729,180.90
February	5,798,604.00	85,729,180.90
March	6,658,632.25	85,729,180.90
April	5,883,737.80	85,729,180.90
May	6,538,422.55	85,729,180.90
June	8,054,375.95	85,729,180.90
July	7,496,202.55	85,729,180.90
August	8,433,002.90	85,729,180.90
September	8,836,040.00	85,729,180.90
October	8,643,188.40	85,729,180.90
November	6,503,028.00	85,729,180.90
December	6,931,255.35	85,729,180.90
Total	**85,729,180.90**	**85,729,180.90**

FIGURE 3-27 All-time Profit alongside Total Profit sliced by Month

Month	Total Profit	January Profit
	119,456.90	5,833,234.25
January	5,833,234.25	5,833,234.25
February	5,798,604.00	5,833,234.25
March	6,658,632.25	5,833,234.25
April	5,883,737.80	5,833,234.25
May	6,538,422.55	5,833,234.25
June	8,054,375.95	5,833,234.25
July	7,496,202.55	5,833,234.25
August	8,433,002.90	5,833,234.25
September	8,836,040.00	5,833,234.25
October	8,643,188.40	5,833,234.25
November	6,503,028.00	5,833,234.25
December	6,931,255.35	5,833,234.25
Total	**85,729,180.90**	**5,833,234.25**

FIGURE 3-28 January Profit measure alongside Total Profit sliced by Month

When we pass Boolean expressions as filters in CALCULATE, they are transformed into table filters with FILTER and ALL combined. Because you only have the Month column visible, and you sort it by the Calendar Month Number column, the following formula will not work correctly. You can see the values it returns in Figure 3-29.

```
January Profit Wrong = CALCULATE([Total Profit], 'Date'[Month] = "January")
```

Month	Total Profit	January Profit Wrong
	119,456.90	
January	5,833,234.25	5,833,234.25
February	5,798,604.00	
March	6,658,632.25	
April	5,883,737.80	
May	6,538,422.55	
June	8,054,375.95	
July	7,496,202.55	
August	8,433,002.90	
September	8,836,040.00	
October	8,643,188.40	
November	6,503,028.00	
December	6,931,255.35	
Total	**85,729,180.90**	**5,833,234.25**

FIGURE 3-29 January Profit Wrong visualized

The formula does not return the expected results because when slicing by Month, Calendar Month Number is also part of filter context because it sorts Month. To make the formula work correctly, either list conditions for both columns or iterate over a table that includes both columns. Either of the following expressions returns the expected result:

// Including conditions for both columns

```
January Profit =
CALCULATE (
    [Total Profit],
    'Date'[Month] = "January",
    'Date'[Month Number] = 1
)
```

// Boolean expressions internally converted to table filters

```
January Profit =
CALCULATE (
    [Total Profit],
    FILTER (
        ALL('Date'[Month]),
        'Date'[Month] = "January"
    ),
    FILTER (
        ALL('Date'[Month Number]),
        'Date'[Month Number] = 1
    )
)
```

// Alternative approach: iterating over a table that includes both columns

```
January Profit =
CALCULATE (
```

```
    [Total Profit],
    FILTER (
        ALL('Date'[Month], 'Date'[Month Number]),
        'Date'[Month] = "January"
    )
  )
)
```

There is another function in the ALL family of functions that we have not yet explored: ALLSE-LECTED. This function receives one optional argument: either a table or one or more columns from one table. According to the official documentation, this function removes filter context from rows and columns of a table, while retaining all other context filters or explicit filters. In Power BI, rows and columns of a table can be extended to mean axes, legends, and so on. To see the effect of ALLSELECTED, follow these steps:

1. Create a new measure with the following formula:

   ```
   Profit AllSelected = CALCULATE([Total Profit], ALLSELECTED('Date'))
   ```

2. Create a table visual with the following fields:

   - **Year**
   - **Total Profit**
   - **Profit AllSelected**

3. Create a slicer with **Year** as its field.

4. Select years 2019–2021, inclusive.

At this stage, you should see figures like those shown in Figure 3-30.

Year	Total Profit	Profit AllSelected
2019	13,886,695.65	64,147,990.55
2020	23,688,699.40	64,147,990.55
2021	26,572,595.50	64,147,990.55
Total	**64,147,990.55**	**64,147,990.55**

FIGURE 3-30 Profit AllSelected used in a table

Note the values displayed by the Profit AllSelected measure; they are the same as the grand total of Total Profit in this table. If we change the year selection, the values will change to the new grand total.

Because the only parameter of ALLSELECTED is optional, you can use it with no parameters as follows:

```
Profit AllSelected = CALCULATE([Total Profit], ALLSELECTED ())
```

Used in this way, ALLSELECTED will consider filters from the entire data model, not just one table or column.

TIME INTELLIGENCE

Time Intelligence in DAX is an umbrella term that often refers to calculations that span over predefined periods of time. DAX has more than 30 built-in functions to handle Time Intelligence. An example of using Time Intelligence is the comparison of different periods this year versus last year, for instance.

Most Time Intelligence functions receive a date column as a parameter and return a table that can be used as a filter in CALCULATE, while a small group of functions return scalar values. The functions that return scalar values are all shorthand and can be rewritten using CALCULATE and one of the functions that return a table.

For the Time Intelligence functions to work correctly, you must have a date table, which is also known as a calendar table. The table should be similar to the Date table from the Wide World Importers data model, where you have a row for each date between the earliest and latest dates in your data model with no gaps. If your data source does not contain such a table, you can create one yourself. We discussed the CALENDAR and CALENDARAUTO functions earlier in this chapter.

Another requirement for the calendar table is either to be part of a one-to-many relationship with a column of type date or be marked as Date table. This way, the Time Intelligence functions will work without needing modifications.

Once your calendar table satisfies the requirements, you can use the Time Intelligence functions correctly. For example, to calculate year-to-date profit, you can use the DATESYTD function and write the following formula:

```
Profit YTD = CALCULATE([Total Profit], DATESYTD('Date'[Date]))
```

If you use this measure alongside the Total Profit measure in a matrix visual and add Year and Month on rows, you can see a visual like in Figure 3-31.

Year	Total Profit	Profit YTD
⊟ **2020**	**23,688,699.40**	**23,688,699.40**
January	1,744,886.60	1,744,886.60
February	1,859,239.60	3,604,126.20
March	1,820,979.55	5,425,105.75
April	1,937,131.40	7,362,237.15
May	1,801,123.05	9,163,360.20
June	1,910,675.85	11,074,036.05
July	1,871,503.60	12,945,539.65
August	1,921,543.15	14,867,082.80
September	2,025,148.55	16,892,231.35
October	2,298,565.50	19,190,796.85
November	2,210,495.70	21,401,292.55
December	2,287,406.85	23,688,699.40
⊟ **2021**	**26,572,595.50**	**26,572,595.50**
January	2,036,105.15	2,036,105.15
February	1,830,820.00	3,866,925.15
Total	**85,729,180.90**	

FIGURE 3-31 Profit YTD shown alongside Total Profit and sliced by Year and Month

Note how the profit amount is being added month by month from January to December 2020, and then it starts at January 2021 again. DATESYTD has an optional second parameter, which is the year-end date. With this parameter, you can specify a custom year-end date such as **30-6** or **6-30**, depending on your locale. This option is often used for calculations involving fiscal or financial years. When omitted, the default option is December 31. For instance, the following measure calculates year-to-date profit for the year ending on June 30. You can see the values it returns in Figure 3-32.

```
Profit FYTD = CALCULATE([Total Profit], DATESYTD('Date'[Date], "30-6"))
```

Year	Total Profit	Profit YTD	Profit FYTD
⊟ **2020**	**23,688,699.40**	**23,688,699.40**	**12,614,663.35**
January	1,744,886.60	1,744,886.60	13,585,711.10
February	1,859,239.60	3,604,126.20	15,444,950.70
March	1,820,979.55	5,425,105.75	17,265,930.25
April	1,937,131.40	7,362,237.15	19,203,061.65
May	1,801,123.05	9,163,360.20	21,004,184.70
June	1,910,675.85	11,074,036.05	22,914,860.55
July	1,871,503.60	12,945,539.65	1,871,503.60
August	1,921,543.15	14,867,082.80	3,793,046.75
September	2,025,148.55	16,892,231.35	5,818,195.30
October	2,298,565.50	19,190,796.85	8,116,760.80
November	2,210,495.70	21,401,292.55	10,327,256.50
December	2,287,406.85	23,688,699.40	12,614,663.35
⊟ **2021**	**26,572,595.50**	**26,572,595.50**	**13,974,742.40**
January	2,036,105.15	2,036,105.15	14,650,768.50
February	1,830,820.00	3,866,925.15	16,481,588.50
Total	**85,729,180.90**		

FIGURE 3-32 Profit FYTD shown alongside Profit YTD and Total Profit

Note how the calculation of year-to-date profit now starts over in July instead of January.

DATESYTD also has two sister functions, DATESMTD and DATESQTD, which return month-to-date and quarter-to-date date tables, respectively. Both functions always receive one parameter only, with no optional parameters.

Because the DATESMTD, DATESQTD, and DATESYTD functions are almost always used as filters for CALCULATE expressions, there are three functions that simplify writing formulas with these functions: TOTALMTD, TOTALQTD, and TOTALYTD. For example, you can rewrite the Profit FYTD formula as follows:

```
Profit FYTD = TOTALYTD([Total Profit], 'Date'[Date], "30-6")
```

The three functions receive two mandatory arguments: a scalar expression and the calendar table date column. The optional third parameter can be used to pass an additional filter. TOTALYTD can also receive an optional fourth parameter, the year-end date. When no third parameter is specified, the year-end date can be used as the third parameter.

With DAX, it is possible to calculate semi-additive measures such as opening and closing balances. For these purposes, there are monthly, quarterly, and yearly functions for both opening and closing balances:

- OPENINGBALANCEMONTH
- OPENINGBALANCEQUARTER
- OPENINGBALANCEYEAR
- CLOSINGBALANCEMONTH
- CLOSINGBALANCEQUARTER
- CLOSINGBALANCEYEAR

Each of the six functions received two required parameters: a scalar expression and the date column of a calendar table. A filter can be passed as the optional third parameter. Also, the yearly functions can receive an optional fourth parameter specifying the year-end date.

For review purposes, calculate the opening and closing month balance of profit as follows, even if the measures make no sense financially:

```
Opening Profit = OPENINGBALANCEMONTH([Total Profit], 'Date'[Date])
Closing Profit = CLOSINGBALANCEMONTH([Total Profit], 'Date'[Date])
```

The OPENINGBALANCEMONTH function calculates the scalar value used as the first parameter for the last day of the previous month. In general, the opening balance functions return the same values as closing balance functions for the previous month. For example, the opening monthly balance for June 2019 will be the same as the closing monthly balance for May 2019. Both measures are shown in Figure 3-33.

The opening and closing balance functions we have just reviewed return scalar values. There are DAX functions that return table functions for the beginning and the end of periods:

- STARTOFMONTH
- STARTOFQUARTER
- STARTOFYEAR
- ENDOFMONTH
- ENDOFQUARTER
- ENDOFYEAR

Each function in this list receives one required parameter: the date column from a calendar table. As before, the yearly functions can also receive a year-end date as an optional parameter. For example, you can rewrite the Closing Profit measure using the ENDOFMONTH function as follows:

```
Closing Profit = CALCULATE([Total Profit], ENDOFMONTH('Date'[Date]))
```

Year	Total Profit	Opening Profit	Closing Profit
2019-05-30	34,291.45		34,114.60
2019-05-31	34,114.60		34,114.60
⊟ June	1,852,081.45	34,114.60	21,593.60
2019-06-01	20,154.40	34,114.60	21,593.60
2019-06-02	42,774.70	34,114.60	21,593.60
2019-06-03	64,974.80	34,114.60	21,593.60
2019-06-04	55,817.10	34,114.60	21,593.60
2019-06-05	106,799.00	34,114.60	21,593.60
2019-06-06	77,676.85	34,114.60	21,593.60
2019-06-07	117,373.55	34,114.60	21,593.60
2019-06-08	92,062.40	34,114.60	21,593.60
2019-06-09	121,370.35	34,114.60	21,593.60
2019-06-10	106,093.95	34,114.60	21,593.60
2019-06-11	54,792.30	34,114.60	21,593.60
2019-06-12	67,971.75	34,114.60	21,593.60
2019-06-13	26,966.30	34,114.60	21,593.60
2019-06-14	22,662.30	34,114.60	21,593.60
2019-06-15	20,865.50	34,114.60	21,593.60
2019-06-16	51,255.25	34,114.60	21,593.60
2019-06-17	64,698.95	34,114.60	21,593.60
2019-06-18	69,447.60	34,114.60	21,593.60
2019-06-19	92,976.90	34,114.60	21,593.60
2019-06-20	41,176.10	34,114.60	21,593.60
2019-06-21	57,260.05	34,114.60	21,593.60
2019-06-22	75,608.05	34,114.60	21,593.60
2019-06-23	38,530.25	34,114.60	21,593.60
2019-06-24	78,323.30	34,114.60	21,593.60
2019-06-25	91,428.25	34,114.60	21,593.60
2019-06-26	62,668.30	34,114.60	21,593.60
2019-06-27	70,870.20	34,114.60	21,593.60
2019-06-28	31,257.25	34,114.60	21,593.60
2019-06-29	6,632.15	34,114.60	21,593.60
2019-06-30	21,593.60	34,114.60	21,593.60
⊟ July	1,442,121.85	21,593.60	38,292.90
2019-07-01	18,608.00	21,593.60	38,292.90
Total	85,729,180.90		

FIGURE 3-33 Opening Profit and Closing Profit shown alongside Total Profit

The Opening Profit measure cannot be rewritten using only CALCULATE and STARTOFMONTH. Use a function that can shift dates because the opening balance of a measure is its closing balance for the previous month. The most often used function is DATEADD, which receives exactly three arguments: the dates column of a calendar table, the number of intervals, and the interval. The interval can be one of the following:

- DAY

- MONTH

- QUARTER

- YEAR

DATEADD is not the only function that can shift dates. There is a similar function that can shift dates, PARALLELPERIOD, that receives the same arguments as DATEADD. However, PARALLELPERIOD cannot receive DAY as the fourth parameter. The difference between the two functions is that DATEADD shifts dates for each date in the current filter context, while PARALLELPERIOD returns a full parallel period as a result. To illustrate the difference between the two functions, create the following two functions:

```
Profit Last Month DateAdd =
CALCULATE (
    [Total Profit],
    DATEADD('Date'[Date], -1, MONTH)
)
Profit Last Month ParallelPeriod =
CALCULATE (
    [Total Profit],
    PARALLELPERIOD('Date'[Date], -1, MONTH)
)
```

The two measures are shown side by side in Figure 3-34.

Note how the two measures display the same results at the month level, but the values are different at date level: DATEADD displays a different value for each date, whereas PARALLELPERIOD shows the same value for each date within one month. Also, note that the value of the DATEADD measure is the same from March 28 to March 31, 2021 because the last date in February 2021 is February 28, 2021, and dates from March 28 to March 31, 2021 are all treated as the last day of the month when compared to the previous month.

In addition to DATEADD and PARALLELPERIOD, the following functions have descriptive names that shift by a predefined period:

- SAMEPERIODLASTYEAR: same as DATEADD(Dates, -1, YEAR)
- PREVIOUSDAY
- PREVIOUSMONTH
- PREVIOUSQUARTER
- PREVIOUSYEAR
- NEXTDAY
- NEXTMONTH
- NEXTQUARTER
- NEXTYEAR

Year	Total Profit	Profit Last Month DateAdd	Profit Last Month ParallelPeriod
2021-02-26	41,140.95	74,405.50	2,036,105.15
2021-02-27	40,045.45	47,150.75	2,036,105.15
2021-02-28	11,026.55	16,600.20	2,036,105.15
⊟ **March**	**2,395,542.40**	**1,830,820.00**	**1,830,820.00**
2021-03-01	7,541.80	7,727.80	1,830,820.00
2021-03-02	39,346.15	122,339.50	1,830,820.00
2021-03-03	33,300.15	74,130.85	1,830,820.00
2021-03-04	40,228.40	110,967.35	1,830,820.00
2021-03-05	136,274.00	103,966.50	1,830,820.00
2021-03-06	97,800.95	35,699.90	1,830,820.00
2021-03-07	23,718.50	96,304.85	1,830,820.00
2021-03-08	115,023.95	63,447.45	1,830,820.00
2021-03-09	163,830.45	80,309.40	1,830,820.00
2021-03-10	108,534.30	57,573.45	1,830,820.00
2021-03-11	113,163.85	61,893.50	1,830,820.00
2021-03-12	87,062.25	23,440.00	1,830,820.00
2021-03-13	43,229.95		1,830,820.00
2021-03-14		119,314.70	1,830,820.00
2021-03-15	114,827.65	123,583.35	1,830,820.00
2021-03-16	77,916.90	56,517.90	1,830,820.00
2021-03-17	84,808.95	122,545.65	1,830,820.00
2021-03-18	39,915.90	124,772.10	1,830,820.00
2021-03-19	59,817.35	57,838.95	1,830,820.00
2021-03-20	52,469.55		1,830,820.00
2021-03-21		95,708.25	1,830,820.00
2021-03-22	108,530.25	54,402.65	1,830,820.00
2021-03-23	337,583.80	11,777.65	1,830,820.00
2021-03-24	159,069.10	74,786.70	1,830,820.00
2021-03-25		59,558.60	1,830,820.00
2021-03-26	82,905.15	41,140.95	1,830,820.00
2021-03-27	72,318.20	40,045.45	1,830,820.00
2021-03-28	61,018.80	11,026.55	1,830,820.00
2021-03-29	46,569.05	11,026.55	1,830,820.00
2021-03-30	38,070.75	11,026.55	1,830,820.00
2021-03-31	50,666.30	11,026.55	1,830,820.00
Total	**85,729,180.90**	**85,609,724.00**	**85,609,724.00**

FIGURE 3-34 Profit Last Month DateAdd and Profit Last Month ParallelPeriod used in a matrix visual

This list of functions receives the date column of a calendar table as the only required parameter. PREVIOUSYEAR and NEXTYEAR can also receive the year-end date as the optional second parameter.

You can combine some Time Intelligence functions. For example, using either DATEADD or PARALLELPERIOD, you can rewrite the Opening Profit measure as follows:

```
Opening Profit DateAdd =
CALCULATE (
```

```
    [Total Profit],
    DATEADD(STARTOFMONTH('Date'[Date]), -1, DAY)
)
```

Note that the order in which you nest functions matters. While the following measure works, it returns incorrect results, as seen in Figure 3-35:

```
Opening Profit DateAdd Wrong =
CALCULATE (
    [Total Profit],
    STARTOFMONTH(DATEADD('Date'[Date], -1, DAY))
)
```

Year	Total Profit	Opening Profit	Opening Profit DateAdd	Opening Profit DateAdd Wrong
2021-01-28	16,600.20	20,693.85	20,693.85	35,545.60
2021-01-29	20,403.55	20,693.85	20,693.85	35,545.60
2021-01-30	16,972.80	20,693.85	20,693.85	35,545.60
2021-01-31	16,146.80	20,693.85	20,693.85	35,545.60
⊟ February	1,830,820.00	16,146.80	16,146.80	35,545.60
2021-02-01	7,727.80	16,146.80	16,146.80	35,545.60
2021-02-02	122,339.50	16,146.80	16,146.80	7,727.80
2021-02-03	74,130.85	16,146.80	16,146.80	7,727.80
2021-02-04	110,967.35	16,146.80	16,146.80	7,727.80
2021-02-05	103,966.50	16,146.80	16,146.80	7,727.80
2021-02-06	35,699.90	16,146.80	16,146.80	7,727.80
2021-02-07	96,304.85	16,146.80	16,146.80	7,727.80
2021-02-08	63,447.45	16,146.80	16,146.80	7,727.80
2021-02-09	80,309.40	16,146.80	16,146.80	7,727.80
2021-02-10	57,573.45	16,146.80	16,146.80	7,727.80
2021-02-11	61,893.50	16,146.80	16,146.80	7,727.80
2021-02-12	23,440.00	16,146.80	16,146.80	7,727.80
2021-02-13		16,146.80	16,146.80	7,727.80
2021-02-14	119,314.70	16,146.80	16,146.80	7,727.80
2021-02-15	123,583.35	16,146.80	16,146.80	7,727.80
2021-02-16	56,517.90	16,146.80	16,146.80	7,727.80
2021-02-17	122,545.65	16,146.80	16,146.80	7,727.80
2021-02-18	124,772.10	16,146.80	16,146.80	7,727.80
2021-02-19	57,838.95	16,146.80	16,146.80	7,727.80
2021-02-20		16,146.80	16,146.80	7,727.80
2021-02-21	95,708.25	16,146.80	16,146.80	7,727.80
2021-02-22	54,402.65	16,146.80	16,146.80	7,727.80
2021-02-23	11,777.65	16,146.80	16,146.80	7,727.80
2021-02-24	74,786.70	16,146.80	16,146.80	7,727.80
2021-02-25	59,558.60	16,146.80	16,146.80	7,727.80
2021-02-26	41,140.95	16,146.80	16,146.80	7,727.80
2021-02-27	40,045.45	16,146.80	16,146.80	7,727.80
2021-02-28	11,026.55	16,146.80	16,146.80	7,727.80
⊟ March	2,395,542.40	11,026.55	11,026.55	7,727.80
2021-03-01	7,541.80	11,026.55	11,026.55	7,727.80
Total	85,729,180.90			

FIGURE 3-35 Opening Profit DateAdd Wrong shown alongside the correct Opening Profit measure

The reason why this is not correct is that the dates are shifted back first, then STARTOFMONTH returns the first date of the month of the shifted date.

If you need to calculate a value for the first or last date in the current filter context, you can use the FIRSTDATE or the LASTDATE function, respectively. Both functions can be used as filters in CALCULATE. The functions do not override the currently selected dates. More specifically, the two functions can be rewritten as follows:

// Same as FIRSTDATE

```
'Date'[Date] = MIN('Date'[Date])
```

// Same as LASTDATE

```
'Date'[Date] = MAX('Date'[Date])
```

If you need to filter by a custom date interval, you can use DATESBETWEEN. The function receives three arguments: the date column of a calendar table, a start date, and an end date. For example, calculate Total Profit between June 10, 2021 and April 5, 2024, inclusive, as follows:

```
Profit Custom Period =
CALCULATE (
    [Total Profit],
    DATESBETWEEN (
        'Date'[Date],
        DATE(2021, 10, 6),
        DATE(2024, 4, 5)
    )
)
```

The measure shows the same value regardless of the selected date.

If your custom time interval is based on days, months, quarters, or years, you can use the DATESINPERIOD function. The function receives exactly three arguments: the date column from a calendar table; a start date; the number of intervals; and the interval, which can be DAY, MONTH, QUARTER, or YEAR. For instance, you can calculate the rolling monthly profit with the following measure:

```
Rolling Monthly Profit =
CALCULATE (
    [Total Profit],
    DATESINPERIOD (
        'Date'[Date],
        MAX('Date'[Date]),
        -1,
        MONTH
    )
)
```

USING INACTIVE RELATIONSHIPS

As discussed earlier, there can be no more than one active physical relationship between two tables. Between the Sale and Date tables there are two active relationships:

- Active one from Sale (Delivery Date Key) to Date (Date)
- Inactive one from Sale (Invoice Date Key) to Date (Date)

By default, all values we aggregate in the Sale table are going to be filtered by Delivery Date Key. To use the inactive relationship, activate it programmatically with DAX using the USERELATIONSHIP function. This function receives two parameters, which are the columns used in a relationship. To calculate Total Profit by Invoice Date Key, you can write the following measure formula, as shown in Figure 3-36.

```
Total Profit by Invoice Date =
CALCULATE (
    [Total Profit],
    USERELATIONSHIP('Date'[Date], Sale[Invoice Date Key])
)
```

Year	Total Profit	Total Profit by Invoice Date
	119,456.90	
2019	13,886,695.65	14,208,987.05
2020	23,688,699.40	23,666,819.70
2021	26,572,595.50	26,322,158.20
2022	21,461,733.45	21,531,215.95
Total	**85,729,180.90**	**85,729,180.90**

FIGURE 3-36 Total Profit by Invoice Date used in a table visual

Note that the Total Profit by Invoice Date measure is blank when Year is blank. This is because no Invoice Date Key value is blank, which means there is no blank row automatically added to the Date table when filtering by Invoice Date Key instead of Delivery Date Key.

The order of the columns used as parameters does not matter, though a relationship must exist between two columns. Otherwise, you will get the error seen in Figure 3-37.

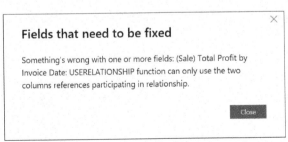

Fields that need to be fixed

Something's wrong with one or more fields: (Sale) Total Profit by Invoice Date: USERELATIONSHIP function can only use the two columns references participating in relationship.

Close

FIGURE 3-37 Error message when using USERELATIONSHIP without a relationship

USING SELECTEDVALUE

The SELECTEDVALUE function receives a column reference as the first parameter, which is required, and SELECTEDVALUE receives a default value as the optional second parameter. The function returns a column value if there is only one in the current filter context. Otherwise, it returns the default value. The function acts as a shortcut for the following syntax:

```
MyParameter Value =
IF (
    HASONEVALUE(MyParameter[MyParameter]),
    VALUES(MyParameter[MyParameter]),
    5
)
```

The HASONEVALUE function checks whether the input column has only one value in the current filter context. If it does, then the VALUES function, which returns a table, is converted into a scalar value because it has only one row and one column. If the input column has more than one value, the default value—in this case, 5—is returned. This function can be useful when you want to change a metric based on the selection. For instance, you can scale the Total Profit value based on the selected value in the Scale column of the Scale table with the following measure:

```
Profit Scaled = [Total Profit] / SELECTEDVALUE(Scale[Scale], 1)
```

If you put the Scale column values on rows in a matrix visual and Total Profit and Profit Scaled as values, you should see a visual similar to Figure 3-38.

Scale	Total Profit	Profit Scaled
1	85,729,180.90	85,729,180.90
1000	85,729,180.90	85,729.18
1000000	85,729,180.90	85.73
Total	**85,729,180.90**	**85,729,180.90**

FIGURE 3-38 Total Profit and Profit Scaled put against the Scale column

Note how Total Profit shows the same value for each Scale value because there is no relationship between Scale and any other table. However, Profit Scaled shows different values because it reads the currently selected value of Scale from the current filter context by using SELECTEDVALUE. Also, note two things:

- First, Total Profit and Profit Scaled have the same value when Scale is 1.
- Second, Profit Scaled at the total level shows the same value as when Scale is 1 because at the total level, there is no filter on Scale; therefore, the default value of 1 is used.

PASSING FILTERS FROM DISCONNECTED TABLES

In some cases, you may need to pass filters from disconnected tables. For example, it might be too expensive to create a column with concatenated keys to create a physical relationship. In this case, it might make sense to use virtual relationships.

One way you can pass filters from one table to another is by using INTERSECT. As discussed earlier, this table function returns a table with rows that exist in both tables.

To see the effect of using a virtual relationship, deactivate the relationship between Customer and Targets and create the following measures in the Targets table:

```
Total Target Amount = SUM(Targets[Target Excluding Tax])
Target Amount Intersect =
CALCULATE (
    [Total Target Quantity],
    INTERSECT (
        VALUES(Targets[Buying Group]),
        VALUES(Customer[Buying Group])
    )
)
```

If you create a matrix visual with Buying Group on rows and Total Target Amount and Target Amount Intersect as values, you will see a visual similar to Figure 3-39.

Buying Group	Total Target Amount	Target Amount Intersect
N/A	180400000	
Tailspin Toys	180400000	55400000
Wingtip Toys	180400000	55700000
Total	**180400000**	**111100000**

FIGURE 3-39 Year, Total Target Amount, and Target Amount Intersect in matrix visual

Note how Total Target Amount has the same value regardless of the Buying Group value. This is because we deactivated the relationship between the Targets and Buying Group table, meaning that filters from the Date table do not reach the Targets table. However, the Target Amount Intersect measure shows different values for each Buying Group because it is being filtered by a virtual relationship created with INTERSECT.

It is important to note that the order in which you pass the parameters to INTERSECT matters. The following measure returns the same values as Total Target Amount, which is the same value for each year:

```
Target Amount Intersect Wrong =
CALCULATE (
    [Total Target Amount],
    INTERSECT (
        VALUES(Customer[Buying Group]),
        VALUES(Targets[Buying Group])
    )
)
```

When you create virtual relationships with INTERSECT, the table you want to pass filters from should come first, and the table you want to filter should come second.

It's also possible to create virtual relationships by using the TREATAS function. The function receives at least two arguments: a table to pass filters from, and one or more columns to pass filters to. For instance, you can rewrite the preceding measures in the following way:

```
Target Amount TreatAs =
CALCULATE (
    [Total Target Amount],
    TREATAS (
        VALUES(Customer[Buying Group]),
        Targets[Buying Group]
    )
)
```

Figure 3-40 shows the INTERSECT and TREATAS measures compared.

Buying Group	Total Target Amount	Target Amount Intersect	Target Amount TreatAs
N/A	180400000		
Tailspin Toys	180400000	55400000	55400000
Wingtip Toys	180400000	55700000	55700000
Total	**180400000**	**111100000**	**111100000**

FIGURE 3-40 Measures with virtual relationships

Note how Total Target Amount still displays the same value for each row. At the beginning of this exercise, we purposefully deactivated relationships between Targets and Buying Group to highlight the effect that virtual relationships can have. Although virtual relationships can be very powerful, if you have an option to create physical relationships, as in our case, it is best to pass filters using physical relationships instead of virtual ones. Your code will be much shorter, and it will also perform much better. If at this point you activate the relationship between Buying Group and Targets again, the same matrix visual will look like the one shown in Figure 3-41.

Buying Group	Total Target Amount	Target Amount Intersect	Target Amount TreatAs
Tailspin Toys	55400000	55400000	55400000
Wingtip Toys	55700000	55700000	55700000
Total	**180400000**	**111100000**	**111100000**

FIGURE 3-41 The same matrix visual after activating relationships

When you are using activated relationships, the Total Target Amount measure displays the same values as the other two measures because the filters from the Customer table now reach the Targets table.

Design and build a large format dataset

In Power BI Premium, you can enable large dataset format, which can bring the following benefits:

- Datasets can grow beyond 10 GB in size.
- There is a default segment size of 8 million rows.
- Write operations are faster when using the XML for Analysis (XMLA) endpoint.

> **NOTE PUBLISHING DATASETS LARGER THAN 10 GB**
>
> Even with the large dataset format configured, you still won't be able to publish datasets larger than 10 GB from Power BI Desktop to Power BI service. To allow datasets to grow beyond the size, you'll need to leverage incremental refresh.

You can enable large dataset format for each dataset individually, or you can set it as default in a Premium workspace.

For a specific dataset:

1. Go to the dataset settings.
2. Expand **Large dataset storage format**.
3. Set the toggle to **On** and select **Apply**, as shown in Figure 3-42.

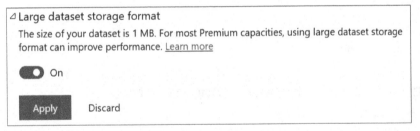

FIGURE 3-42 Large dataset storage format in dataset settings

To set large dataset storage format as default in a Premium workspace:

1. Go to the workspace settings.
2. Go to the **Premium** section.
3. From the **Default storage format** drop-down list, select **Large dataset storage format**, as shown in Figure 3-43.
4. Select **Save**.

FIGURE 3-43 Workspace Premium settings

Note that with the large dataset storage format, downloading the PBIX file from the Power BI service may not work.

Design and build composite models, including aggregations

By using composite models, you can optimize the performance of data sources that use the DirectQuery mode by using aggregations. For instance, if you're using DirectQuery, with a fact table containing data for each customer, and you report on values for all customers combined, you can create an aggregation at the total customers level. If you need to report data on individual customers, you can still use the original table, and Power BI will automatically determine whether it should use the aggregation or the original table.

> **NOTE REPRODUCING THE STEPS**
>
> Working in DirectQuery mode requires a database, so there's no corresponding companion file. Setting up a database is not tested on the exam; if you have access to a database, the steps to create and manage aggregations are going to be similar as described in this section.

An aggregation table can be a table created in a variety of ways:

- Imported M query
- Calculated table in DAX
- Another table in DirectQuery mode

Once you have a suitable table, you can turn it into an aggregation table as described next. The aggregation table should contain at least some of the same keys and columns you want to aggregate, and it does not have to come from the same source as the detail table.

For example, let's say you're using the Sales table in DirectQuery mode, and you have an aggregation table called SalesAllCustomers, which is the same as Sale, except it doesn't have detailed information on each customer. Managing aggregations involves the following steps:

1. Right-click any table in the **Data** pane.
2. Select **Manage aggregations**.
3. In the **Aggregation table** drop-down list, select **SalesAllCustomers**. You'll see the options presented like in Figure 3-44.

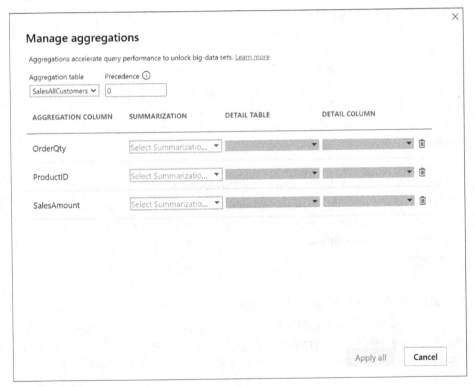

FIGURE 3-44 Manage aggregations

4. For each column, you can select the appropriate summarization and the corresponding detail table and column, if relevant:

- **Count**—This can only be used for count, not distinct count.

- **GroupBy**—This is used for relationship keys.
- **Max**—Corresponds to the maximum value.
- **Min**—Corresponds to the minimum value.
- **Sum**—Corresponds to sum.
- **Count table rows**—Counts rows in a table.

5. Once you make all selections, select **Apply all**, and Power BI will hide the aggregation table.

Queries that can be resolved by using the aggregation table will use the aggregation table. In case the aggregation is insufficient—in our example that involved reporting values for individual customers—the detail table will be used automatically.

You can use multiple aggregation tables if needed—in this case, tables with higher precedence will be used first.

Design and implement enterprise-scale row-level security and object-level security

A common business requirement is to secure data so that different users who view the same report can see different subsets of data. In Power BI, this can be accomplished with the feature called *row-level security (RLS)*.

Row-level security restricts data by filtering it at the row level, depending on the rules defined for each user. To configure RLS, you first need to create and define each role in Power BI Desktop, and then assign individual users or Active Directory security groups to the roles in the Power BI service.

> **NOTE ROW-LEVEL SECURITY AND LIVE CONNECTIONS**
>
> Defining roles in Power BI only works for imported data and DirectQuery. When you connect live to a Power BI dataset or an Analysis Services data model, Power BI will rely on row-level security configured in the source, and you cannot override it by creating roles in Power BI Desktop.

Creating roles in Power BI Desktop

To see the list of roles configured in a dataset in Power BI Desktop, select **Manage roles** from the **Modeling** ribbon in the **Report** view. To create a new role, select **New** in the **Roles** section. You'll then be prompted to specify table filters, as shown in Figure 3-45.

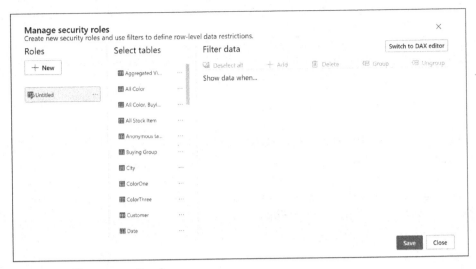

FIGURE 3-45 Manage security roles

When you create a role, you have the option to change the default name to a new one. It's important to give roles user-friendly names because you'll see them in the Power BI service, and you need to be able to assign users to the correct roles.

If you select the ellipsis next to a role, you'll be presented with the following options:

- **Rename**—Use this option to rename the currently selected role; you can also rename a role by double-clicking its name.
- **Duplicate**—This option creates a copy of the currently selected role.
- **Delete**—This option deletes the currently selected role.

For each role, you can define a DAX expression to filter each table. When row-level security is configured, these expressions will be evaluated against each row of the relevant table, and only those rows for which the expressions are evaluated as true will be visible.

To create a filter, select a table in the **Select tables** section, then select **Add**. You can configure a filter by using the user interface, or you can switch to DAX editor and enter your own expression.

For example, in the Wide World Importers data model that we previously developed, you can create the following roles:

1. Create a new role and rename it to **Southeast**.
2. Select **City** > **Add**.
3. Select **Sales Territory** instead of City in the drop-down list.
4. Enter **Southeast** next to **equals**.
5. Duplicate the **Southeast** role and rename it to **Plains**.
6. Change the filter in the **Plains** role to **Plains**.
7. Select **Save** > **Close**.

We can now test the roles in Power BI Desktop.

Viewing as roles in Power BI Desktop

In Power BI Desktop, you can check what the users with specific roles will see even before you publish your report to the Power BI service and assign users to roles. For this, once you have at least one role defined, select **View as** on the **Modeling** ribbon in the **Report** view. You'll then see the **View as roles** window shown in Figure 3-46.

FIGURE 3-46 View as roles

Note that you can view as several roles simultaneously. This is because you can allocate a single user or a security group to multiple roles in the Power BI service; in this case, the security rules of the roles will complement each other. For example, if you select both the **Plains** and the **Southeast** roles, you'll see data for both territories. For this reason, you should always have clear names for your RLS roles.

EXAM TIP

You should know the effect of combining multiple security roles for a single user based on the description of security filters of each role.

When viewing data as roles, you'll see the bar at the top shown in Figure 3-47.

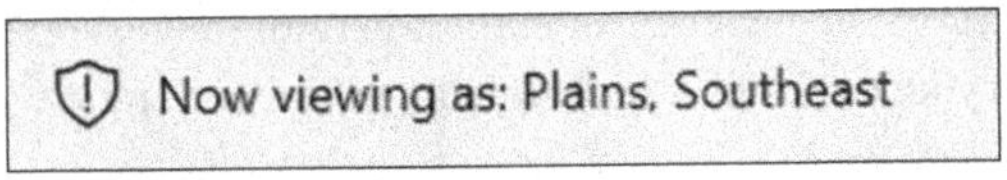

🛡 Now viewing as: Plains, Southeast

FIGURE 3-47 Now viewing report as

> **IMPORTANT** **APPLICATION OF ROW-LEVEL SECURITY**
>
> The filters applied by row-level security are applied only at query time and not at processing time. The implication of this is that the filters won't change the values of calculated columns and calculated tables.

Another option in the **View as roles** window is **Other user**. With this option, you can test dynamic row-level security, which is covered next.

Dynamic row-level security

The roles we've created so far have been static, which means that all users within a role will see the same data. If you have several rules that specify how you should secure your data, this approach may mean you have to create a number of roles as well as update the data model every time a new role should be introduced or an old one removed.

There is an alternative approach, called *dynamic row-level security*, which allows you to show different data to different users within the same role.

> **NOTE** **DYNAMIC ROW-LEVEL SECURITY**
>
> Because dynamic row-level security can use a single role, this approach is preferable in large-scale implementations of Power BI where there are many users who need to see different data.

For this approach, your data model must contain the usernames of people who should have access to the relevant rows of data. You'll also need to pass the active username as a filter condition. Power BI has two functions that allow you to get the username of the current user:

- **USERNAME**—This function returns the domain and login of the user in the domain\login format.
- **USERPRINCIPALNAME**—Depending on how the Active Directory was set up, this function usually returns the email address of the user.

To see how dynamic row-level security works in our Wide World Importers data model, first create a new security role:

1. Select **Manage roles** on the **Modeling** ribbon.
2. Create a new security role and call it **Dynamic RLS**.
3. For the **Dynamic RLS** role, specify the following expression in DAX editor for the **Employee** table:

```
[Email] = USERPRINCIPALNAME()
```

4. Select **Save** > **Close**.

Now you can test the new role:

1. Select **View as** on the **Modeling** ribbon.
2. Select both **Other user** and **Dynamic RLS**.
3. Enter **jack.potter@wideworldimporters.com** in the **Other user** box.
4. Select **OK**.
5. Go to the **Data** view.
6. Select the **Employee** table.

Note that the Employee table is now filtered to just Jack Potter's row, as shown in Figure 3-48.

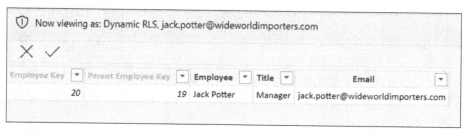

FIGURE 3-48 Employee table viewed as Jack Potter

Although this may be good enough for us in certain cases, it's a common requirement for managers to see the data of those who report to them. Since Jack is a manager, he should be able to see data of the salespersons who report to him. For that, we can create a new role called **Dynamic RLS (hierarchy)** with the following table filter DAX expression:

```
PATHCONTAINS(
    PATH(
        Employee[Employee Key],
        Employee[Parent Employee Key]
    ),
    LOOKUPVALUE(
        Employee[Employee Key],
        Employee[Email],
        USERPRINCIPALNAME()
    )
)
```

This table filter DAX expression keeps those rows where Jack is part of the hierarchy path, which relies on the Employee table having both the ID and parent ID columns.

After you make this change, the Employee table will show four rows: Jack's row and three rows of the salespersons who report to Jack, as seen in Figure 3-49.

Employee Key	Parent Employee Key	Employee	Title	Email
20	19	Jack Potter	Manager	jack.potter@wideworldimporters.com
16	20	Archer Lamble	Salesperson	archer.lamble@wideworldimporters.com
15	20	Taj Shand	Salesperson	taj.shand@wideworldimporters.com
14	20	Lily Code	Salesperson	lily.code@wideworldimporters.com

FIGURE 3-49 Employee table viewed as Jack Potter

So far, you've created the roles in Power BI Desktop. Once you publish the report, you'll have to assign users or security groups to roles in Power BI service separately.

Object-level security

In some cases, instead of or in addition to rows, you'll want to secure objects—columns or tables, or both. Hiding columns or tables won't make the objects secure, since anyone who can view a model will be able to view hidden objects. Furthermore, perspectives aren't a security feature, so we can't use a perspective to secure objects. Instead, we can use object-level security, which we can configure in Tabular Editor.

For example, let's say we want to hide the Targets table from some group of people, which we can do in the following way:

1. In Power BI Desktop, create a new role called **Hide Targets**.

2. Launch Tabular Editor as an external tool.

3. In Tabular Editor, select the **Targets** table.

4. In table properties, expand the **Object Level Security** section.

5. From the drop-down list next to the **Hide Targets** role, select **None**. At this stage, the Targets table properties should look like in Figure 3-50.

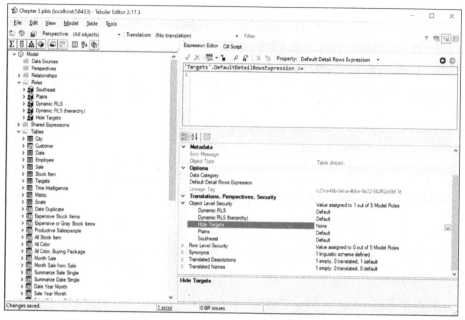

FIGURE 3-50 Table properties of Targets table in Tabular Editor

6. Save changes to the model by pressing **Ctrl+S**.

We can now test the role:

1. In Power BI Desktop **Report** view, select **Modeling** > **View as**.

2. Select the **Hide Targets** role and select **OK**.

Note that you don't see the Targets table in the Report view anymore, even if it shows hidden objects. Additionally, any visuals that were based on data from the Targets table will show errors.

Also note that measures based on secured columns or tables will be automatically secured as well, so we'll only need to work on securing columns and tables.

Finally, keep in mind that you cannot combine different roles that use row-level security and object-level security. If you need to secure both rows and objects at the same time, you must create a role that includes security rules for both rows and objects.

Assigning security roles membership

Once you've configured row-level security roles in Power BI Desktop, you can publish your report to the Power BI service and add members to each role. To do so, go to the dataset security settings by hovering over a dataset in the list of workspace items and selecting **More options** > **Security**. If you don't have any roles defined in the dataset, you'll see the message in Figure 3-51.

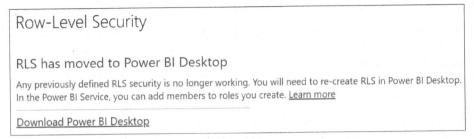

FIGURE 3-51 RLS has moved to Power BI Desktop message

If you've created RLS roles defined in the dataset, you'll see a page like the one shown in Figure 3-52.

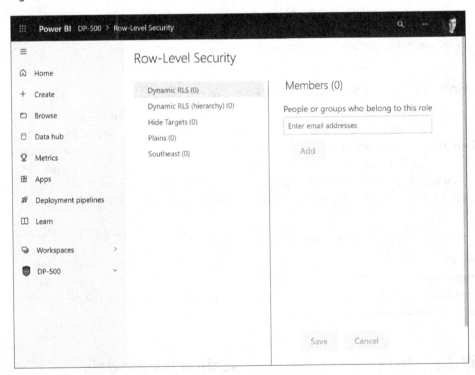

FIGURE 3-52 Row-level security role membership

On the left side of the Row-Level Security page, you can see a list of all roles in the dataset. The numbers in brackets show how many members each role has. On the right, you can view, add, and remove members for a selected role.

To add a member to a role, first select a role on the left, and then enter email addresses or security groups in the **People or groups who belong to this role** field. After you enter new members, select **Add** > **Save**. The changes will be applied immediately.

To remove a member from a role, select the cross next to the member and then select **Save**.

When you use row-level security in Power BI, you can use an email address for each user. Although this solution works, it can be hard to maintain. For example, consider that you have several datasets that use RLS based on the same rules and it's viewed mostly by the same users. If a new user joins your company and you need to give them access to those datasets, you will have to update the row-level security settings for each dataset.

In cases like this, you can assign security groups as members of row-level security roles. When a new user joins the company, you will have to add them to the security group only once. The same principles apply to sharing content in Power BI.

> **NEED MORE REVIEW? CREATING SECURITY GROUPS**
>
> Instructions on how to create security groups are outside the scope of this book. For more details, see "Create a group in the Microsoft 365 admin center" at *https://docs.microsoft.com/en-us/microsoft-365/admin/create-groups/create-groups*.

Viewing as roles in the Power BI service

As we saw with the View as feature in Power BI Desktop, you can test roles in the Power BI service. For this, you need to hover over a role on the Row-Level Security page and select **More options** (the ellipsis) > **Test as role**. You will then see the way a report appears to the members of the role. If needed, you can test a combination of roles or view as a specific user by selecting **Now viewing as** in the blue bar at the top and selecting the desired parameters. Once you are satisfied with how the roles work, you can select **Back to Row-Level Security**.

> **IMPORTANT ROW-LEVEL SECURITY AND WORKSPACE ROLES**
>
> Row-level security does not work on users who have the Contributor, Member, or Admin role in the workspace in which the dataset resides. Those who have edit rights will always see the whole dataset regardless of the security settings, even though the Test as role feature may show a filtered dataset.

Skill 3.2: Optimize enterprise-scale data models

Data models in the enterprise environment occasionally grow sufficiently large to affect the report performance, and sometimes users may complain about the poor experience they have. There can be many reasons for poor performance, and in this section, we'll explore several ways in which you can optimize your data models.

This skill covers how to:

- Identify and implement performance improvements in queries and report visuals
- Troubleshoot DAX performance by using DAX Studio
- Optimize a data model by using Tabular Editor 2
- Analyze data model efficiency by using VertiPaq Analyzer
- Implement incremental refresh (including the use of query folding)
- Optimize a data model by using denormalization

Identify and implement performance improvements in queries and report visuals

Sometimes you may notice that the report performance is not optimal. Power BI Desktop has a feature called Performance Analyzer, which you can use to trace the slow-performing visuals and to see the DAX queries behind them.

To turn on Performance Analyzer, go to the **Report** view and select **View** > **Performance analyzer**. This opens the Performance Analyzer pane shown in Figure 3-53.

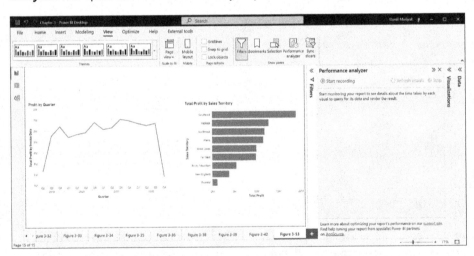

FIGURE 3-53 Performance Analyzer

Performance Analyzer works by recording traces, and it then shows you how long each visual took to render. To start recording traces, select **Start recording**. After that, you need to perform some actions, such as applying filters, that will recalculate the visuals, or you can select **Refresh visuals** to refresh the visuals as they are. You'll then see the rendering duration for each visual.

To identify the slowest visuals, you can sort visuals in the Performance Analyzer pane by selecting the arrow next to **Duration (ms)**.

Each visual that contains data has a DAX query behind it, which you can copy by expanding the line of the visual in the Performance Analyzer pane and selecting **Copy query**. You can analyze the query further in DAX Studio, for example. It's also possible to export all traces by selecting **Export**.

To clear the Performance Analyzer pane, select **Clear**. Once you're done recording traces, select **Stop**.

Troubleshoot DAX performance by using DAX Studio

DAX Studio can be helpful when you are trying to analyze the performance of measures and queries. If you select **Query Plan** before running a query, you will see the physical and logical query plans. If you select **Server Timings**, you'll see how much time was spent in the formula and storage engine, the number of storage engine queries, and the degree of parallelism, as shown in Figure 3-54.

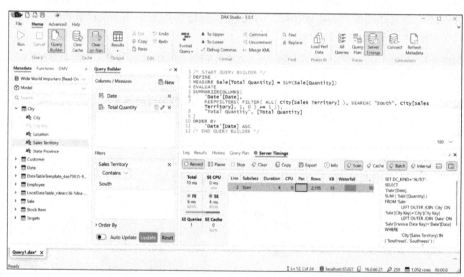

FIGURE 3-54 Server Timings in DAX Studio

As mentioned in Skill 3.1: Design and build tabular models, it can be useful to clear cache before running your queries to ensure that the performance differences aren't due to cached results.

Optimize a data model by using Tabular Editor 2

Best Practice Analyzer (BPA) in Tabular Editor 2 allows you to optimize your model by checking your model for adherence to the rules you add. You can access BPA by selecting **Tools** > **Best**

Practice Analyzer. BPA can check your model for adherence to the rules you add. Before you can use BPA, you have to add BPA rules by selecting **Tools** > **Manage BPA Rules** > **Add**. If you don't want to create your own rules, you can load them from a file or URL. For example, the following URL contains some BPA rules developed in Microsoft: https://raw.githubusercontent.com/microsoft/Analysis-Services/master/BestPracticeRules/BPARules.json.

Once you add rules and open Best Practice Analyzer, you should see a list of rule violations, as shown in Figure 3-55.

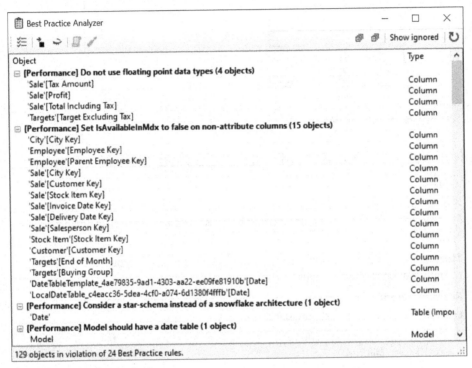

FIGURE 3-55 Best Practice Analyzer

To fix some rule violations, you can right-click a line and select **Apply fix**; other times you may need to apply a fix manually.

Analyze data model efficiency by using VertiPaq Analyzer

DAX Studio can show you the relative size of each column and table in your data model when you select **Advanced** > **View Metrics**. Figure 3-56 shows an example of model metrics, also known as VertiPaq Analyzer.

Note that size is only relevant to imported data. In addition to table and column size, you can view relationships, partitions, referential integrity violations, encoding, and other model information.

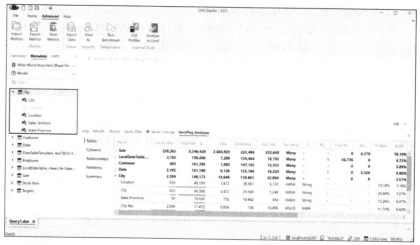

FIGURE 3-56 VertiPaq Analyzer in DAX Studio

Implement incremental refresh (including the use of query folding)

Power BI allows you to work with datasets well in excess of gigabytes even after Power BI automatically compresses data. However, when you refresh large datasets, you may run into the following issues:

- **Speed**—Dataset refreshes may take a very long time, preventing you from displaying the information in a timely manner.

- **Resource usage**—Transferring and transforming large amounts of data may use up precious RAM, CPU, and network bandwidth.

- **Reliability**—Long-running queries to data sources may time out or fail, resulting in dataset refresh failures.

By using incremental refresh, you can address all these issues at once: you'll only refresh a subset of data, resulting in quicker, more reliable refreshes with lower resource consumption.

While you can set a different incremental refresh policy for each table in your dataset, to set an incremental refresh policy, you'll need to filter a table based on dates. Therefore, usually you'll configure incremental refresh for fact tables that hold time-series data—for example, sales records.

For incremental refresh to work in Power BI service, you need to configure the former in Power BI Desktop, which involves the following steps:

1. Create the RangeStart and RangeEnd parameters.
2. Filter by using the RangeStart and RangeEnd parameters.
3. Define incremental refresh policies.

Creating the RangeStart and RangeEnd parameters

The first step in configuring incremental refresh in Power BI Desktop is to create the RangeStart and RangeEnd parameters that will be used to filter dates. These parameter names are reserved and case-sensitive—other parameter names won't work properly for incremental refresh. You create the parameters in Power Query Editor in the following way:

1. In Power Query Editor, select **Manage parameters** > **New parameter**.

2. Configure the RangeStart parameter as follows:

   - Name: **RangeStart**.
   - Type: **Date/Time**.
   - Current value: **01/01/2023**. Power Query may change the input format of this value later, depending on your system settings.

3. Above the list of parameters, select **New** and create the RangeEnd parameter as follows:

   - Name: **RangeEnd**.
   - Type: **Date/Time**.
   - Current value: **31/12/2023**, or **12/31/2023** if your system uses the MDY date format. At this stage, the parameters should look like those shown in Figure 3-57.

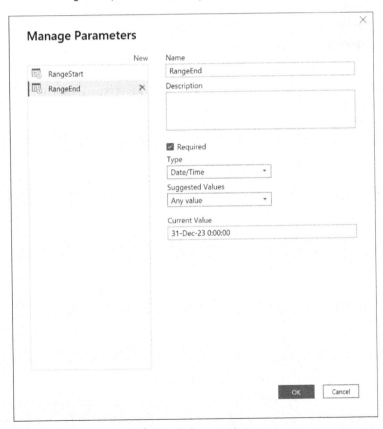

FIGURE 3-57 RangeStart and RangeEnd parameters

4. Select **OK**.

The choice of the current values only matters in Power BI Desktop because parameter values will be automatically overridden in Power BI service.

Filtering by using the RangeStart and RangeEnd parameters

The RangeStart and RangeEnd parameters are needed to filter based on dates. For example, let's say you have a table called Sale that has a date/time column called OrderDate, and you want to incrementally refresh the latest sales records based on OrderDate. In this case, you can apply the filters by implementing the following steps:

1. In Power Query Editor, select the **Sale** table from the list of queries.

2. Select the filter button on the **OrderDate** column header and select **Date/time filters** > **Custom filter**.

3. For the first condition, select

   - **is after or equal to** from the first drop-down list
   - **Parameter** from the second drop-down list
   - **RangeStart** from the third drop-down list

4. For the second condition, select

   - **is before** from the first drop-down list
   - **Parameter** from the second drop-down list
   - **RangeEnd** from the third drop-down list

5. Ensure the logic between the conditions is set to **And**. At this stage, the filter conditions should match the ones shown in Figure 3-58.

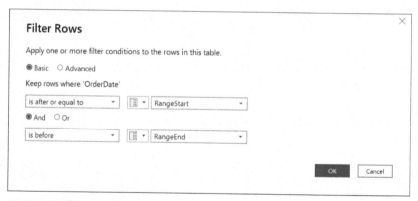

FIGURE 3-58 Filter conditions

6. Select **OK**.

7. Close Power Query Editor by selecting **Close & apply**.

While you can also use "is after" and "is before or equal to" as filter conditions, it's important that one of the conditions is a strict inequality, while the other one is not strict. In other words, if you set one condition to be "is after or equal to" and the other to "is before or equal to", then you'll run into issues, because the edge values will be allocated to different partitions.

> **NOTE FILTERING DATES**
>
> Even though the RangeStart and RangeEnd parameters must be of type Date/Time, the column you filter can be a different type. For example, it's common for data warehouses to store dates as integers, such as 20230523 for May 23, 2023. In this case, you can employ a custom function to convert the parameter values to the required data type, and then you can use the Power Query Advanced Editor to filter the table by using the converted values.

Defining incremental refresh policies

With the RangeStart and RangeEnd parameters now filtering the table for which we want to apply an incremental refresh—in our example, Sale—we can now define an incremental refresh policy in the following way:

1. In the **Data** pane of Power BI Desktop, right-click the table you want to refresh incrementally.
2. Select **Incremental refresh**.
3. Ensure the correct table is selected in the **Table** drop-down list and switch the **Incrementally refresh this table** toggle so it's on.
4. Select the periods for which you want to store and refresh data. Note that you can select different periods for storing and refreshing data. In our example, we can store the last 10 years of data and refresh the last 15 days of data. At this stage, your incremental refresh settings should look as shown in Figure 3-59.
5. Select **Apply**.

When defining an incremental refresh policy, you can also use the following options:

- **Detect data changes**—To make incremental refreshes even more efficient, Power BI can check the maximum value of a date/time column you specify, and data will be refreshed only if the value changes. This column should not be the same column that you filter by using the RangeStart and RangeEnd parameters.

- **Only refresh complete periods**—You can use this setting to exclude incomplete periods from refreshes. In some cases, reporting incomplete periods does not make business sense. For example, if scheduled refresh takes place at 6 a.m. in the morning and there's some data for the day, then displaying the current day's figures may be misleading to report users. Excluding incomplete periods may be appropriate in this case.

- **Get the latest data in real time with DirectQuery**—You can partition tables in such a way that the latest data is in DirectQuery mode, while the old data is imported.

You can define a different incremental refresh policy for each table in your data model while still using the same RangeStart and RangeEnd parameters.

Once you publish your dataset to Power BI service, the data will be refreshed incrementally. The first refresh may take longer to refresh the whole dataset, but subsequent refreshes will benefit from incremental refresh and will be faster.

Incremental refresh and real-time data   ✕

ⓘ These settings will apply when you publish the dataset to the Power BI service. Once you do
    that, you won't be able to download it back to Power BI Desktop. Learn more

1. Select table

| Sale | ⌄ |

2. Set import and refresh ranges

⬤ Incrementally refresh this table

Archive data starting | 10 | | Years | ⌄ | before refresh date

Data imported from 1/1/2013 to 2/26/2023 (inclusive)

Incrementally refresh data starting | 15 | | Days | ⌄ | before refresh date

Data will be incrementally refreshed from 2/27/2023 to 3/13/2023 (inclusive)

3. Choose optional settings

☐ Get the latest data in real time with DirectQuery (Premium only) Learn more

☐ Only refresh complete days Learn more

☐ Detect data changes Learn more

4. Review and apply

| | Archived | | **Incremental Refresh** | |
| 10 years before
refresh date | | | 15 days before
refresh date | | Refresh date |

[Apply] [Cancel]

FIGURE 3-59 Incremental refresh

Query folding

Incremental refresh is only effective when query folding occurs—that is, when filtering by dates results in the data source returning a reduced set of data. If query folding does not occur, then filtering happens after Power BI retrieves all data, making incremental refresh policies useless. When you define an incremental refresh policy, Power BI Desktop will try to verify whether query folding occurs. If it's unable to confirm query folding, then you'll see a message as shown in Figure 3-60.

Incremental refresh and real-time data   ✕

⚠ Unable to confirm if the M query can be folded. It is not recommended to use incremental
   refresh with non-foldable queries. Learn more

FIGURE 3-60 Query folding warning

Note that query folding may still occur, though you'll need to confirm it yourself by using query diagnostics. We reviewed query diagnostics in Skill 2.2: Ingest and transform data by using Power BI.

Optimize a data model by using denormalization

While Power BI can work with a variety of schemas, it works best with star schemas. Therefore, you should strive to denormalize snowflake schemas into star schemas. The closer to the source you get denormalized data, the better performance you get in most cases. If you need to denormalize in Power Query and the merge operation is slow, you can refer to Skill 2.2: Ingest and transform data by using Power BI to learn Power Query performance improvement skills.

Note that in some cases a flat table will deliver better performance than snowflake schema. The price you may pay in this case is reduced user-friendliness for report builders, since all fields are going to be in the same table. Additionally, for some you may need to write more complex DAX, especially if you used to have more than one fact.

Chapter summary

- You may want to use DirectQuery when data frequently changes and you need to report the latest data. Another reason to use DirectQuery is when there's too much data to import into a model.

- Power BI Desktop supports various external tools, such as DAX Studio and Tabular Editor. You can use DAX Studio to write DAX queries and troubleshoot query performance, and you can use Tabular Editor to develop your model and apply best practice rules.

- Calculation groups are special tables in Power BI that allow you to write less DAX and apply the same calculations to any selected measure. You can create calculation groups in Tabular Editor.

- DAX is a functional language that you can use to create measures, calculated columns, calculated tables, and calculation groups. You can also write queries in DAX that start with EVALUATE.

- A large dataset format is a feature in the Power BI service that may improve the dataset read and write operation performance.

- Composite models allow you to combine DirectQuery and imported data. You can define aggregations to improve the user experience in some cases.

- In Power BI, you can secure data in two ways. Row-level security will show specific rows to different groups of people, and object-level security will hide some columns or tables from some groups of people. You can define roles in Power BI Desktop and assign members in the Power BI service.

■ Performance Analyzer in Power BI Desktop allows you to analyze the performance of visuals. Once you know which visuals are the most problematic, you can copy the underlying query for further analysis.

■ In DAX Studio, you can analyze the query performance by seeing how much time is spent in formula and storage engines. You can make changes to your formulas, clear cache, and see if your changes made any difference to performance.

■ The Best Practice Analyzer (BPA) feature of Tabular Editor allows you to check whether your data model adheres to a set of rules. You can define rules yourself or use someone else's rules.

■ In DAX Studio, you can view the model metrics and see which columns or tables consume the most space. You can then optimize the data model size, knowing that the number of distinct values in a column is the largest contributor to the data model size.

■ When working with large datasets, you can configure incremental refresh to only refresh the latest data while storing the old data. Incremental refresh policies are defined in Power BI Desktop and then applied automatically in the Power BI service. To define an incremental refresh policy for a table, you need to use RangeStart and RangeEnd date/time parameters to filter the table you want to refresh incrementally, and then set the periods for which you want to store and refresh data.

■ Instead of using snowflake data models, you should strive to use star schemas. You can denormalize in Power Query if needed.

Thought experiment

In this thought experiment, demonstrate your skills and knowledge of the topics covered in this chapter. You can find the answers in the section that follows.

Situation setup

1. You need to optimize a measure. Which tool should you use?

    A. Query diagnostics in Power Query

    B. Performance Analyzer

    C. DAX Studio

    D. Tabular Editor

2. Your report uses a dataset in DirectQuery mode. Some users complain that their basic reports take a long time to load. How can you improve performance?

    A. Configure incremental refresh.

    B. Build a composite model and configure an aggregation table.

    C. Remove some columns from the dataset.

3. You created a bar graph with Color on the axis and Quantity on the values. The visual is shown in Figure 3-61.

Quantity by Color

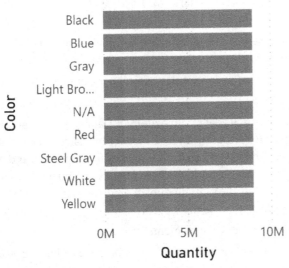

FIGURE 3-61 Bar graph showing Quantity by Color

Upon further checking, you find out that black stock items sold 1.1 million units. How can you fix the graph? The solution should use minimal effort and consider that you may want to analyze sales by metrics other than Quantity.

A. Create the following measure:
```
Total Quantity =
CALCULATE (
    SUM ( Sale[Quantity] ),
    TREATAS ( VALUES ( 'Stock Item'[Stock Item Key] ), Sale[Stock Item Key] )
)
```

B. Create an active physical relationship between Sale and Stock Item.

C. Create the following measure:
```
Total Quantity =
CALCULATE (
    SUM ( Sale[Quantity] ),
    INTERSECT( Sale, 'Stock Item' )
)
```

4. You want to create a line chart showing Quantity by the invoice date. You notice that there is a relationship between the Date from the Date table and the Invoice Date Key from the Sale table, but the relationship is inactive. All other visuals in your report will be analyzing values by delivery date. How should you approach this problem?

A. Create the following measure:

```
Quantity by Invoice Date =
CALCULATE (
    SUM ( Sale[Quantity] ),
    USERELATIONSHIP ( 'Date'[Date], Sale[Invoice Date Key] )
)
```

B. Delete the relationship based on the delivery date and activate the relationship based on the invoice date.

C. Activate the relationship based on invoice date, keeping the other relationship as is.

D. Use the TREATAS function.

5. You work on a dataset that sources its data from Azure SQL Database. The main fact table contains daily sales data for the last five years. To make the dataset refresh more efficiently, you configure incremental refresh for the table by filtering the sales data column. Upon checking the refresh history in the Power BI service, you notice that the refresh always takes approximately the same amount of time, suggesting that incremental refresh doesn't happen. What could be the reason?

A. Azure SQL Database doesn't support incremental refresh.

B. One of the transformation steps breaks query folding before date filtering happens.

C. The date/time range parameters are called RangeFrom and RangeTo.

D. The storage mode is set to Import.

Thought experiment answers

1. The answer is **C**. In DAX Studio, you can see the query plan as well as server timings when executing DAX queries that include the measure you want to optimize. DAX is used after you load data, and query diagnostics are a Power Query feature, so option A is wrong. Neither Performance Analyzer nor Tabular Editor can provide a detailed breakdown of why a measure is slow, so options B and D are also wrong.

2. The answer is **B**. Aggregate tables can be used to answer queries that don't need a lot of details. You cannot configure incremental refresh in DirectQuery mode, so option A is wrong. Option C is incorrect because the dataset uses DirectQuery, and removing columns won't affect the performance of the visuals that are already in the report.

3. The answer is **B**. Creating a physical relationship is the least arduous solution and will let you avoid creating virtual relationships like in answer A. While the measure from option A will solve the problem of incorrect values, you will need to write a similar measure for each different metric you want to analyze. The measure formula from option C will not work because Sale and Stock item have a different number of columns. Option D involves too much effort and only solves the problem at hand; if you want to analyze quantity by individual stock items, this approach will fail.

4.   The answer is **A**. Because this is going to be a one-off visual, creating a measure that activates the relationship at query time solves the problem and involves the least effort. If you delete the relationship based on delivery date, as option B suggests, other visuals that use the Date table will display the wrong values. Following option C is not possible because no more than one relationship can be active at a time. Using TREATAS as suggested in option D will result in the wrong figures.

5.   The answer is **B**. For incremental refresh to work, query folding must take place. Otherwise data is filtered after it's loaded, and the refresh time will be the same as without incremental refresh. Option A is incorrect because Azure SQL databases do support incremental refresh. Option C is incorrect because the date/time parameters used for incremental refresh must be called RangeStart and RangeEnd—other names won't work. Option D is incorrect because incremental refresh is designed for imported data, not other storage modes.

## CHAPTER 4

Explore and visualize data

Exploring and visualizing data is a critical step in your data projects. It is essential in order to get a good grasp of how the data is structured and what the data means. This can be a particularly challenging problem when the amount of data is large. Azure Synapse Analytics and Power BI provide the tools you need in order to explore and visualize your data right where you manipulate it.

Skills covered in this chapter:

- Skill 4.1: Explore data by using Azure Synapse Analytics
- Skill 4.2: Visualize data by using Power BI

Skill 4.1: Explore data by using Azure Synapse Analytics

Azure Synapse Analytics encompasses many of the features you need when it comes to your data projects. On top of being able to query and transform your data, you also have powerful visualization capabilities that will help you, no matter the size of your dataset. Moreover, there are many ways to produce visuals, which will give you the flexibility you need to be productive.

> **This skill covers how to:**
> - Explore data by using native visuals in Spark notebooks
> - Explore and visualize data by using the Azure Synapse SQL results pane

Explore data by using native visuals in Spark notebooks

As a reminder, Spark is one of the compute engines present in Azure Synapse, along with SQL. The particularity of Spark is that it's a distributed in-memory framework. It combines batch and streaming, machine language (ML) and graph analysis, and also has some capabilities for data visualization. In this section we will review how to visualize your data by using the show() and display() functions, the Spark SQL magic command, and Python as well as R libraries.

The show() and display() functions

The show() and display() functions are functions that you can call in a cell of the notebook. The display() function is powerful because it gives access to a range of visualizations. Let's discuss how to use it.

1. Open your Synapse Studio.

2. In **Manage** > **Apache Spark pools**, check if you have a Spark pool; otherwise, create one.

3. In order to use the same dataset we used in Chapter 2, navigate to **Data** > **Linked** > **Azure Data Lake Storage Gen2** > **Primary data store**.

4. Find the taxi dataset.

5. Right-click **New notebook** > **Load to Dataframe**.

6. Attach your Spark pool.

7. Execute the cell.

As you can see, the primary visualization is a table. But you can also switch to more advanced visualizations, as shown in Figure 4-1. We will dive deeper into the chart visualizations later in this chapter.

VendorID	lpep_pickup_datetime	lpep_dropoff_datetime	store_and_fwd_flag	RatecodeID	PULocationID
2	2022-01-01 00:14:21	2022-01-01 00:15:33	N	1.0	42
1	2022-01-01 00:20:55	2022-01-01 00:29:38	N	1.0	116
1	2022-01-01 00:57:02	2022-01-01 01:13:14	N	1.0	41
2	2022-01-01 00:07:42	2022-01-01 00:15:57	N	1.0	181
2	2022-01-01 00:07:50	2022-01-01 00:28:52	N	1.0	33
1	2022-01-01 00:47:57	2022-01-01 00:54:09	N	1.0	150
2	2022-01-01 00:13:38	2022-01-01 00:33:50	N	1.0	66
2	2022-01-01 00:43:00	2022-01-01 00:49:20	N	1.0	40
2	2022-01-01 00:41:04	2022-01-01 00:47:04	N	1.0	112
2	2022-01-01 00:51:07	2022-01-01 01:09:31	N	1.0	256

FIGURE 4-1 Data visualization with the display() function

The show() function, although similar in appearance, is more basic. It's built into Apache Spark itself and can be very useful for exploring your data in a raw fashion. To learn how to use the show() function, try the following:

1. Add a new cell to your notebook.

2. Add the following Python code:

```
df[['lpep_pickup_datetime', 'passenger_count', 'trip_distance', 'tip_amount',
'total_amount']].limit(10).show()
```

3. Execute the cell.

You should see the output of the show() function as displayed in Figure 4-2.

```
+--------------------+--------------+-------------+----------+------------+
|lpep_pickup_datetime|passenger_count|trip_distance|tip_amount|total_amount|
+--------------------+--------------+-------------+----------+------------+
| 2022-01-01 00:14:21|           1.0|         0.44|       0.0|         4.8|
| 2022-01-01 00:20:55|           1.0|          2.1|       0.0|        10.8|
| 2022-01-01 00:57:02|           1.0|          3.7|       4.6|       23.15|
| 2022-01-01 00:07:42|           1.0|         1.69|       0.0|         9.3|
| 2022-01-01 00:07:50|           1.0|         6.26|      5.21|       31.26|
| 2022-01-01 00:47:57|           1.0|          1.3|       0.0|         8.3|
| 2022-01-01 00:13:38|           1.0|         6.47|       0.0|        23.8|
| 2022-01-01 00:43:00|           1.0|         1.15|       0.0|         7.3|
| 2022-01-01 00:41:04|           1.0|          1.3|       0.0|         7.3|
| 2022-01-01 00:51:07|           1.0|         4.75|      4.21|       25.26|
+--------------------+--------------+-------------+----------+------------+
```

FIGURE 4-2 Data visualization with the show() function

The show() and display() functions provide convenient, out-of-the-box ways to explore your data in a notebook. But there's much more, so read on.

Spark SQL magic command

Spark magic commands are commands used to interact with the Spark cluster from the notebook. One of the most common use cases for them is the ability to run Spark code interactively in multiple languages. Spark supports Scala, Python, R, and C# in Azure Synapse. Here you'll learn how to visualize data with Spark SQL using the %%sql magic command.

Before that, though, we need to create a view that we can query with Spark SQL. To do so, create a new cell and type the following code:

```
from pyspark.sql.functions import *
from datetime import datetime
from dateutil import parser
df.select('passenger_count', 'trip_distance', 'tip_amount', 'fare_amount',
 'total_amount',
dayofmonth(col('lpep_pickup_datetime')).alias('day_of_month')).
createOrReplaceTempView("taxi")
```

Then we can use the following code:

```
%%sql
SELECT

    day_of_month,
    MIN(tip_amount) AS minTipAmount,
    MAX(tip_amount) AS maxTipAmount,
    AVG(tip_amount) AS avgTipAmount,
    AVG(fare_amount) AS avgFareAmount,
     AVG(total_amount) as avgTotalAmount
FROM taxi
GROUP BY day_of_month
ORDER BY day_of_month ASC
```

Here, the %%sql magic command will make use of the Spark SQL engine and directly display the results in a table, as shown in Figure 4-3.

day_of_month	minTipAmount	maxTipAmount	avgTipAmount	avgFareAmount
1	0	75	1.9611616954474116	16.002441130298305
2	0	40	1.7483466666666672	14.299073333333363
3	-0.66	28.66	1.5047041166380781	13.20706260720414
4	-0.01	75	1.6725588914549672	14.07353810623559
5	-0.66	22.26	1.5995927401505097	13.658003541390018
6	-0.66	21.26	1.577410714285714	13.64385629251703
7	0	25	1.6636626637554586	13.161517467248926

FIGURE 4-3 Data visualization with the Spark SQL magic command

Here we can also toggle the **Chart** option. Then select **View options** and select the following values:

- **Chart type:** Column chart
- **Key:** day_of_month
- **Values**: avgTipAmount
- **Series Group:** Leave blank
- **Aggregation:** Avg
- **Stacked:** Checked

Then click Apply. The result will be a column chart showing the tip amount and fare amount stacked per day, as shown in Figure 4-4.

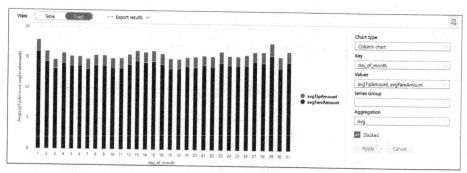

FIGURE 4-4 Data visualization in the Chart pane with Spark SQL

You can select multiple chart types, which makes the Chart pane a good tool for a quick data exploration.

Python libraries

The Python language is well known for being rich in data visualization libraries. The most famous of them is Matplotlib. Let's review one way to use it with our taxi dataset.

In the existing notebook, create a new cell and import Matplotlib as well as pandas:

```
import matplotlib.pyplot as plt
import pandas as pd
```

In a new cell, create our visualization. Here we'll make a histogram showing the counts of tip amounts, as seen in Figure 4-5.

```
ax1 = df[['tip_amount']].toPandas().plot(kind='hist', bins=25, facecolor='lightblue')
ax1.set_title('Tip amount distribution')
ax1.set_xlabel('Tip Amount ($)')
ax1.set_ylabel('Counts')
plt.suptitle('')
plt.show()
```

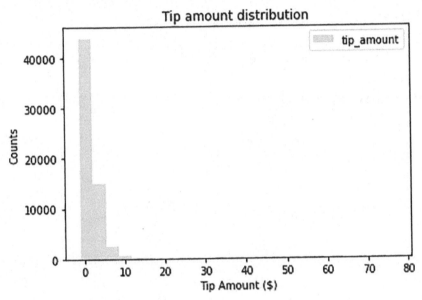

FIGURE 4-5 Data visualization with Python

Matplotlib is extremely rich in terms of chart types. When used in conjunction with pandas, there are about 10 different plot types you can use. This is again a great tool in your toolbox to visualize your data.

Explore and visualize data by using the Azure Synapse SQL results pane

Azure Synapse SQL, in a similar fashion as Spark SQL, offers data visualization capabilities. They are useful if you are already exploring and transforming your data with Azure Synapse SQL. This feature is available both in the serverless pool and the dedicated pool.

To review how to explore data in Azure Synapse SQL, let's do the following:

1. Open your Synapse Studio.

2. In order to use the same dataset we used in Chapter 2, navigate to **Data** > **Linked** > **Azure Data Lake Storage Gen2** > **Primary data store**.

3. Find the taxi dataset.

4. Right-click **New SQL Script** > **Select TOP 100 rows**.

5. Make sure the script is connecting to your built-in engine.

6. Click Run.

This should take a few second to run. In the **Results** pane, select Chart. Set the chart options as follow:

- **Chart type:** Line
- **Category column:** (none)
- **Legend (series) columns:** trip_distance
- **Legend position:** bottom – center
- **Legend (series) label:** Leave blank
- **Category label:** Leave blank

You should see the chart shown in Figure 4-6.

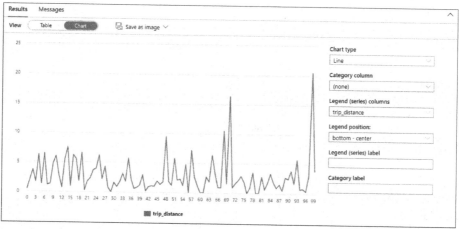

FIGURE 4-6 Line chart with Azure Synapse SQL

Skill 4.2: Visualize data by using Power BI

Data visualization is at the heart of Power BI. In this section, we'll discuss several skills that may be necessary to address some of the challenges of operating in the enterprise environment, such as providing the consistent formatting across the reports and designing reports with accessibility in mind.

We'll also explain how you can create R and Python visuals, enable visual personalization, and set up automatic page refresh. In some cases you may need to query Power BI datasets by using the XMLA endpoint or create paginated reports, and we'll review both skills in this section as well.

> **NOTE COMPANION FILE**
>
> Most of the visuals shown in this chapter are available in the companion PBIX file.

This skill covers how to:

- Create and import a custom report theme
- Create R or Python visuals in Power BI
- Connect to and query datasets by using the XMLA endpoint
- Design and configure Power BI reports for accessibility
- Enable personalized visuals in a report
- Configure automatic page refresh
- Create and distribute paginated reports in Power BI Report Builder

Create and import a custom report theme

Power BI offers many ways to customize the look of your reports, one of which is formatting. While the Power BI team designed a default theme that works in many circumstances, in many cases you may want to apply different formatting to your reports. Large companies often have their own brand books or at least a preferred color palette, and to be brand-compliant, your reports will need to follow the brand guidelines.

For example, you may want to select a particular font face for your reports; formatting each visual to apply the formatting is tedious, error-prone, and time-consuming. Even though you could use Format Painter, doing so will still be laborious and may not always produce the desired results. When you want your reports to be formatted in your way of choosing by default, you can use a custom report theme, which will save you a lot of time and apply formatting consistently for all new visuals and pages.

> **NOTE APPLYING A REPORT THEME**
>
> You can apply a report theme only in Power BI Desktop, not in the Power BI service. Dashboard themes, which are outside the scope of this book, are applied in the Power BI service.

In addition to the default theme, Power BI Desktop includes several other themes that you can see by selecting **View** > **Themes**, as shown in Figure 4-7. Furthermore, you can select **View** > **Themes** > **Theme gallery** to download more themes.

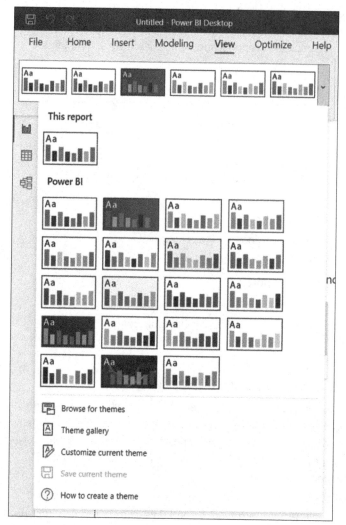

FIGURE 4-7 Themes in Power BI Desktop

When using themes, you should keep in mind that the theme will format only those formatting options that you didn't specify manually. If you want to revert the manually applied formatting to the theme formatting, you'll need to select **Reset to default** in the formatting options.

You can also create your own theme in a few ways:

- Power BI Desktop theme editor
- Edit a theme JSON file
- Third-party tools

Power BI Desktop theme editor

You can create your own way by customizing the current theme directly in Power BI Desktop. To open the theme editor, shown in Figure 4-8, select **View** > **Themes** > **Customize current theme**.

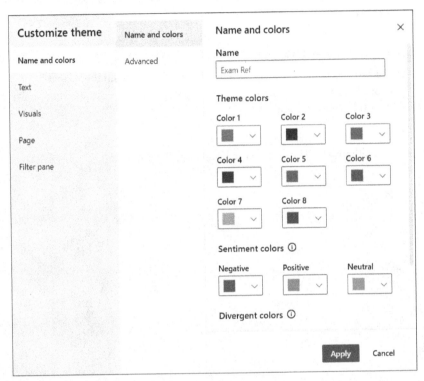

FIGURE 4-8 Customize theme

The Power BI Desktop theme customization feature allows you to customize several categories of properties:

- **Name and colors**—Theme name, theme colors, sentiment color, divergent colors, and structural colors.
- **Text**—General font options, as well as options specific to titles, cards and KPIs, and tab headers in the key influencers visual
- **Visuals**—Background, border, header, and tooltip formatting options
- **Page**—Wallpaper and page background colors and transparency
- **Filter pane**—Formatting options of the filter pane and filter cards

Once you've made your customizations, select **Apply** to apply your changes to the current report theme.

Edit a theme JSON file

Note that the built-in theme editor does not contain all available properties you can format, and to apply some formatting by default, you'll need to edit the theme file, which is a JSON file.

If you want to export the current theme file from Power BI Desktop, you can select **View** > **Themes** > **Save current theme**.

> **NOTE SAVE CURRENT THEME GRAYED OUT**
>
> If you cannot save the current theme, it's likely because you're using a default theme and made no customizations to it. To export a default theme, apply at least one customization; even editing the report theme is sufficient.

If you open a Power BI theme file in a text editor, it will look like this:

```
{
    "name": "Exam Ref",
    "textClasses": {
        "label": {
            "fontSize": 12
        }
    },
    "dataColors": [
        "#0A89FF",
        "#0B1EAA",
        "#E7652D",
        "#78008A",
        "#DB329E",
        "#7A4ED4",
        "#ECC305",
        "#D4303C"
    ],
    "visualStyles": {
        "*": {
            "*": {
                "background": [
                    {
                        "transparency": 100
                    }
                ]
            }
        },
        "page": {
            "*": {
                "background": [
                    {
                        "color": {
                            "solid": {
                                "color": "#FFFFFF"
                            }
                        }
                    },
```

```
                    "transparency": 100
             }
        ]
      }
    }
  }
}
```

You can then make changes in the file, save it, then import in Power BI Desktop by selecting **View** > **Themes** > **Browse for themes** and selecting your theme JSON file. If the theme file was created correctly, you'll see the message shown in Figure 4-9; otherwise, you'll get an error message.

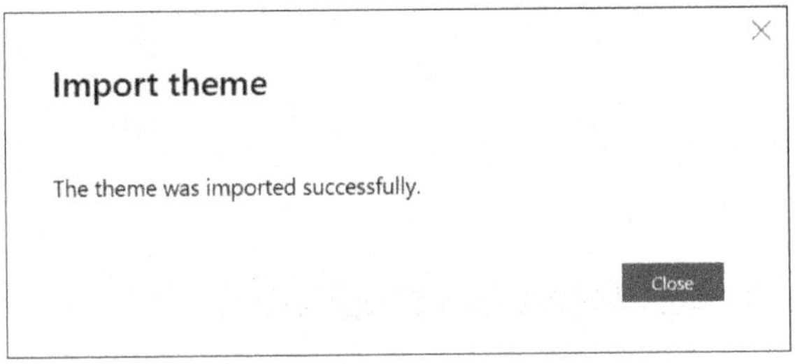

FIGURE 4-9 Import theme message

When editing a theme JSON file, you only need to specify the properties you want to change—other properties will be inherited from the base theme included in Power BI Desktop when you created your report.

When you want to apply the same formatting to a class of properties, you can use the asterisk to denote *all items within the class.*

> **NOTE**   **REPORT THEME PROPERTIES**
>
> The full list of all properties available for formatting is outside the scope of this book. For more details, see the section "Properties within each card" in "Use report themes in Power BI Desktop" at *https://learn.microsoft.com/en-us/power-bi/create-reports/ desktop-report-themes#properties-within-each-card.*

If you need to edit the theme you imported, you can either export your theme and edit the JSON file, or customize the theme in Power BI Desktop if the properties you want to edit are supported. Note that editing in Power BI Desktop only changes the properties you edit; theme properties not editable in Power BI Desktop will not be changed, and you won't lose the theme properties you don't see.

Third-party tools

In addition to the Power BI Desktop theme editor and manually editing JSON files, you can use third-party tools to create custom report themes. For example, you can use the PowerBI.

Tips Theme Generator available at https://themes.powerbi.tips. As you can see in Figure 4-10, the theme generator offers a user interface that allows editing of more properties than the built-in Power BI Desktop theme editor.

FIGURE 4-10 PowerBI.Tips Theme Generator

If you need to edit a theme already created in PowerBI.Tips Theme Generator, you'll need to edit it manually as described earlier in this section.

Create R or Python visuals in Power BI

If you're looking to add some visualization that's not available by default, one option is to create an R or Python visual. Incorporating an R or Python visual can be a powerful addition to the standard visuals in Power BI.

Requirements for R or Python visuals

You can create an R or Python visual only in Power BI Desktop, and for that you'll need to have them installed on your machine first.

> **NOTE INSTALLING R OR PYTHON**
>
> The exam does not test your ability to install R or Python; therefore, this book assumes you've already installed each engine.
>
> If you need to install R, you can download it from CRAN at *https://cran.r-project.org*.
>
> To install Python, you can download it from the official repository at *https://www.python.org/downloads*.

Once you've install R or Python, you'll need to ensure that the correct home directory is specified in Power BI Desktop in **File** > **Options and settings** > **Options** > **R scripting** or **Python scripting**, respectively. Figure 4-11 shows the R and Python script options side by side.

FIGURE 4-11 R and Python script options

As you can see in Figure 4-11, R and Python settings are very similar. For both R and Python, you can select the home directory that contains R and Python, respectively, as well as which integrated development environment (IDE) you want Power BI Desktop to launch for each language. Finally, scripting options also allow you to change the temporary storage location, which is sometimes used when visuals automatically install additional packages.

Work in script editors

To start creating an R or Python visual, select the R or Python visual from the **Visualizations** pane. If this is the first time you're creating a script visual in the report, you'll be prompted to enable script visuals like in Figure 4-12.

Enable script visuals

This Power BI Desktop file contains script visuals. Only enable script visuals if you trust the author and source, or after you review and understand their scripts.

Enable   Review   Cancel

FIGURE 4-12 Enable script visuals

Script visuals may contain code with security or privacy risks. You should enable script visuals only if you trust the creator and source of the visual. You need to enable script visuals only once in a report development session, even if you create both R and Python visuals.

Once you select **Enable**, you'll need to add some fields into the **Values** area in the **Visualization** pane to your visual. You'll then see the script editor, where you can enter code. Figure 4-13 shows the Python script editor as an example.

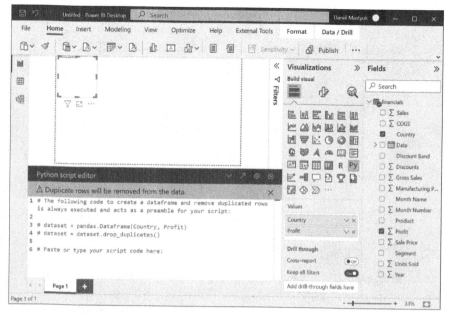

FIGURE 4-13 Python script editor

Power BI creates a table structure (DataFrame) called dataset with the fields you add from your data to the visual. The default summarization of fields is *Don't summarize*. You can then write or paste code that results in a visual, and then select the run button in the upper-right corner of the script editor to run the script and display the visual.

If desired, you can use an external IDE to write your scripts: for example, R Studio or Visual Studio Code. To launch IDE, select the diagonal arrow button in the upper-right corner of the script editor. For example, Figure 4-14 shows Visual Studio Code launched as a Python IDE.

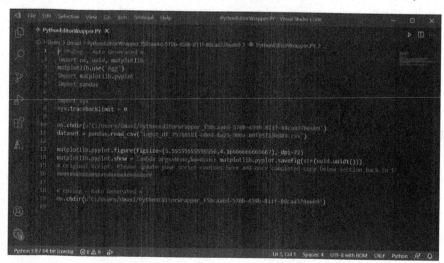

FIGURE 4-14 Visual Studio Code

Note that the IDE contains more code than the Power BI script editor. For example, you can see that for Python, Power BI imports several modules, and it's useful to know that Power BI does not rename them, so you know how you can use the modules in your code. If desired, you can re-import modules and rename them in your code.

Exporting the code from IDE to Power BI Desktop automatically is not supported. Once you're done writing your code in the IDE, you'll need to copy it and paste it back to the Power BI script editor.

Create R visuals

Even if you want to create R visuals not based on any data from your data model, you still need to add at least one field to your visual to start writing your script. To test your R settings and whether R visuals will be displayed, you can create a visual that displays data generated inline. For example, you can add any data field to your R visual and paste the following code:

```
library(ggplot2)
ggplot(iris, aes(Sepal.Length, Petal.Length, colour=Species)) + geom_point()
```

Once you run the script, you should see a visual like the one in Figure 4-15.

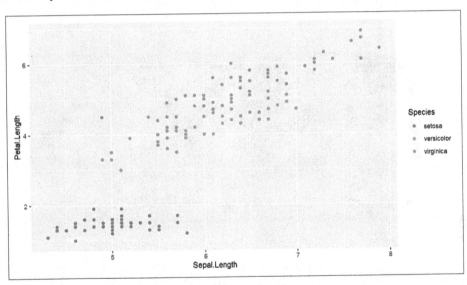

FIGURE 4-15 R visual example

If you use an R visual, in many cases you'll likely want to use your own data. As mentioned earlier, once you add your data fields to the visual, they'll be kept in the dataset DataFrame, and you can then use the DataFrame in your visual. For instance, the following script uses data from the Power BI Desktop sample dataset to plot profit by country:

```
# The following code to create a dataframe and remove duplicated rows is always
executed and acts as a preamble for your script:
```

```
# dataset <- data.frame(Country, Profit)
# dataset <- unique(dataset)

# Paste or type your script code here:

# Run in R Studio: install.packages("maps")
library(maps)
library(ggplot2)

world_map <- map_data(map = "world")

ggplot(dataset) +
  geom_map(aes(map_id = Country, fill = as.factor(Profit)), map = world_map) +
  geom_polygon(data = world_map, aes(x = long, y = lat, group = group), colour =
'black', fill = NA) +
  expand_limits(x = world_map$long, y = world_map$lat) +
  scale_fill_brewer(name = "Profit", palette = "Blues") +
  theme_void() +
  coord_fixed()
```

After you run the code, you'll see a graph like the one in Figure 4-16.

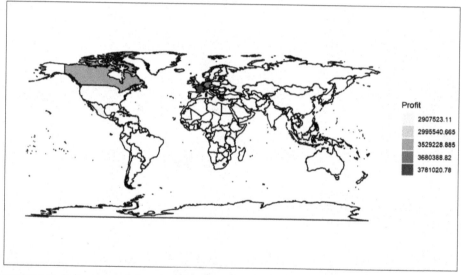

FIGURE 4-16 R visual example based on data from data model

When creating R visuals, you should keep in mind the following limitations:

- You can only plot up to 150,000 rows.

- The output size is limited to 2 MB.

- The timeout for plotting is 5 minutes.

- Only plotting to the default device is supported.

- R visuals can't be used to filter other visuals.

- R visuals use the default field names and don't support renaming fields.
- Not all R packages are supported in the Power BI service.

> **NOTE SUPPORTED R PACKAGES**
>
> To view the list of supported packages and their versions, see the section "R packages that are supported in Power BI" in "Create visuals by using R packages in the Power BI service" at *https://learn.microsoft.com/en-us/power-bi/connect-data/service-r-packages-support*.

Create Python visuals

As with R visuals, to test whether Python visuals work for you regardless of data, you can create a visual that doesn't use data from your data model like so:

```
import matplotlib.pyplot as plt

plt.bar(x=['a', 'b'], height=[1, 2])

plt.show()
```

If the visual works as it should, you'll see a graph like the one in Figure 4-17.

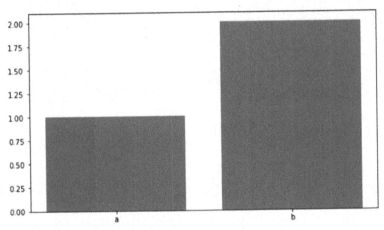

FIGURE 4-17 Python visual example

Python visuals are mostly useful with your own data, and once you add all fields of interest, you can use the dataset DataFrame to create your Python visual. For example, the following script works with the financial data sample from Power BI Desktop:

```
# The following code to create a dataframe and remove duplicated rows is always
# executed and acts as a preamble for your script:

# dataset = pandas.DataFrame(Country, Product, Sales, COGS, Units Sold, Profit)
# dataset = dataset.drop_duplicates()
```

```
# Paste or type your script code here:

import matplotlib.pyplot as plt
import seaborn as sns

dataset = dataset.fillna("Other")

p = sns.pairplot(dataset, hue="Product", palette="husl")
p._legend.remove()
plt.legend(loc="best", title="Product")
plt.tight_layout()

plt.show()
```

When you run the script, you'll get a visual like the one in Figure 4-18.

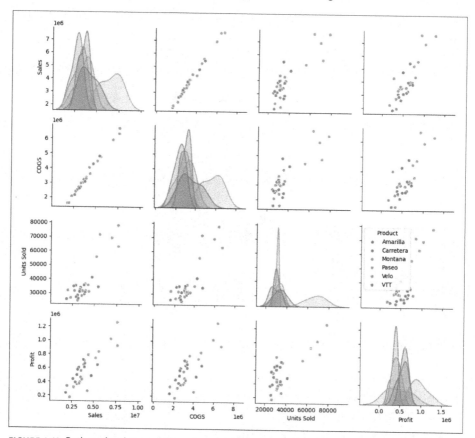

FIGURE 4-18 Python visual example based on data from Power BI

Python visuals have similar limitations to R visuals:

- You can only plot up to 150,000 rows.
- The timeout for plotting is 5 minutes.

- Only plotting to the default device is supported.
- Python visuals can't be used to filter other visuals.
- Python visuals use the default field names and don't support renaming fields.
- Not all Python packages are supported in the Power BI service.

> *NOTE* **SUPPORTED PYTHON PACKAGES**
>
> To view the list of supported packages and their versions, see the section "Python packages that are supported in Power BI" in "Learn which Python packages are supported in Power BI" at *https://learn.microsoft.com/en-us/power-bi/connect-data/service-python-packages-support.*

Connect to and query datasets by using the XMLA endpoint

As mentioned in Chapter 1, you can connect to Power BI datasets residing in a Premium capacity by using the XMLA endpoint. You can use a Power BI dataset as a semantic layer and use tools other than Power BI to query your datasets by using the XMLA endpoint.

> *NOTE* **POWER BI PREMIUM CAPACITIES**
>
> In this section, "Premium capacity" loosely refers to datasets in Embedded, Premium, and Premium per user workspaces. You can also connect to datamarts in the same way.

Connect to a dataset

To connect to a Power BI dataset, use the connection string from the workspace or dataset settings. For example, if your workspace is called *Dev Workspace*, you can use the following connection string in place of the server address:

```
powerbi://api.powerbi.com/v1.0/myorg/Dev%20Workspace
```

In case you want to connect to a different tenant where you're a guest, you can replace *myorg* with the domain of the tenant, such as *contoso.com*.

There are several tools you can use to connect to a Power BI dataset, one of which is DAX Studio, covered in Chapter 3. You can connect to a Power BI dataset in DAX Studio by performing the following steps:

1. Open DAX Studio.
2. Select **Home** > **Connect**. Figure 4-19 shows the Connect options. If you connected to a workspace before, the Tabular Server field may be pre-filled.

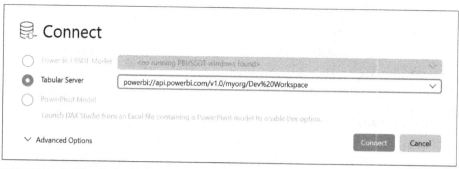

FIGURE 4-19 DAX Studio Connect options

3. In **Tabular Server**, enter the workspace connection string.

4. Select **Connect** and sign in to your account.

Figure 4-20 shows DAX Studio once you connect to a workspace.

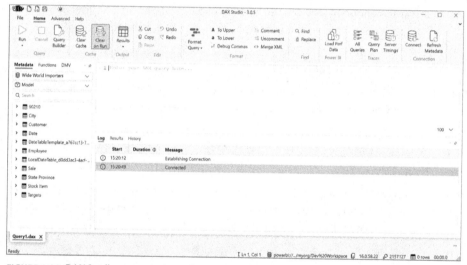

FIGURE 4-20 DAX Studio connected to a Power BI workspace

You can see the workspace you're connected to at the bottom of the screen. Note how in the **Metadata** pane on the left, you can select the dataset in the workspace if there are multiple datasets. If you wanted to connect to a specific dataset in the first place, you could specify the Initial Catalog option in the Connect Advanced Options.

Query a dataset

Once you connect to a dataset from a querying tool such a DAX Studio, you can query it. While DAX is usually used to create calculations, such as measures and calculated columns, you can also write queries by using DAX. DAX queries must return tables, and they differ from calculated tables in the syntax: you'll need to use EVALUATE in front of a table expression. For example, the following DAX query returns a list of countries:

```
EVALUATE
VALUES('Sample'[Country])
```

After you write the query, select **Run** in DAX Studio. Figure 4-21 shows the result of the query.

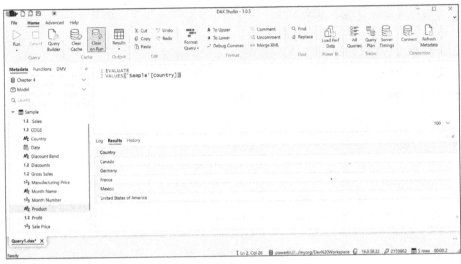

FIGURE 4-21 DAX Studio showing a list of countries

EVALUATE is the only required statement in DAX query. A DAX query can include multiple EVALUATE statements, and they'll return separate result sets. You can add optional keywords to your DAX queries, as shown next.

DEFINE

In the DEFINE section, you can specify query-level variables, measures, columns, and tables. The following query defines a query-level measure called *Total Profit* and a query-level column called *Country Letter* and uses them to show the profit by the first letter of a country:

```
DEFINE
    MEASURE 'Sample'[Total Profit] = SUM('Sample'[Profit])
    COLUMN 'Sample'[Country Letter] = LEFT('Sample'[Country], 1)
EVALUATE
SUMMARIZECOLUMNS(
    'Sample'[Country Letter],
    "Profit", [Total Profit]
)
```

Note that you can override the existing measures by using query-level measures for the duration of the query, but you cannot override the existing columns or tables by using query-level columns or tables. Query-level measures don't affect model measures outside of the query.

When you define a variable in the DEFINE section, there's no need to use RETURN:

```
DEFINE
    MEASURE 'Sample'[Total Profit] = SUM('Sample'[Profit])
    COLUMN 'Sample'[Country Letter] = LEFT('Sample'[Country], 1)
    VAR CountryProfit =
        SUMMARIZECOLUMNS(
        'Sample'[Country Letter],
        "Profit", [Total Profit]
    )
EVALUATE
    CountryProfit
```

While you can have multiple EVALUATE statements in a DAX query, you can only have one DEFINE statement.

ORDER BY

ORDER BY sorts the result table by the specified columns or DAX expressions evaluated in the row context of the result table. In case of columns, they must be part of the result table. The default order is ascending; you can specify ASC or DESC for ascending or descending order, respectively. For example, the following query returns a list of countries sorted in descending order:

```
EVALUATE
VALUES('Sample'[Country])
ORDER BY
'Sample'[Country] DESC
```

Each ORDER BY clause corresponds to its own EVALUATE statement.

START AT

START AT skips all values before the values you specify, the order of which corresponds to the order of columns in the ORDER BY section. You can enter fewer values than there are columns in ORDER BY. For example, the following query returns the list of countries in descending order and their profit, skipping all countries before Mexico:

```
EVALUATE
SUMMARIZECOLUMNS(
    'Sample'[Country],
    "Profit", SUM('Sample'[Profit])
)
ORDER BY
'Sample'[Country] DESC
START AT "Mexico"
```

The values you specify in START AT can be values or parameters. As with ORDER BY, each EVALUATE statement has its own ORDER BY and START AT clauses.

PARAMETERS

If you want to parameterize a query, you can prefix a parameter name with the **@** character and use it in a query. For example, the following query filters the list of countries with profit over the user-specified amount:

```
EVALUATE
FILTER(
    SUMMARIZECOLUMNS(
        'Sample'[Country],
        "Profit", SUM('Sample'[Profit])
    ),
    [Profit] > @TargetProfit
)
```

When you run this query in DAX Studio, you'll be prompted to enter the parameter value and select its data type, as shown in Figure 4-22.

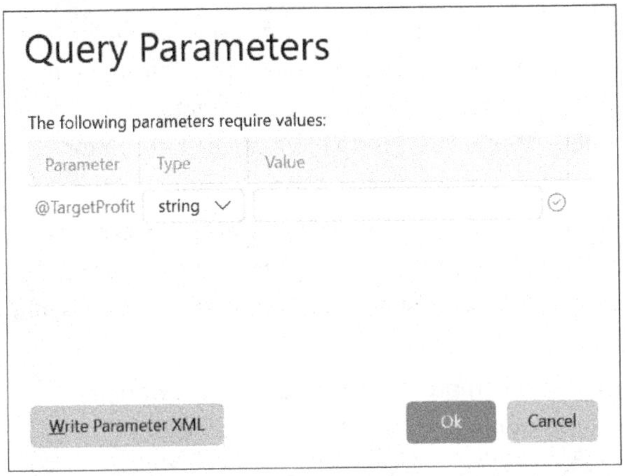

FIGURE 4-22 DAX Studio Query Parameters dialog box

Depending on how you run your parameterized queries, you may need to explicitly change the data type of the parameter in the query, as sometimes a parameter may be typed as text. The following query will type the parameter as a number even if it's originally typed as text:

```
EVALUATE
FILTER(
    SUMMARIZECOLUMNS(
        'Sample'[Country],
        "Profit", SUM('Sample'[Profit])
    ),
    [Profit] > CONVERT(@TargetProfit, DOUBLE)
)
```

Parameterized queries can be especially useful with paginated reports in Power BI.

Design and configure Power BI reports for accessibility

When you're designing a report, it's always best to know what business users want out of the reports you create, because it may be different from what you have in mind. Therefore, it's a good idea to gather feedback from end users in the initial stages of building the report so that you don't have to make as many edits in the future. Adopting techniques such as human-centered design can be useful to embed a feedback loop during this process.

Acknowledging that not all users will have the same technical skill level, you should strive for consistency across pages in your reports. For example, if you have the same slicers on different pages, place them in the same position to make them more user-friendly. In the same way, it's best to use the same font size and font face for visual titles.

Avoid putting too much information into too few visuals. If you have a few very complex visuals, consider splitting your visuals into several simpler visuals and then grouping them among common themes and relevance.

You want to aim for the key insights to be immediately shown to your users. If key information becomes visible only after interaction with the report, consider making the information easier to access by moving it to a more obvious location. Additionally, important information should not be exclusively presented in tooltips, because accessing them will be difficult for users who don't use a mouse.

Including a home page with information about the report, when it was last refreshed, and navigation tips may be useful for users to refer to. By regularly reviewing your report for readability and updating formatting options as new data becomes available, you ensure that users can clearly understand your report.

You can make your Power BI reports accessible to more users, including those who may have visual or physical impairments. There are several ways to make your reports more accessible, without the need for specialized design:

- Page names, titles, and labels
- Markers
- Alternative text (alt text)
- Tab order
- Report theme and color selection

Page names, titles, and labels

Titles of visuals and report page names help users navigate the report. As much as possible, avoid using jargon or acronyms in titles of visuals and page names, because new or external users may not be familiar with the terminology you use. For example, instead of "PY," consider spelling out "Prior Year," and instead of "Amount," consider using the exact metric name that's familiar to business users.

You should ensure that visuals are easy to understand by including data labels and axis titles where relevant. If you're using data labels and each data point has a label, consider decluttering your visual by removing the value axis. Because each point is labeled, displaying the axis in this case does not add any value.

When formatting data labels, you can choose to show them only for some measures by customizing them in the **Format** pane. You can also position data labels below or above data points to improve readability—for example, when you have multiple lines on a chart.

Markers

If you use colors to distinguish different series of values, consider using markers of different shapes, because not all people see colors in the same way. You can turn markers on for line, area, combo, and scatter charts. In the **Shapes** section of the **Format** pane, you can enable markers and select their color, shape, and size. You can also customize markers for each series.

Alt text

As we discussed previously, you can set alt text for visuals in the **General** section of the **Format** pane when a visual is selected. Alt text will be read out to users of screen readers.

It's advisable to add alt text for all nondecorative visualization items, thus ensuring that report users can understand what you are showing even if they can't see the visuals.

A visual's alt text should contain the information you want the report user to take away from it. Calling out a specific data point may be risky because users can apply filters to Power BI reports. Conditional formatting is appropriate when you want to call out some insights dynamically.

Tab order

Some users may navigate your reports by using their keyboard. The default order in which they will navigate visuals may not match the perceived order. To change the tab order, in the **Report** view select **View** > **Selection** > **Tab order**.

> **NOTE LAYER ORDER**
>
> The layer order of visuals on a page, configured in the **Selection** pane, determines which visual is shown in the front and which one is shown in the back in case visuals overlap. Layer order does not correspond to tab order—they are different concepts.

You can change the tab order of visuals in the **Selection** pane in two ways:

- Drag and drop the items within the list.
- Select an item and use the up and down arrows.

It's advisable to hide decorative elements, such as shapes, from the tab order. To do so, select the number to the left of the visual in the tab order list. Figure 4-23 shows the **Selection** pane where a shape is hidden from the tab order.

When you hide decorative elements from tab order, they aren't available for selection by keyboard users, and this improves the navigation experience.

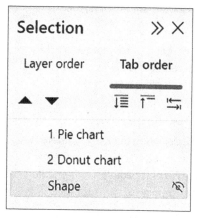

FIGURE 4-23 Tab order in the Selection pane

Report theme and color selection

In general, the colors you choose should have sufficient contrast between text and background to make text legible and easy to read.

> **NOTE** **CONTRAST RATIO AND ACCESSIBILITY**
>
> There are many tools on the web that you can use to check color contrast. One of them is Accessible Colors, located at *https://accessible-colors.com.*

Some color combinations may be difficult to discriminate for users who have color vision deficiencies. For example, avoid green and red on the same page if you want to make your reports accessible. There are other undesirable color combinations, and it's always best to check whether your colors are accessible by using a color accessibility tool.

Power BI includes several predefined color themes, which you can see in the **Themes** grouping of the **View** ribbon. You can also create and import your own theme to facilitate the process of building reports.

> **NEED MORE REVIEW?** **ACCESSIBILITY IN POWER BI**
>
> If you'd like to read further about creating accessible reports in Power BI, including more examples and illustrations, see "Design Power BI reports for accessibility" at *https://docs.microsoft.com/en-us/power-bi/create-reports/desktop-accessibility-creating-reports.*

Enable personalized visuals in a report

Even if you follow all best practices when you create a Power BI report, in some cases users may want to see different visuals because they have different preferences, like different chart types, or they may want to look at something that wasn't originally shown in the report. Instead of addressing all user queries yourself, you can enable visual personalization in reports, allowing users to change visuals to some extent. To allow users to personalize visuals, you'll need to enable the feature in the report and, optionally, create one or more new perspectives in your dataset.

Enable visual personalization

By default, users cannot personalize visuals; enabling the experience is a two-step process. First, you need to enable the feature for the report:

- In Power BI Desktop, go to **File** > **Options and settings** > **Options** > **Current file** > **Report settings** > **Personalize visuals** and select **Allow report readers to personalize visuals to suit their needs**.

- In the Power BI service, go to the report settings and ensure that **Allow report readers to personalize visuals to suit their needs** is toggled on.

Once you enable the visual personalization at report level, all visuals can be personalized by default. You can turn off the feature at the page or the visual level.

To turn off the feature at page level, go to the page format settings and toggle **Personalize visual** to **Off**.

To turn off the feature for a specific visual, perform the following steps:

1. Select the visual.

2. In the **Visualizations** pane, select **Format your visual** > **General** > **Header icons** > **Icons**.

3. Toggle **Personalize visual** to **Off**.

When report readers personalize visuals in the Power BI service, their experience will be similar to Figure 4-24.

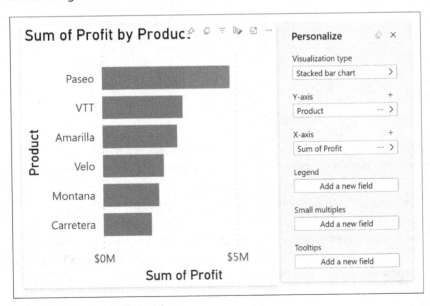

FIGURE 4-24 Personalization options

The visual options that a report reader can personalize will depend on the visual type. If your users want to save their personalized visuals, you should direct them to save personal bookmarks, because personalized visuals aren't saved by default.

Create perspectives

By default, when personalizing a visual, a report reader will see all the fields available to them. In case of large models, seeing all the fields may be overwhelming, especially when some fields are technical and aren't meant to be seen by end users. To reduce the number of fields available to a user when personalizing a visual, you can use perspectives.

A *perspective* is a reduced list of fields created for a better user experience. You can create perspectives in Tabular Editor, covered in Chapter 3. To create a perspective, connect Tabular Editor to your model, right-click **Perspectives**, select **New Perspective**, and enter the new perspective name. At this point, you'll see the new perspective, as shown in Figure 4-25.

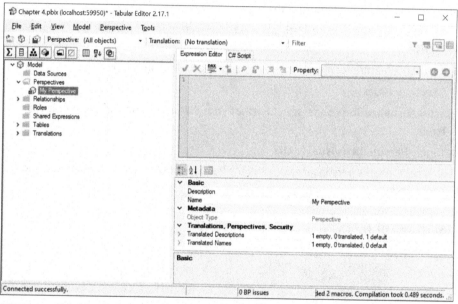

FIGURE 4-25 Tabular Editor with a new perspective

Once you have created a perspective, you can start adding fields to it by right-clicking a field or table, selecting **Show in Perspectives**, and selecting the perspective to add the field or table to.

After you save changes in Tabular Editor, you'll need to go back to the report and make use of the new perspective. Go to the page format options, select **Personalize visual**, and select your new perspective from the **Report-reader perspective** drop-down list. Note that you select a perspective for each page individually; if desired, you can select **Apply to all pages** to set the same perspective for all existing report pages. New pages will still have Default fields selected by default.

Configure automatic page refresh

When you're using DirectQuery, it's often desirable to have your report visuals refreshed automatically to reflect the latest data. This capability is especially important when you monitor near-real-time data, such as data coming from sensors or streaming data.

You can set up automatic page refresh in the **Visualizations** pane by selecting **Format your report page** and toggling **Page refresh** to **On**. Power BI will then refresh all visuals on a page at the rate that depends on the refresh type you select. Power BI supports two types of automatic page refresh: fixed interval and change detection.

> **IMPORTANT** **AUTOMATIC PAGE REFRESH IN POWER BI SERVICE**
>
> For automatic page refresh to work in the Power BI service, the feature must be enabled by the tenant administrator. Change detection also requires Premium capacity.

Fixed interval

In some scenarios, you may want to refresh your visuals at a constant rate—for example, 30 seconds. For this, you need to select **Auto page refresh** from the **Refresh type** drop-down list and set the refresh interval, which can be in multiples of seconds, minutes, hours, or days. This type of page refresh is suitable for some scenarios, but it may put unnecessary strain on the server because it will refresh data even if there are no changes.

You can select **Show details** to see the actual refresh rate and when data was last refreshed. When logged into your Power BI account, you can see whether the feature is enabled by your Power BI tenant administrator and the minimum interval allowed by your administrator.

Fixed interval automatic page refresh is configured for each page individually. Figure 4-26 shows a page set to refresh every 10 seconds.

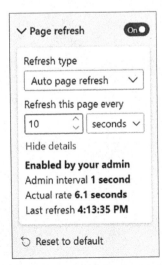

FIGURE 4-26 Page refresh set to 10 seconds

Change detection

The change detection type of refresh can be more efficient than the fixed interval automatic page refresh because visuals are refreshed only when there's a change in data. Change detection uses a measure you define to check whether there are changes in the data—if the value of a measure is different from last time, then the visuals will be refreshed.

You can select one measure per model that will be used to detect changes. Unlike fixed interval automatic page refresh, which can be configured for each page separately, you can define only one change detection measure per model, though you can use change detection for some pages and fixed interval refresh for other pages.

To set up change detection as the preferred refresh type for a page, select **Change detection** from the **Refresh type** drop-down list in the **Page refresh** section of the page format settings.

Next, to configure the change detection measure, select **Add change detection** from the **Page refresh** section. Alternatively, you can select **Change detection** on the **Modeling** ribbon, or right-click a field in the **Fields** pane and select **Change detection**. Figure 4-27 shows the available options.

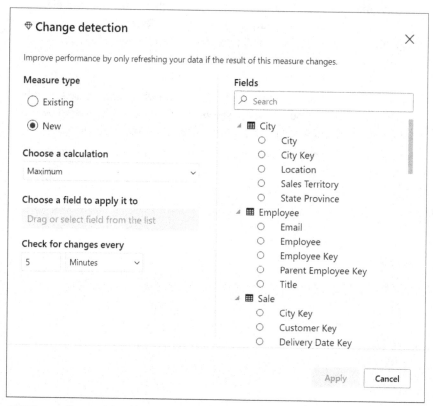

FIGURE 4-27 Change detection

When selecting the change detection measure, you can select an existing measure or a new one by defining your own calculation. For new calculations, you can select a column and use one of the following aggregations, depending on the data type:

- Count
- Count (Distinct)
- Minimum
- Maximum
- Sum

In addition to the measure, you must select how often Power BI should check for changes, which can be multiples of seconds, minutes, or hours.

After you select the measure and check frequency, select **Apply**.

Create and distribute paginated reports in Power BI Report Builder

While the reports you create in Power BI Desktop can be printed, they're primarily meant to be used online in the Power BI service or mobile apps. Usually, the reports are formatted to fit well on a computer or mobile phone screen, and different report pages often serve different purposes.

There are valid use cases for printing reports and sharing them offline. For example, someone may want to print a sales performance report that shows each region on a different page and distribute the report before a meeting. For cases like this, a *paginated report* would be a good fit. Paginated reports are created by using software called Power BI Report Builder.

> **NOTE**   **INSTALLING POWER BI REPORT BUILDER**
>
> You can download the Power BI Report Builder installer from the Microsoft Download Center at *https://aka.ms/pbireportbuilder*.

Like normal Power BI reports, paginated reports can be created by using data from various data sources, and you can even use a Power BI service dataset as a data source.

> **NOTE**   **DOWNLOADING RDL FILES**
>
> To download an RDL file from Power BI service, you must have a dataset already published.

To start creating a paginated report based on a Power BI dataset, go to a workspace, hover over a dataset, and select **More options** > **Create paginated report**. When you open the RDL file, you should see blank canvas with placeholder text like in Figure 4-28.

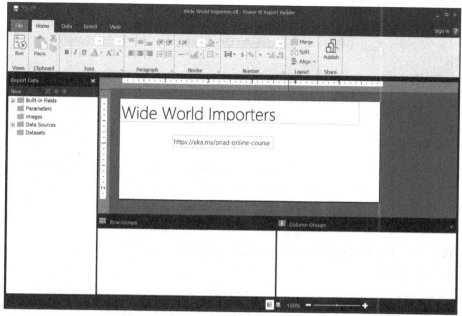

FIGURE 4-28 Power BI Report Builder

The RDL file will already contain a data source—the Power BI dataset you downloaded the RDL file from. To create a report, you'll need to add one or more datasets to your paginated report. Once finished, you can select **Publish** on the **Home** ribbon and select a workspace to publish to.

> **NEED MORE REVIEW?**   **CREATING PAGINATED REPORTS**
>
> Specific steps required to complete a paginated report are outside the scope of this book. For a step-by-step tutorial, see "Tutorial: Create a paginated report and upload it to the Power BI service" at *https://learn.microsoft.com/en-us/power-bi/paginated-reports/paginated-reports-quickstart-aw*.

Chapter summary

- Use the multitude of tools in Azure Synapse Spark in order to explore and visualize your date—in particular the show() and display() functions, the Spark SQL magic command, and the Python libraries.
- You can also use the Azure Synapse SQL engines, whether dedicated or serverless, to visualize your data. This is possible with the built-in visualization features in the Results pane that give you access to powerful chart capabilities.

- You can change a report by selecting one of the preset themes or defining your own theme. To create your own theme, you can use Power BI Desktop, edit a JSON file, or use a third-party tool.

- Power BI supports R and Python visuals, which must be installed separately. R and Python visuals can be used to display visuals that aren't available in Power BI by default.

- You can connect to Power BI datasets by using the XMLA endpoint. To query a dataset, you can write queries in DAX.

- You can make your Power BI reports more accessible by carefully selecting page names, titles, and labels. You should use different markers for different categories and not rely on color as the only way to discriminate categories. For each visual, you can set alternative text and its tab order. You should use colors that provide sufficient contrast between font and background, and you can use report themes to make working with colors easier during the development.

- Users can personalize visuals if you enable the feature in a report. To improve the visual personalization experience, you can create perspectives in Tabular Editor.

- When using DirectQuery, you can configure automatic page refresh for each page separately. Power BI supports two types of automatic page refresh: fixed interval and change detection. Change detection works by checking for changes in the value of a measure you define.

- You can create paginated reports by using Power BI Report Builder and publishing them to Power BI service. Paginated reports are a great fit for reports meant to be printed and shared offline.

Thought experiment

In this thought experiment, demonstrate your skills and knowledge of the topics covered in this chapter. You can find the answers in the section that follows.

1. Your organization is heavily using Synapse SQL for the data transformation needs. Which way would you recommend for data exploration? The solution must minimize the learning curve for the data analysts.

   A. Using the powerful Matplotlib library

   B. Using the built-in display() function

   C. Using the Spark SQL magic command

   D. Using the chart capabilities in the Results pane

2. You need to ensure that all new reports created in your organization follow the same formatting guidelines consistent with the corporate branding. How should you address the problem? The solution should minimize the overall time spent on formatting.

   A. Direct users to the brand portal so they know what font and colors should be applied.

B. Tell users to use the Format Painter to copy formatting between visuals for consistency.

C. Create a report template with a corporate theme.

3. You need to ensure that users can effectively navigate your reports by using the keyboard. Which property should you configure?

A. Bookmarks

B. Layer order

C. Mobile layout

D. Tab order

4. You have a report used by hundreds of users, and some business users prefer different visuals than the ones you included. At the same time, some users rely on your visuals for presenting during periodic meetings. How should you address the needs of those who need different visuals? The solution must keep the default views as much as possible.

A. Create new report pages with new visuals.

B. Enable visual personalization.

C. Create new reports.

D. Direct people to use Analyze in Excel.

5. Your team requested you to create a report that shows each company product on a page. Some team members intend to print the report and distribute the printouts during meetings. Currently there are about a dozen products, although new products are sometimes introduced and old ones discontinued. How should you approach the problem?

A. Create a paginated report.

B. Create a single-page report with a single-select product slicer.

C. Create a report with one page per product.

Thought experiment answers

1. The answer is **D**. Using the chart capabilities in the Results pane is the only answer that leverages Synapse SQL. All the other answers are wrong because they require using Synapse Spark, which would make it more difficult for the data analysts.

2. The answer is **C**. Creating a report from a template that already includes a theme will mean that all new reports have the same formatting applied, and it won't require any extra effort from report builders. Option A may result in inconsistent formatting due to different report builders applying guidelines differently. Option B still requires the knowledge of corporate branding requirements, and it will demand more manual effort compared to a corporate Power BI template with a theme included.

3. The answer is **D**. Tab order determines the order in which users switch between visuals when using the keyboard. Bookmarks—option A—aren't helpful for navigating within each page. Layer order—option B—determines the order in which visuals are layered and may be different from Tab order. Mobile layout—option C—is used to create mobile reports.

4. The answer is **B**. Visual personalization will allow those who want to change visuals to do so. Creating new reports or report pages, as options A and C suggest, may introduce confusion as well as extra work in case some changes are required. Analyze in Excel—option D—may result in unforeseen differences between the standard and custom reports, as well as extra development time compared to personalized visuals.

5. The answer is **A**. A paginated report can have as many pages as there are products, dynamically changing whenever the list of product changes. Option B, a single-page report, is inadequate because it will require a lot of manual effort to print out pages on all products. Option C, a multiple-page report, is also wrong because whenever there's a change in the list of products, you'll need to revisit your report and add or remove pages.

Index

Symbols

A

D

dashboard, Power BI, settings, 17
data asset. *See also* data source
    Azure Data Lake, connecting to Microsoft
    Purview, 5–6
    Azure SQL database, connecting to Microsoft
    Purview, 4–5
    browsing, 9–10
    identifying, 8
    registering, 3–4
    requesting access, 10–11
data governance, 1, 2. *See also* Microsoft Purview
data model/ing, 101
    composite, 190–192
    DAX Studio, 103–104
    denormalization, 209
    DirectQuery, 102
        advantages, 102
        disadvantages, 102–103
    efficiency, 203
    importing data, 102
    optimizing, 202–203
    tabular
        calculation item properties, 107
        create calculation groups, 105–108
        DAX functions, 107–108
    Tabular Editor 2, 104–105
data source
    adding to a gateway, 28–29
    DirectQuery, 102
    foldable, 77
    gateway, user management, 29–30
    identifying data loading performance
    bottlenecks, 73
    performance improvements, 76–77
    privacy settings, 79–83
data types
    DAX, 109–110
    M, 84–86
    Power Query
        list, 84–85
        record, 84–85
        table, 86–87
data visualization. *See also* report
    Azure Synapse SQL results pane, 219–220
    color, 240
    magic commands, 217–218
    markers, 239
    personalization, 241–242
    perspective, 242
    Power BI, 220–221
        create and import a custom report theme,
        221–222
        edit a theme JSON file, 224–225
        theme editor, 223
        third-party theme tools, 225–226
    Python, 226
        creating, 231–233
        Matplotlib, 218–219
        requirements, 226–227
        work in script editors, 226–227
    R, 226
        creating, 229–231
        requirements, 226–227
        work in script editors, 226–227
    Spark show() and display() functions, 216–217
dataflow
    creating, 78
    Power BI settings, 18
    transforming data, 79
datamart settings, Power BI, 19
dataset
    connecting to, 233–234
    large format, 189–190
    querying, 234–235
    security, Power BI settings, 19
    shared, 51–52
DATATABLE function, 163–165
date and time functions, 118–119
DATEADD function, 181
DATESBETWEEN function, 184
DATESINPERIOD function, 184
DATESYTD function, 177–178
DATEVALUE function, 109
DAX, 101, 108
    calculated columns
        binning, 123–126
        circular dependencies, 131–132
        formulas, 111–113
        grouping values, 120–126
        versus measures, 169
        primary key, 131–132
        sort by another column error, 121–122
        using functions in, 113–119
        variables, 127–128

J-K

L

M

Q

Plug into learning at

MicrosoftPressStore.com

The Microsoft Press Store by Pearson offers:

- Free U.S. shipping

- Buy an eBook, get three formats – Includes PDF, EPUB, and MOBI to use with your computer, tablet, and mobile devices

- Print & eBook Best Value Packs

- eBook Deal of the Week – Save up to 50% on featured title

- Newsletter – Be the first to hear about new releases, announcements, special offers, and more

- Register your book – Find companion files, errata, and product updates, plus receive a special coupon* to save on your next purchase

Discounts are applied to the list price of a product. Some products are not eligible to receive additional discounts, so your discount code may not be applied to all items in your cart. Discount codes cannot be applied to products that are already discounted, such as eBook Deal of the Week, eBooks that are part of a book + eBook pack, and products with special discounts applied as part of a promotional offering. Only one coupon can be used per order.

 Pearson